CONTENTS

ACKNOWLEDGEMENTS

For Karen, Hannah and Barney

Thanks are due to everyone who has provided the help, support and hard work needed to get this book completed.

Mark Walsh

The publishers gratefully acknowledge the following for permission to reproduce photographs and other material. Every effort has been made to trace copyright holders, but if any material has been inadvertantly overlooked, the publishers will be pleased to correct this at the earliest opportunity.

Alamy: title page br, 107, 112t, 190, 191,

Getty Images: title page tl, tr, br, 16, 30, 31t, 33, 57,66, 70, 106, 146cl, c, 159, 165, 169,

iStock: 19, 31c, 112b, 117, 119, 124, 137, 147bl, cb, 148b, 149, 154, 157, 158, 167, 170, 180, 182, 184, 187, 188, 195, 197, 207, 209, 210, 213, 215, 218, 221, 224, 226, 227, 229, 231, 235, 237, 239, 240

St John Ambulance: 228

INTRODUCTION

Welcome to GCSE Health and Social Care for OCR!

The aim of this book is to help you to develop the knowledge and understanding that you will need to complete your GCSE Health and Social Care course. The book covers the following units:

- **Unit 1 – Health, Social Care and Early Years Provision**
- **Unit 2 – Understanding Personal Development and Relationships**
- **Unit 3 - Promoting Health and Wellbeing**
- **Unit 4 – Safeguarding and Protecting Individuals**

You need to complete the first two units if you are taking the GCSE Single Award qualification. You need to complete all four units if you are taking the GCSE Double Award qualification. Each of the units in the book provides you with opportunities to develop the knowledge and understanding that will be needed to successfully complete the coursework assignments and external assessments that are part of your GCSE Health and Social Care award.

Features of the book

The book closely follows the specification (syllabus) of your GCSE Health and Social Care award. This means that all of the topics and issues referred to in the course specification are fully covered. You will find the following features in the book:

- **Chapter introduction** – This is short, introductory section at the start of each chapter that tells you what the chapter is going to focus on.

- **Over to you!** – These are activities that aim to get you thinking about an issue or topic. These short activities can usually be completed on the spot without doing any more research. You should try as many of them as you can as they are designed to boost your thinking and learning skills.

- **Investigate...** – These activities are designed to extend your knowledge and understanding by encouraging you to find out a bit more about a topic or issue that you have been learning about. Finding information in other books or on the Internet will help you to deepen and extend your knowledge and understanding of health and social care.

- **Knowledge Check** – This is a list of questions about the topic you have been studying. You should try to answer as many of these as you can to check your learning and understanding of the topics you have been studying. You might also want to try answering the unit 2 and 4 questions again when you are revising for your externally assessed examinations.

- **Chapter checklist** – You will find this feature at the end of each chapter. It provides you with an opportunity to think about what you have been studying and to check that you have covered everything you need to. The chapter checklist also provides you with brief information on how the topics you have been studying are assessed.

Assessment

The OCR GCSE Health and Social Care award is assessed through both coursework assignments and external tests.

- **Unit 1 Health, Social Care and Early Years Provision** is assessed through an assignment set by OCR and marked by your tutor, with a total of 60 marks.

- **Unit 2 Understanding Personal Development and Relationships** is externally assessed through a 1 hour written exam, with a total of 60 marks.

- **Unit 3 Promoting Health and Wellbeing** is assessed through an assignment set by OCR and marked by your tutor, with a total of 60 marks.

- **Unit 4 Safeguarding and Protecting Individuals** is externally assessed through a 1 hour written or computer-based exam, with a total of 60 marks

I've tried to write a book that helps you to gain a good, clear understanding of a range of care topics and also to give you a taste of what to expect from a career in the health and social care sector. Taking a GCSE Health and Social Care course gives you an opportunity to decide whether this is an area of work that you are suitable for and interested in pursuing. Hopefully, you'll think about taking your interest in health and social care further when you've worked through the book and completed your GCSE. Good luck with your course!

Mark Walsh

Health, Social Care and Early Years Provision

Introduction

This unit is about the range of care needs individuals have and the care services that are provided to meet these needs. You will learn about:

- the range of care needs of different service user groups

- the types of services that are provided to meet service user needs

- the ways services have developed and how they are organised

- ways of obtaining care services

- reasons people sometimes don't get the care services that they need

- the jobs and skills of people who work in health, social care and early years services

- the principles of care and values that care workers put into practice through their work with service users.

If you are thinking about working in the health, social care or early years field, this unit will help you to understand how the care system works and the different jobs that are available within it. Understanding what care services are available and how they work will also help should you or a member of your family need to use services in the future.

Chapter 1

The range of care needs of major client groups

Key issue: Who needs to use care services and why?

Health, social care and early years services are provided to meet the care needs of major client groups. Chapter 1 outlines the health, development and social care needs of the following major client groups:

- Babies and children
- Adolescents
- Adults
- Older people
- People with disabilities.

You will learn about the physical, intellectual, emotional and social needs that members of these client groups have. Chapter 1 will also explain how health, social care and early years services respond to the needs and demands of these client groups. By the end of the unit you should understand why individuals may need to use health, social care and early years services.

Client groups

Care services are planned for groups of people who have the same type of problems or similar unmet needs. These groups of people are known as **client groups**. A **service user** is a member of a client group who actually receives a care service. Care organisations in the United Kingdom provide health care, social care and early education services that meet the physical, intellectual, social and emotional needs of major client groups. Some of the services that are provided for a client group are **universal services**, such as general health care provided by GPs (family doctors). These services are suitable for all members of the client group. However, care organisations like the NHS also develop **targeted services**, such as child and adolescent mental health services and adult spinal rehabilitation services, for members of client groups who have particular care and development needs. The groups of service users you need to know about are:

- Babies and children
- Adolescents
- Adults

- Older people
- People with disabilities.

As you can see, these groups cover the whole of the human life span – from newborn babies to very old people. The general needs of human beings of all ages are described below (see Figure 1.1). A person whose physical, intellectual, emotional and social needs are satisfied is likely to experience positive health, wellbeing and personal development.

Figure 1.1 - Examples of PIES needs.

Type of needs	Examples of needs
Physical needs	<ul><li>A balanced diet and sufficient fluids</li><li>Warmth</li><li>Shelter</li><li>Exercise</li><li>Sleep and rest</li><li>Good hygiene</li><li>Protection from harm, illness and injury</li></ul>
Intellectual needs	<ul><li>Interesting and purposeful activities</li><li>Learning opportunities</li><li>Mental challenges and new experiences</li></ul>
Emotional needs	<ul><li>Love, support and care</li><li>A sense of safety and security</li><li>Self-confidence and self-esteem</li></ul>
Social needs	<ul><li>Attachment to a trusted carer</li><li>Relationships with other people</li><li>A sense of identity and belonging within a community</li></ul>

A person's **physical needs** must be satisfied for them to be physically healthy. A person's **intellectual needs** are those things they require to develop their knowledge, skills and abilities. A person's **emotional and social needs** are the things they require to develop relationships and experience emotional wellbeing and good mental health.

The hierarchy of needs

Whilst all human beings have a common range of physical, intellectual, emotional and social needs, the precise nature of these needs vary across the different client groups. This is because a person's needs, and their ability to meet them, change as they move from one life stage to another. Care organisations recognise this and tailor their services to meet the particular health care, social care and developmental needs of each client group.

Abraham Maslow (1908 – 1970), an American psychologist, developed a way of thinking about human needs that is still very influential in care work. He suggested that a person's needs are best understood as a pyramid or hierarchy, arranged in levels of importance (see figure 1.2). He believed that physical needs were the most important because a person must meet these, or have help from other people to meet them, to survive. Maslow suggested that human beings of any age are motivated to have to meet needs higher up the pyramid only when they have met lower level needs. As you study and understand the different stages of human development, you will notice that as people become more capable of meeting certain needs, the focus of their personal development shifts to other levels of need. For example, during infancy parents and care practitioners prioritise physical and safety needs as these are essential for an infant's development. During childhood, physical and safety needs are still important but are usually being met quite successfully. As a result, a child's social needs become more of a priority.

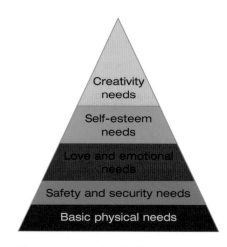

Figure 1.2 Maslow's hierarchy of needs.

Babies

A newborn baby is dependent on others, usually their parents, to provide them with the things they need for health, wellbeing and development. To be healthy and to develop normally, infants require a lot of practical, hands-on care from their parents and from care professionals during the early stages of infancy. A lot of the care needs of babies result from their physical dependence and vulnerability to harm. Infants become less dependent in some ways as they grow and develop into toddlers. However, a 2-year-old toddler still depends on their parents to meet most of their physical, intellectual, emotional and social needs.

Figure 1.3 The care needs of infants.

Case study

Luke is 2 months old. He had a normal birth. After a range of checks by the midwife and doctor at the hospital, his parents took him home the day after his birth. As a young baby, Luke is totally dependent on others for basic care and protection from harm. Luke's mum breastfeeds him several times during the day and night. She and his dad take it in turns to change his nappy, wash him and comfort him when he starts crying. Luke's parents have to make sure that he is fed properly, that he is kept warm but that he doesn't get too hot and that he is kept clean and comfortable. Luke won't be able to meet these needs on his own until he is several years older.

- List any other basic needs that are not mentioned in the case study that you think Luke has. (Hint - what else does he need to be a healthy baby?)
- Identify two things that Luke's mum or dad do to meet his physical needs.
- Which care worker usually visits a mother and baby at home shortly after the birth to check that the baby is healthy and growing well?

Children

Children need less basic care from their parents than infants as they learn how to meet some of their own basic needs. For example, children learn how to feed, wash and dress themselves in early childhood. Even so, children still need a lot of help and support from parents and care practitioners to develop:

- self-care skills (washing, dressing, going to the toilet)
- physical strength and stamina (play and outdoor activities)
- intellectual skills (basic reading, writing and numeracy)
- language skills (talking, reading and writing)
- social skills (friendships and relationships with other children and adults)
- emotional control and appropriate behaviour (at home and with others).

A range of health, social care and early years services are available for children who experience ill-health, social or emotional difficulties, developmental problems or who have disabilities. These services provide specialist forms of care that are targeted at the particular needs of children.

Over to you!

How might the basic care needs of a child be different to those of an adult and an older person?

Case study

Anna is three and a half years old. She has recently begun attending a playgroup two mornings a week. Anna's mum helps to run the playgroup. She thinks that attending playgroup is good for Anna's development. When she's at the playgroup, Anna meets and plays with up to ten other children. Anna enjoys playing with sand and water, climbing and using the trampoline. She now joins in games with other children. Her mum says that Anna has learnt how to make new friends and is much less shy than she was before she started going to playgroup.

- Give an example of one physical, one intellectual, one emotional and one social need that a child could meet through going to playgroup.
- What new skills or abilities might playgroup help Anna to develop?
- Explain how play might help Anna to develop intellectual skills.

Health, Social Care and Early Years Provision

Adolescents

Adolescents have care needs that are different to those of children and adults. During adolescence young people go through **puberty**. This involves major physical growth and development but doesn't normally involve teenagers experiencing major health problems as a result of it. However, some teenagers do develop additional health needs that require specialist care and treatment. For example, teenage girls may require health care services for problems related to **menstruation** and many adolescents seek help for skin problems, such as acne, that often occur during puberty. Adolescents can also benefit from receiving information, advice and guidance from health promotion workers. This helps them make informed choices about aspects of their lifestyle and health behaviour such as smoking, exercise, contraception, drugs, alcohol and unprotected sex.

During adolescence young people often require support to help them with their rapidly changing social and emotional development. For example, young people may require:

- support to help manage relationships with parents and other adults
- experiences that build up confidence, self-esteem and assertiveness
- opportunities to express opinions and explore feelings
- the chance to make personal decisions about the future
- opportunities to develop knowledge and skills useful for adult life and work
- opportunities to socialise, develop and express personal identity
- advice and guidance about relationships, sex and sexuality.

Services to meet the particular health, social care and development needs of adolescents are less common than similar services for children or adults. Adolescents are often required to use children's services until they are 16 years old and then services for adults after their 16th birthday. However, some local areas do now provide specialist targeted services as awareness has grown about the specific needs of adolescents.

 Case study

Gina is fifteen years old. She says that can't wait to leave school and get a job. Gina currently has a difficult relationship with her parents. She complains that they treat her like a child and are too strict with her. Gina believes that she is mature enough to make decisions for herself. Gina's parents complain that she has become 'very difficult' and that she no longer listens to what they tell her. They insist that she doesn't go out after school during the week and won't let her stay at a friend's house at the weekend. Gina feels too angry with her parents to talk to them about any of these things at the moment.

- Who could help Gina to express how she feels?
- What kind of physical care needs do adolescents like Gina have?
- Why do you think parents have difficult relationships with their children during adolescence?

Adults

Adulthood is a life stage where people are expected to be able to meet their own physical, intellectual, emotional and social needs. However, there are always situations where people need help in meeting their needs, such as when they experience problems with their physical or mental health or social problems as a result of changes to their circumstances.

Percentages

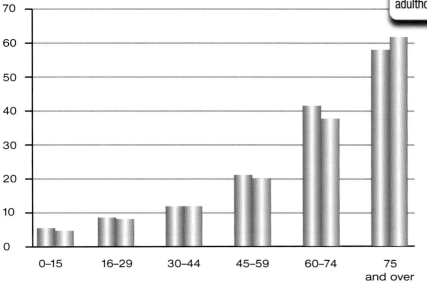

Figure 1.4 – Prevalence of limiting long-term illness by age and sex, UK 2001. Source ONS.

Adults may require health care services for much the same reasons as children and adolescents. However, adults are more likely than children and adolescents to experience serious diseases and disorders, such as cancers and mental health problems, which require a broader range of specialist medical treatment and care. Some health problems, like heart disease, respiratory disorders or arthritis, may develop into chronic

Case study

"My name is Nadine Burton. I'm twenty-six years old and have one child, Leon, who is now nine months old. I've used care services quite a lot recently, mainly because of stress, and for Leon. I saw my GP (family doctor) when I felt under pressure and I wasn't sleeping well. I thought that he could give me something to help me sleep. Leon was waking up in the night and I had to get up to feed him all the time. I was tired all day and I wasn't coping very well. My neighbours then started complaining about Leon's crying. It made me feel depressed. The GP got me some help from social services. They arranged for me to go to a mother and baby group. I now get to meet other new mums and we chat. I find it helps me to relax a bit. The GP also arranged for the Health Visitor to keep coming to see me. She gives me advice about feeding and caring for Leon and she's friendly. Things are getting easier now. Well, the neighbours have stopped complaining, anyway!"

- Which client group is Nadine a member of now?
- Which client group is Leon a member of?
- Give two reasons why Nadine needed help from care services.
- Explain how the care and support provided to Nadine helps to meet her social and emotional needs.

conditions and require the person to use care services throughout their adult life. The same situation is also true of social care services. Some adults may require help and support, such as temporary housing, for a short period, whilst other more vulnerable people need ongoing support to help them to cope with the stresses and difficulties in their life or with a permanent disability.

A wide range of health and social care services are available for adults who experience ill-health, social or emotional difficulties. These services provide specialist forms of care that are targeted at the diverse health, social care and development needs of adults.

Older people

Older people aged 65+ are a major client group for health and social care services. This isn't because all older people are frail, incapable or unwell. However, the gradual effects of the ageing process do mean that many older people tend to experience a reduction in their ability to cope with the demands of daily life and become more vulnerable to ill-health, social isolation and loneliness. Individuals in later adulthood are more likely than younger adults to experience physical health problems that affect their **daily living skills**. Older people may require health services because they develop a condition or illness that reduces their ability to perform everyday tasks such as washing, dressing or shopping for food. Many older people also struggle to live on a reduced income once they retire and stop earning an income. This again can reduce their quality of life by restricting what food they can buy, how much they are able to socialise and even whether they can afford to heat their homes in the winter. As a result, later adulthood is a life stage when many individuals become more vulnerable and require the support of health and social care services to help them to meet their physical, intellectual, emotional and social needs.

Some older people live active, healthy lives whilst others become vulnerable and require lots of support.

Over to you!

Can you think of any care services that are targeted at older people? What needs are these services aiming to meet?

Case study

Mrs Jean Baker is 78 years of age. Until a year ago she spent most of her time looking after her house and her husband Peter, aged 80. Peter Baker had a severe heart attack a year ago and has been in hospital ever since. Mrs Baker tries to visit him whenever she can but is finding life on her own very difficult. She feels that she needs help to cope with her housework and general chores like shopping. Mrs Baker has also been feeling unwell recently and has been lonely since her husband was admitted to hospital.

- What do you think Mrs Baker's care needs are?
- How could Mrs Baker be given more emotional support?
- Name two types of care service which are provided to meet the needs of older people.

Health, Social Care and Early Years Provision

People with disabilities

Some forms of health, social care and early years services are developed and provided to meet the needs of people with specific conditions or problems. These include:

- People with learning disabilities
- People with mental health problems
- People with physical disabilities
- People with sensory impairments (visual or hearing).

Whilst these groups of service users have many of the same universal care needs as other people of a similar age, their particular problems require specialist care provision because of the need to also take account of the individual's disability or mental health problem. Learning and physical disabilities, mental health problems and sensory impairments can affect the personal development of people in all life stages. For example, an individual's particular disability or impairment may result in specific care needs because it disrupts, slows down or limits some aspect of their personal development so that the individual requires additional, specialist forms of help and support, such as medication, psychological therapy, special education or equipment or residential care services, to enable them to function to the best of their ability.

Over to you!

What kinds of specific care needs do you think an adult might have if they lost their eyesight in an accident?

Investigate ...

Use the Internet to find the websites of the RNID (www.rnid.org.uk) and the RNIB (www.rnib.org.uk). Find out what help is available for visually and hearing impaired people.

Specific needs	Targeted services	
Learning difficulties	● Day centres ● Supported housing	● Employment support ● Specialist education and training
Sensory impairments	● Adapted housing ● Hearing/guide dogs	● Adapted daily living equipment ● Occupational therapy
Mental health problems	● In-patient units ● Community nurses ● Day centres	● Supported employment ● Psychotherapy
Physical disability	● Residential care ● Transport services	● Occupational therapy ● Community support workers

Figure 1.5 Targeted services for individuals with special needs.

Case study

Richard is thirty-two years old and has Down's syndrome. He lives at home with his parents and attends a day centre where he has made some friends. Richard has learnt to wash, dress and feed himself but requires help and support to adapt to new people and changes in his routine. Richard's parents and carers say that he is not able to make decisions for himself or live independently at the moment. Even so, Richard says that he'd like to be a bus driver and get married one day.

- What kinds of care needs do you think Richard has at the moment?
- Explain how going to the day centre could help to meet Richard's needs.
- How do you think Richard could be helped to become more independent?

Permanent and temporary needs

We have seen that people have care needs in every life stage. However, it is important to distinguish between the temporary care needs that a person has and the more permanent, ongoing needs that can also develop.

A person may have **temporary care needs** because they become unwell or experience some social or developmental problems at a particular point in their life. This is usually the case where a person develops an acute (short term) illness or has an accident that requires treatment. When the person recovers or gets over their problems, their need for care will end. The same is true during infancy, childhood and early adolescence. Parents and other adults may provide forms of physical care and social, emotional and intellectual support for an individual until they are able to meet their needs independently. In this sense, we all have temporary care needs during the early parts of life.

An individual can develop, or be born with, **permanent care needs** because they have a **chronic** (ongoing) health problem or condition that affects their ability to function independently. For example, a person with chronic kidney disease may need regular **dialysis** (removal of waste products from the blood) for the rest of their life unless they receive a kidney transplant. Similarly, a child born with Down's syndrome is likely to need specialist health and social care support throughout their life because their learning difficulties will limit their social and intellectual development and prevent them from developing the skills needed for independent living.

Over to you!

Identify the last time you needed others to provide you with care. How temporary were your care needs?

Social policy goals

The government is responsible for funding, and in many cases providing, a range of health, social care, education and welfare services for the population of the United Kingdom. The main purpose of these services is to provide help for people 'in need'. One of the key challenges for any government is to identify the main health and social problems facing society (such as child protection, obesity and substance misuse, for example). They do this by commissioning research studies and reports into a wide range of health and social care issues and also by collecting and analysing data to identify which groups are most 'in need'. Once reports and data are available, the government produce social policies which set out how they intend to tackle the problems that have been identified. The social policies that are produced will include a range of targets or goals that need to be achieved in order to deal with the problems faced by those who are 'in need'.

Since 1997, the New Labour government has produced a range of social policies relating to health care and early years services. Some of these are described in figure 1.6.

There are a wide range of social policy goals that affect all areas of health, social care and early years service provision. The NHS, local authorities and voluntary organisations typically develop and adapt the services they provide in order to try and achieve the targets or goals set by each of the government's social policies.

Focus	Social policy goal	Government action
Early years	● To reduce child poverty ● To improve early learning opportunities for all	● Development of Sure Start Children's centres ● Employment and child care support for lone parent and low income families. ● Employment of a range of family and child care support workers ● Increased nursery places for children under 4 years of age
Health care	● To reduce deaths and illness from heart disease, cancers, strokes, accidents and suicide ● To tackle inequalities in health experience between different groups in the population	● Reduction in waiting times for hospital appointments ● Employment of more health care staff in the NHS ● Development of more primary care and walk-in services to improve access to health care ● A change in focus to preventative health care services

Figure 1.6 Social policies on health care and early years.

Assessing population care needs

Social policies are one of the factors that influence the development of health, social care and early years services. Another factor, closely related to the development of social policies, is the range of care, development and support needs that exist within a local population. NHS Strategic Health Authorities are regional organisations that are responsible for implementing the government's social policies in specified local areas. They work directly with Primary Care Trusts and alongside Local Authorities to assess the health care, social care and early years support needs of the local population so that they can provide an appropriate range of care services. When the range of care needs within a local population are known the local NHS Primary Care Trust will commission health care services for all service user groups whilst the Local Authority has the responsibility for commissioning social care and early years services for vulnerable people and young children. The data required to assess health needs is generally obtained from hospital and GP records and from surveys carried out in local communities.

Over to you!

Find out the name and website address of your local Primary Care Trust. Have a look on their website for information about the Joint Strategic Needs Assessment. This will tell you about population care needs in your local area.

Ensuring equality for diverse service users

British society is diverse. This means that the population is made up of people with differing ethnic and cultural backgrounds and groups of people with differing gender, sexuality and social class characteristics. Health, social care and early years service providers have a duty to provide care services that meet the particular needs of all potential service users. This means that they must find ways of responding to diversity. However, care service providers also have to ensure that everyone is treated fairly and equally. In particular, all service users should have equal access to care services and no group should be discriminated against within the care system. Care services try to ensure equality for diverse service users by:

- Developing equal opportunities polices that apply to service users and care practitioners.
- Adopting an equal opportunities approach when employing care workers so that the care organisation has staff who are representative of the local community.

UNIT 1

- Providing care staff with equalities and diversity training to raise awareness of these issues.

- Using translation and interpreter services to ensure that information is available in the languages used by members of the local community and in formats that are accessible to them.

- Encouraging care practitioners to use an anti-discriminatory practice approach that challenges any form of unfair discrimination and seeks to promote fair and equal treatment for all service users.

- Ensuring that all care practitioners understand and use care values in their work with service users.

Chapter checklist

The box below summarises the areas covered in chapter 1. Tick the areas that you feel you understand and would be confident about when writing your assignment for this unit. If there are any areas that you don't understand or are not confident about, you will need to return to them before you begin to plan or write your assignment.

Knowledge Check

1 What is a client group?
2 Why are care services planned for client groups?
3 What are the four types of need?
4 What can happen when a person has unmet needs?
5 What is a 'chronic' health problem?
6 Name two client groups that have non-adult members.
7 Why do babies need a lot of care?
8 Name two skills that babies develop before their first birthday.
9 Can you think of any other basic or specialist types of care a child might need to be healthy and happy?
10 How are the care needs of an adolescent different to those of an adult?
11 Which age range are 'adult' care services aimed at?
12 Why do some older people require help from care services?

Client groups	❏		
Types of need		Children	❏
Physical	❏	Adolescents	❏
Intellectual	❏	Adults (early/middle)	❏
Emotional	❏	Later adulthood	❏
Social	❏	Individuals with specific needs	❏
Permanent	❏		
Temporary	❏	**Assessing population health needs**	❏
Client group care needs		**Social policy goals**	❏
Infants	❏	**Ensuring equality for diverse groups**	❏

Assessment Guide

Your learning in this unit will be assessed through a controlled assessment task. This will be set by the OCR awarding body and marked by your tutor.

The assignment will require you to produce a report based on an investigation into health, social care or early years services in your local community. For example, you could choose to investigate services in the:

- health sector – such as a health centre or hospital (private or NHS).
- social care sector – such as a local authority day centre for older people or a private residential home.
- early years sector – such as a nursery, paediatric service or children's centre focusing on the needs of 0–8 year old children.

When you have decided which sector your investigation will be based on, you will need to think about the health, care and development needs of clients who use the service you are focusing on.

Chapter 1 has covered the range of needs that different client groups have as well as how care services are planned to meet these needs. Studying and referring back to chapter 1 should provide you with the background information needed to complete this part of the controlled assessment task.

Chapter 2

Obtaining services and barriers to health, social care and early years services

Key issue: How can people gain access to care services and what can prevent people from being able to use the services they need?

People who have care needs generally need to obtain appropriate services or forms of support to meet these needs. But how can people gain access to care services when they require them? Chapter 2 focuses on the different ways of obtaining health, social care and early years services. You will learn about different methods of referral, including:

- Self-referral
- Professional referral
- Third-party referral.

Chapter 2 also outlines the different barriers that can prevent people from accessing the care services they need. These include:

- Physical barriers, including stairs, lack of lifts and lack of adaptations
- Psychological barriers, including social stigma and fears about loss of independence
- Financial barriers, including means-testing, charges and fees
- Geographical barriers, including poor transport links and distance
- Cultural barriers, including different cultural beliefs about who should provide care
- Language barriers, including difficulties in using English
- Resource barriers, including staff shortages, postcode lottery, lack of funding and heavy local demand for services.

A number of different laws protect an individual's right to access the care services they require. You should know about the main provisions of these laws and the client groups they affect. By the end of the chapter you should have a good understanding of the different ways of gaining access to care services, rights to access and some of the barriers that service users can face in trying to obtain the care they need.

Access to care services

An individual may need to access health, social care or early years services because they are at a point in their life where they require:

- care

- practical or developmental support
- advice or guidance
- treatment or therapy.

People use care services when they have health problems, require social support or have unmet development needs. National and local care services are provided to meet the needs of the different client groups.

Local care organisations try to plan and develop services that meet local care needs. To do this, care organisations need to know who lives in their area and what kinds of health, social care and development needs they have. For example, to provide maternity services, local health care organisations need to know how many women of childbearing age live in their area and how many children are likely to be born in a year.

The referral system

Service users can access health, social care and early years services in a number of ways. All types of care services use a **referral** system to manage the process of providing their care services. There are three different forms of referral:

- **Self-referral** occurs when a person applies for a care service themselves. Making an appointment to see your GP (family doctor), phoning **NHS Direct** for advice and information or going to an opticians for an eye-test are all ways of making a self-referral to health care services.

- **Professional referral** occurs when a care worker puts someone who has come to see them in touch with another care professional. An example of a professional referral occurs where a GP refers a patient to a counsellor for therapy.

- **Third party referral** occurs when a person who is not a care professional applies for a care service on behalf of someone else. For example, if a woman telephoned the local social services department to request home care services for her mother, this would be a third-party referral.

Referral to health care services

Primary health care services are the front-line 'family doctor' or health centre services that are available in all local areas. People usually obtain primary health care services by self-referring or through a third party referral. Everyone has a right to register with a GP and obtain primary health care services. If someone does not have a GP, their local health authority is expected to find them one within two working days.

Secondary health care services are more specialist hospital-based services. Some secondary health care services, such as accident and emergency (A&E) and genito-urinary medicine (GUM) clinics, can be obtained by self-referral. However, most secondary health care services are obtained through a GP's professional referral. This applies to both in-patient care (the patient stays in hospital) and out-patient services (the patient lives at home and comes to a hospital clinic occasionally).

To make a professional referral, a GP will contact a hospital consultant requesting an appointment or an admission for their patient. There is usually a waiting list system. The GP will tell the

Over to you!

For each of the following examples identify:

- the client group involved
- the type of referral(s) involved in each situation.

1 Mrs Arkwright is 78 years old and is frail. Her home carer noticed that she has a bad cough. The home carer rang Mrs Arkwright's GP, asking him to make a home visit.

2 Rosie Abdi, a social worker, has received a phone call about a three-year-old child who is being left alone during the day. The call came from a neighbour of the child's parents. Rosie has asked the family's GP to accompany her on a visit to the child's home.

3 Mr Ghupta, aged 35, has a long-term mental health problem. He takes himself to his local health centre or to the local hospital's accident and emergency department when he feels unwell and needs treatment.

1 Ellisha, aged 29, is five months pregnant. Her GP has made an appointment for her to have an ultrasound scan at the local hospital.

2 Jim has had a bad back for three days. His wife has made him an appointment with a private sector osteopath.

hospital consultant how urgent the referral is. In cases of serious emergency the patient will be admitted to hospital on the same day.

Referral to social care services

Access to social care can be by self, third-party or professional referral. Referrals to statutory organisations, like social services departments, will usually be dealt with by a duty social worker. It's their job to find out what exactly the situation is and what is needed.

An assessment of need is carried out on everyone who is referred to social services. An individual will receive social care services if a need is identified and they also meet the **eligibility criteria** to obtain services. The person carrying out the assessment will usually be a care co-ordinator or social worker. If the person referred to social services is a child, a special assessment would be carried out to see if the child is 'at risk' and in need of child protection services. If this isn't the case, an assessment will be carried out to establish whether the child is 'in need'. Appropriate services and support will then be provided.

Voluntary and private sector social care services

A lot of domiciliary, day and residential care is available directly from voluntary and private agencies. A self or third party referral can be used to gain access to these services. Most agencies carry out their own assessments. The only eligibility criteria are that:

a   the person has the ability to pay, and

b   the agency have the staff to supply the service.

Referral to early years services

For the most part access is by parents applying direct to a private or voluntary sector service provider, such as a private nursery or childminder. A child will usually be offered a place if they are considered suitable, the parents are able to afford the fees and there is a space available. The availability of spaces is usually the main issue affecting access to voluntary sector early years services. Affording the cost of services is usually the main issue affecting access to private sector early years services.

Legislation and access to care services

The Human Rights Act 1998 (updated 2000) is an important equality law that gives people who live in the UK a range of basic human rights. The right to life and the right to freedom from unfair discrimination can be used to gain access to care services. The Act helps people who have disabilities or who feel they are being discriminated against to assert their rights to care. This now includes the right not to be evicted from a care home if the owners believe that the individual's care needs have become too expensive for them to meet.

The Mental Health Act 2007 applies in England and Wales. It enables care practitioners to return a mentally unwell person to hospital if they are not complying with treatment in the community. The Act also provides a range of protections for people who are unwilling to have certain treatments, such as electroconvulsive therapy, and ensures that a person can only be detained in hospital if appropriate treatment is available for them.

The **Children Act 1989** was introduced to protect children who are 'at risk' of harm from neglect abuse or other forms of injury. Under the Act, local authorities are required to ensure that children's welfare is protected and that services are provided to meet the needs of children identified as 'at risk'. The **Children Act 2004** amended and updated the 1989 Act in order to ensure that service providers worked in a more integrated, collaborative way and covers care for all children, including disabled and looked after children living in foster care and in local authority children's homes. The Act also gives local authorities flexibility in the way they meet children's needs.

The **Disability Discrimination Act 2005** gave disabled people protection from unfair discrimination for the first time. The Act requires providers of goods and services, facilities and premises to make 'reasonable adjustments' to allow disabled people to gain access. Access to the premises, facilities and services of health, social care and early years providers is covered by this law.

Nursing and Residential Care Homes Regulations 1984 (amended 2002) affects the setting up and running of care homes. The regulations ensure that people who live in care homes have the right to be protected from danger and harm. Residential homes are also inspected and must keep detailed information on residents and staff who work at the home. The 2002 amendments to these regulations set a range of legally enforceable minimum standards, such as room sizes, and access to bathroom facilities

Barriers to accessing services

There are occasions where people have a need for a care service, but they are unable to get it. Some of the most common 'barriers' to obtaining health care services are set out in figure 1.7.

Figure 1.7 Barriers to access.

Obtaining services and barriers to health, social care and early years services

Physical barriers

Physical barriers to healthcare services generally involve problems with the 'built environment'. That is, some people can't get into the places where care services are provided whilst others are unable to leave their own homes to go to the places where care is available. Physical 'barriers' within buildings, such as outside steps or narrow doorways, may prevent an individual from entering or leaving. For example, a wheelchair user would be unable to get care services at a health centre that only had steps up to the front door. A parent pushing a child in a pram would also struggle and may be put off from using this health centre. Other physical barriers, such as internal stairs, narrow corridors and doorways and a lack of lifts or adapted toilet facilities, sometimes occur within buildings and can prevent disabled and older people from using services.

Psychological barriers

Not everyone has a positive attitude towards managing their personal health and wellbeing or using care services. Some people avoid going to see their doctor because they are embarrassed, lack concern about their personal health or are frightened to find out what might be wrong with them. For example, the incidence of testicular cancer is higher than it should be partly because men are often reluctant to conduct self-examinations or seek help early if they find anything unusual. You may also know someone who is too scared to go to their doctor or dentist. Problems such as alcoholism, drug misuse, eating disorders, obesity, sexually transmitted diseases and mental health difficulties are sometimes seen as embarrassing or shameful. These negative feelings and beliefs may lead to people suffering from these problems not seeking help as early as they should.

Older people and disabled people with health and social care problems may also be frightened that they will lose their independence if they reveal a health problem or tell a care practitioner that they are finding it hard to cope at home. Similar psychological barriers can prevent people from accessing social services when they need them. In particular, some people feel that there is a stigma (or sense of shame) attached to using social service departments, so they will avoid doing so, even if they have a clear need. Accepting help from voluntary organisations or informal support groups can also be a problem for people who see these services as a form of 'charity'.

Financial barriers

Health, social care and early years services are sometimes only available to people if they pay some or all of the cost involved in providing them. For example, unless you fall into an exempt group you will have to pay **charges** for NHS prescriptions, eye tests and dental services. The financial cost of these and other services can act as a barrier to care for some people. For example, when free eye testing for people over 65 was withdrawn in 1989 there was a dramatic fall in the number of older people having eye tests. The British Medical Association claimed that this led to serious eye diseases and potential blindness going undetected. These free eye tests have now been reintroduced.

 Over to you!

How do you think these physical barriers could be overcome to allow wheelchair users to gain access to care services?

Over to you

Why do you think there is a stigma attached to receiving help or support from local authority social services departments? How might care practitioners and care organisations help people to overcome the stigma of accepting 'charity'?

The range of health, social care and early years services provided by companies and individual practitioners who make up the private sector are only available to people who can afford to pay the fees for these services. Some people pay into insurance schemes or are given health insurance by their employers to cover these costs. However, many of the people who would otherwise have to pay out of their own pocket are put off by the cost of private sector fees. As a result financial barriers do prevent some people from obtaining some forms of health, social care and early years services that they would otherwise benefit from.

In social care, adult services are **means-tested**. This means that service users have their income and savings assessed before services are provided. Those who fall below the financial limit imposed by social services are eligible for services. People who have more money or savings than the limit have to pay some or all of the cost of the service they want. As a result, some people can be put off applying for social care services by the costs involved or by having to disclose financial information.

The health, social care and early years services provided by the private sector are only available to those people who can afford to pay for them. Some people have health insurance or employers who pay for or subsidise medical and child care costs. Those who don't have the money or an employer to subsidise them are likely to see the costs of private sector services as a financial barrier to them gaining the services they require.

Geographical barriers

Health, social care or early years services may be difficult to obtain if they are located several miles away from where a potential service user lives. This is a particular problem for people who live in rural (country) areas. The problem is made even worse for people who rely on public transport. Sometimes people have to travel very long distances to obtain specialist health care treatment that isn't available in their own health district. As a result the geographical location of services may act as a barrier to people getting the care they need. Health facilities, social care provision and early years services that are difficult to get to are not likely to be used by people who do not have easy access to their own transport. Some of the ways in which health and social care care organisations try to overcome geographical barriers include:

- holding regular surgeries in more remote areas
- developing mobile clinics, toy libraries and visiting counselling services
- employing community-based staff to travel to areas that have poor access to services
- using information and communications technology, including the Internet, email and webcams, to put care workers and service users in touch with each other.

Cultural and language barriers

The UK is a multicultural country in which people, particularly recent immigrants, speak a variety of languages. In areas where there are large numbers of people from minority ethnic communities, health and social care authorities try to ensure that

Investigate ...

How much are prescriptions and eye test charges for adults now? Find out how much adults have to pay for these services and who is eligible for free or reduced cost prescriptions and eye-tests.

Over to you!

If a friend told you that they were having problems with their teeth but was reluctant to go to see a dentist because 'it costs too much', what could you do or say to enable them to overcome the financial barrier that is preventing them from getting the care they need?

language barriers are overcome by providing multi-lingual signs, interpreters and bilingual staff. However, health and care information is not always available in the languages that some people speak or in the formats needed by people who have eyesight or hearing problems. People who are unable to speak or have limited understanding of English, or who have hearing or visual impairments can therefore struggle to find care that meets their cultural, language and communication needs. People will not use care services where they are unable to make themselves understood or which lack sensitivity to their cultural needs. Ways of overcoming these barriers include:

- cultural awareness training for care workers
- employing care workers with diverse cultural backgrounds that reflect those of the service user population
- using multi-lingual interpreter and advocacy services
- producing information in different languages and different formats to make them accessible to all service users.

Resource barriers

The resources that organisations require before they can provide care services include:

- skilled staff
- buildings (including in-patient beds) and equipment
- money to pay for running costs and staff wages.

Service users sometimes find that care organisations have staff shortages or don't have enough money to provide the care services that they need when they need it. As a result, lack of human or financial resources can mean service users have to go on a waiting list for treatment. The area where a service user lives can also affect their ability to access care services. If a person lives in an area that has staffing shortages or a lack of funding for care services, they may have to wait longer or may even find that a particular service isn't available to them. By contrast, another person living nearby but in a different health authority area may get the treatment or services they require. This situation is known as the **postcode lottery**.

As the main providers of social care services, local authorities have to manage their resources carefully. When their budget is cut or restricted, a local authority may increase the eligibility criteria for services. For example, in the past many local authorities would help someone who was quite independent but who needed a home help to do some cleaning and shopping for them. Nowadays, these services are not available in many areas and someone must require personal care on a daily basis before they became eligible for a home help.

In many areas of the UK, there is a shortage of early years nursery education and day nursery places. Although there is no charge for state-run services in most cases, few people are eligible for them. As a result there is often great local demand for voluntary and private sector places. The limited number of places combined with the high demand for them is another example of a resource barrier that may prevent people from accessing the services they require.

Knowledge Check

1 What kind of referral is used most often to obtain primary health care services?

2 Who does a GP need to contact to make a professional referral for specialist hospital services?

3 Explain how language barriers can prevent some people from gaining the care services they need.

4 How do you think physical barriers could be overcome to allow wheelchair users to gain access to care services?

5 Why do you think there is a stigma attached to receiving help or support local authority social services departments?

6 What is a means-test?

7 Which type of care worker usually deals with a referral to a social services department?

8 Explain what has to happen before an adult can receive social care services from the local authority.

9 Describe two ways in which a person living in a rural area may face geographical barriers when they require health care services.

Chapter checklist

The box below provides a summary of the areas covered in chapter 2. Tick the areas that you feel you understand and would be confident about when writing your assignment. If there are any areas that you don't understand or are not confident about, you will need to return to them before you begin planning or writing your assignment.

Methods of referral
Self-referral ❑
Professional referral ❑
Third-party referral ❑

Legislation
Human Rights Act 1998 ❑
Mental Health Act 2007 ❑
Children Act 1998 and 2004 ❑
Disability Discrimination Act 2005 ❑
Nursing and Residential Care
   Homes Regulations 1984 ❑

Barriers to accessing services
Physical barriers ❑
Psychological barriers ❑
Financial barriers ❑
Geographical barriers ❑
Cultural / language barriers ❑
Resource barriers ❑

Assessment Guide

Your learning in this unit will be assessed through a controlled assessment task. This will be set by the OCR awarding body and marked by your tutor.

The assignment will require you to produce a report based on an investigation into health, social care or early years services in your local community. For example, you could choose to investigate services in the:

● health sector – such as a health centre or hospital (private or NHS)

● social care sector – such as a local authority day centre for older people or a private residential home

● early years sector – such as a nursery, paediatric service or children's centre focusing on the needs of 0–8 year old children.

As part of your investigation you will need to find out about:

● the different ways in which people can gain access to the services you are focusing on

● possible barriers to access

● what the care organisation has done to remove barriers to access.

Your report will also need to show that you understand the possible effects of barriers on clients and the impact that legislation has had on promoting access to the services you are investigating.

Chapter 2 has covered methods of obtaining care services, barriers to access and legislation that is designed to promote access to care services. Studying and referring back to chapter 2 should provide you with the background information needed to complete this part of the controlled assessment task.

Chapter 3

The provision of health, social care and early years services

Key issue: What types of care services are povided to meet client group needs

A range of care services are available to meet the health, social care and development needs of people in each of the major client groups. Chapter 3 will describe the types of services that are available and the way they are organised. You will learn about different types of care service providers, including:

- Statutory services (NHS Trusts and Local Authorities)
- Private services (companies and self-employed practitioners)
- Third sector services (charities, local support groups and not-for-profit organisations)
- Informal services (family, friends and neighbours).

Care service providers often work together in order to meet the complex care needs of some service users. Chapter 3 will explain how partnerships and multi-agency working are used to achieve this. By the end of the unit you should have a good understanding of the range of health, social care and early years services that are provided in the United Kingdom.

How are care services organised?

You probably know about a number of health, social care and early years services in your local area. There may be a hospital, health centre, family doctor service, nursery or residential home near to where you live, for example. You or members of your family may have used some of these services recently. Local care services like those mentioned are provided by a range of different organisations and self-employed care workers. One way of understanding how care services are provided is to look at how they are organised into statutory, private, informal and third sector care providers.

The statutory care sector

The government is responsible for controlling and running the part of the care system known as the **statutory sector**. This part of the care system includes organisations such as the **National Health Service** (NHS) and **Local Authorities** (local councils). These organisations provide a lot of health, social care and early years services throughout the United Kingdom. By law the government has to provide some types of care services. The laws that set out

Over to you!

Make a list of all the health and social care services you have received. Divide your list into health, social care and early years services.

Emergency services are provided by the statutory sector.

these duties are also called 'statutes' - this is where 'statutory' comes from.

The private sector

The **private sector** is made up of care businesses, such as private hospitals, high street pharmacists and nurseries, and self-employed care practitioners, such as childminders, counsellors and osteopaths, for example. Private sector organisations and self-employed practitioners usually charge people a fee for the health, social care or early years services that they provide. Private sector care providers work to make a profit as well as to meet service users care needs.

In the UK, the private sector offers fewer services and has fewer organisations and service users than either the statutory or voluntary sectors. Private sector organisations focus more on health and early years services than on social care. Many of the services that are provided in the private sector cannot easily be obtained in the statutory system and are specialist, non-emergency services. Day care nurseries and osteopathy services are examples.

The third sector

The care system in the United Kingdom includes a large number of charities, local support groups and not-for-profit organisations. These are known as the third sector or sometimes as the independent sector. The third sector is made up of organisations that provide their care services because they see a need for them. Third sector care organisations are independent of government. They don't have a legal (or 'statutory') duty to provide care service but do it voluntarily. The sector is also called 'voluntary' because many of the organisations have workers who are unpaid volunteers. *MENCAP* is an example of a third sector organisation that recruits volunteers to work with people who have learning disabilities. Third sector organisations provide a large range of social care and early years services in the UK that are non-profit making as well as independent from government.

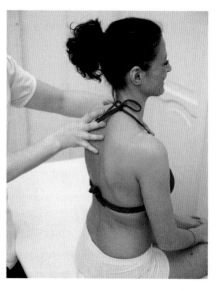

Osteopaths work in the private sector.

Origins of the third sector

The third sector began in the nineteenth century when there were very few care services for ordinary people. At the time most care services had to be paid for and were too expensive for all but the rich. Charities and voluntary organisations grew out of the campaigns and donations of a few rich **philanthropists**. These were wealthy individuals, like Joseph Rowntree, who wanted to help their local communities and reduce the poverty and suffering they saw around them.

The third sector now consists of large, national organisations, like MENCAP, Help the Aged and National Society for the Prevention of Cruelty to Children (NSPCC), and a large number of much smaller groups that work for a cause in their local area. An example would be a support group for single parents or a playgroup that aims to meet the developmental needs of local toddlers.

Joseph Rowntree, 1836–1925.

Most playgroups are run by unpaid volunteers.

Most third sector organisations are **registered charities**. This means that they obtain money for their services through donations and fund-raising. Some third sector organisations also receive government grants and small payments from service users, but they put this income back into running their services and don't try to make a profit. Third sector organisations often recruit unpaid volunteers who provide their time and skills for free. However, larger not-for-profit and voluntary organisations also employ and pay some people to work as care practitioners, managers and administrative staff.

The informal sector

The **informal sector** consists of the very large number of unpaid people who look after members of their own family, their friends or their neighbours who have care needs. Because these people are not trained, employed or paid to provide care, they are known as informal carers. Informal carers provide a lot of care for infants and children, older people and people with disabilities.

Care providers in each of the four sectors make an important contribution to the overall delivery of care services in the UK. A care provider will usually focus on providing either health care, social care or early years services. However, there are overlaps between these types of care service and in practice different care organisations and self-employed practitioners often work together to provide a range of care services for clients who have complex needs.

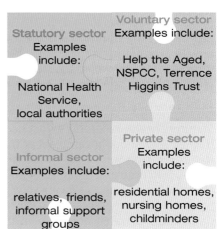

Figure 1.8 The four care sectors.

Case study

Sophie is 17 years of age and has Down's syndrome. Sophie's condition has affected her health and personal development throughout her life and will mean that she has lifelong care and support needs. Sophie currently receives care and support from a range of care practitioners who work together to meet her complex needs. Dr Hill is Sophie's GP. He works at a local health centre that is funded and run by the National Health Service (NHS). Alison Rasheed is a specialist learning disability social worker, employed by the local authority, who organises and monitors the special education and social care services that Sophie uses. Sophie attends the Stepping Stones day centre three days each week where she takes part in a range of education and leisure activities. The centre was established and is still managed MENCAP. Sophie's parents pay for her to attend a riding school that provides specialist classes for people with learning disabilities on Thursdays. Sophie is still very reliant on her parents for day-to-day care and support. They provide practical and emotional support in a variety of ways to help Sophie to develop her daily living skills.

- Which of the care practitioners working with Sophie are employed by the statutory sector?
- Identify the voluntary sector care service that Sophie uses.
- Which of the services mentioned is part of the private sector?
- What type of care do Sophie's parents provide for her?

Knowledge Check

1 Name the four main care sectors.

2 Which care sector is funded and run by the government?

3 What is distinctive about the third sector?

4 Explain why voluntary organisations developed in the late nineteenth century.

5 Do third sector organisations only employ volunteers?

6 How do private sector organisations differ from third sector organisations?

7 Describe two examples of private sector care services.

8 Who provides care in the informal sector?

Providers of health care services

Most health care services in the United Kingdom are now provided by the **statutory sector**. Private sector organisations and private practitioners also provide a significant range of health cares services. The voluntary and informal sectors provide very few health care services.

Statutory health care services

Statutory health care services first became available in 1948. This is when the Labour government at the time founded the National Health Service (NHS). The NHS was launched to tackle widespread problems of ill-health and to provide free services for all in the UK. Before this health services were not available to all people. Some voluntary services existed but most people had to pay a doctor privately or join an insurance scheme if they wanted health care services. This meant that most people didn't receive good health care because they couldn't afford to pay.

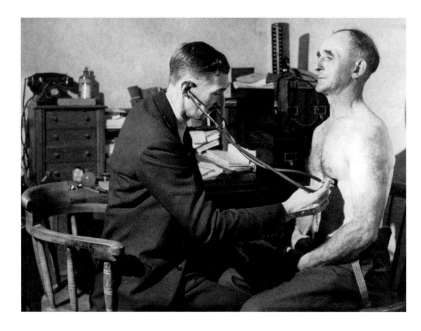

The early years of NHS care.

National and local structures

The government of the UK is made up of politicians who are members of the political party that has won the last general election. Making sure that health care services are provided is one of the main tasks that every government has. Government politicians and civil servants make decisions about how statutory health care services should be organised and paid for throughout the country. The politician who has overall responsibility for this is called the **Secretary of State for Health**. England, Wales, Scotland and Northern Ireland each have different Secretaries of State for Health. They are each responsible for planning and making decisions about NHS services in their country (see figure 1.9 – national and local health care structures in the UK).

The government is the main provider of the money for statutory health care services. This government money (also called 'funding') is used to employ thousands of people in a wide

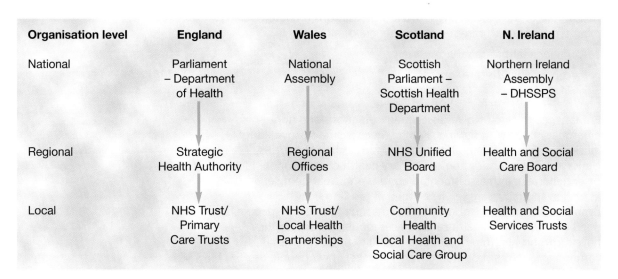

Organisation level	England	Wales	Scotland	N. Ireland
National	Parliament – Department of Health	National Assembly	Scottish Parliament – Scottish Health Department	Northern Ireland Assembly – DHSSPS
Regional	Strategic Health Authority	Regional Offices	NHS Unified Board	Health and Social Care Board
Local	NHS Trust/ Primary Care Trusts	NHS Trust/ Local Health Partnerships	Community Health Local Health and Social Care Group	Health and Social Services Trusts

Figure 1.9 National and local health care structures in the UK.

variety of care jobs, buy equipment and keep the statutory health care system running. The government funds most hospitals, GP practices and community health services in the United Kingdom. The actual planning and monitoring of local statutory health care services is carried out by regional bodies. These are called Strategic Health Authorities in England and Wales, Local Health Boards in Scotland and Unified Health and Social Services Boards in Northern Ireland (see figure 1.9).

Types of NHS provider

NHS health centres provide many care services for the local community.

Most of us will use statutory health care services at some point in our lives. We might need emergency hospital care or more likely we will have a less severe illness and go to our GP (family doctor) for help. The statutory health care services that we use will be provided by an NHS Trust organisation. Every area of the UK has an NHS Trust that takes responsibility for providing statutory health care in their locality. **NHS Trust** organisations provide two main types of health care service for people of all ages:

- primary health care services
- secondary health care services.

Primary health care services

Primary health care involves assessment, diagnosis and non-emergency treatment services. Primary health care is provided for all client groups in community settings, such as health centres, clinics and service user's homes. Primary health care providers offer general health assessment, diagnosis and treatment services as well as specialist care services aimed at tackling health problems like smoking, obesity and stress reduction. Some people need to use primary health care services regularly because they have a **chronic** health problem or a disability that requires continuing treatment or monitoring. However, most people use primary health care services on an occasional basis for minor illnesses.

Figure 1.10 Examples of primary health care services.

Primary care services are usually provided by a **primary health care team** (PHCT). A GP (or family doctor) is often the leader or co-ordinator of the team. Other team members include practice nurses, district nurses, community psychiatric nurses and health visitors. Team members meet regularly to discuss patients and co-ordinate their work with them.

Secondary health care services

The specialist types of care and treatment that are provided in a hospital or a specialist clinic are known as **secondary care**. Hospital care services focus on very specific, and often complex, health problems rather than on general, everyday problems. For example, large general hospitals usually have an accident and emergency (A&E) department that deals with life-threatening as well as minor injuries, a theatre or surgical department that deals with operations and a maternity unit that deals with childbirth. All of these departments provide specialised health care services.

As well as providing complex care and treatment services, hospitals often have specialist services such as laboratories and radiography (x-ray) departments that are used to diagnose (identify) health problems that GPs and other primary care workers are unable to identify because they don't have the specialist facilities or knowledge.

Most secondary health care is provided by **NHS Trust hospitals**. These are government-funded organisations that have a legal responsibility to provide health care services locally. There are a number of different kinds of hospital:

- District General Hospitals provide a wide range of secondary health care services for the whole population of an area. For example, they provide services for seriously ill adults and children who need an operation or treatment that involves contact with specially trained doctors and nurses.

- Local community hospitals usually provide a more limited range of treatments for a smaller number of people in an area. They often have facilities for people to be seen as out-patients and have far fewer beds than district general hospitals.

Over to you!

Teenagers often feel that their health needs should be taken more seriously. Suggest two services that you think primary health care workers should offer to teenagers at your local health centre. Briefly explain your reasons.

Over to you!

Make a list of the types of events or situations that can result in people needing urgent care or treatment from secondary health care services.

- National Teaching Hospitals and Specialist Units provide highly specialist medical, surgical and psychiatric treatment for patients who come from all over the country. Their expertise is available to both in-patients and out-patients. Two examples of this kind of hospital are Great Ormond Street Hospital for Sick Children and the Royal Homeopathic Hospital in central London.

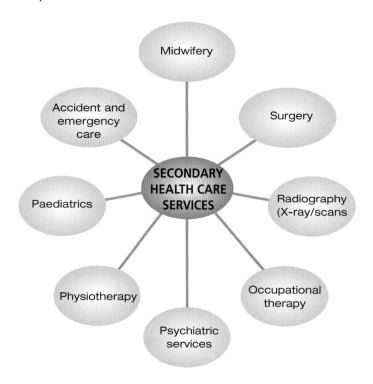

Figure 1.11 Examples of secondary health care services.

Investigate ...

Using information available through the Internet, leaflets or booklets produced by your local NHS Trust, investigate the services offered by your nearest NHS Trust hospital. What kinds of specialist care and treatment are provided for children? Does the hospital specialise in any other kinds of health care service? Summarise your findings in either a poster or a leaflet.

Case study

Ashok is nine years old. Last Christmas Ashok was admitted to a children's hospital when he fell over on his new rollerblades. Ashok broke his ankle and banged his head hard against the pavement. He stayed in the children's hospital for three days whilst tests were done and his ankle was put in plaster. Ashok felt frightened and lonely in hospital and was glad to go home after his short stay.

- What care needs did Ashok have a result of his accident?

- What effect did being in hospital have on Ashok's emotional wellbeing?

- List as many childhood illnesses as you can think of and try to identify the kinds of care or treatment that are provided to deal with them.

Integrated children's services

Integrated children's services are a new feature of statutory services that have been developed throughout the UK since the Children Act (2004) was passed. This piece of legislation is the result of a government policy called *Every Child Matters*. The *Every Child Matters* policy put forward the idea of linking together (integrating) all of the services that children come into contact with. The importance of integrating children's services became very clear following the death of Victoria Climbie, an 8-year-old girl, in 2000. Victoria died as a result of severe physical abuse that was caused by her aunt and her aunt's boyfriend who were supposed to be caring for her. Victoria's death occurred despite the fact that care professionals from several different care organizations had come into contact with her. The fact that the different care professionals who had concerns about Victoria didn't communicate with each other or take responsibility for stopping what was happening occurred because of a lack of **multi-agency** and **partnership working**.

Integrated children's services now offer joined-up health, social care and education services to vulnerable children and their families through children's centres, extended schools, youth clubs and health care clinics. A local integrated children's service will typically:

- be the first point of contact for all enquiries from children, families and professionals
- receive and make referrals for services for children
- identify, refer and monitor vulnerable children.

The care practitioners who are employed by an integrated children's service:

- assess service user's needs
- give information and advice
- receive and make referrals for emergency and preventive services
- complete and manage information about a child and their family.

Integrating children's services is seen as a way of protecting vulnerable children and of improving the opportunities and life experiences of the poorest and most disadvantaged children. Examples of integrated children's services include:

- **Sure Start Children's Centres** (0–5 years) that offer child care, health and family welfare services
- **Extended schools** (primary and secondary) that offer out-of-hours activities, parenting support, child care, community health services, adult learning and recreational activities
- **Multi-agency disability** teams that provide a single point of referral, assessment and treatment for children and young people with physical, learning or sensory disabilities.

Integrated children's services are a new form of statutory care provision that combines health, social care and early years provision in order to target the needs of vulnerable children and families. As a result these services break down the traditional organisational barriers between health, social care and early years services.

Private health care services

Private sector health care organisations include a number of large care businesses, such as *BUPA* and *Nuffield Hospitals*. These organisations provide complex health care services, including surgery, in their own private hospitals. It is also possible to pay for care as a private patient in a ward or unit of some NHS hospitals. The private sector also includes a wide range of self-employed private practitioners who offer specialist forms of

Investigate ...

Identify the location of your nearest Sure Start Children's Centre. Find out:

- What services are available at the centre
- Who the services are provided for
- Which health, social care and early years professionals work at the centre
- What the aims and objectives of the centre are
- What the benefits of using the centre are to service users.

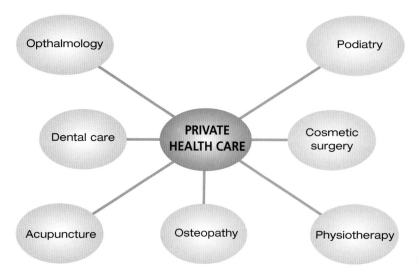

Figure 1.12 Examples of private health care services.

health care through a private practice. Many dentists, physiotherapists and counsellors work as private practitioners, for example. Sometimes a private practitioner offers clients an alternative service to those freely available from local statutory or voluntary sector organisations. In other circumstances they offer specialist services that are not available in the statutory or voluntary sector. An example might be osteopathy or acupuncture. Private sector health care clients pay for their care through health insurance or pay the costs directly from their own finances.

Outsourcing of indirect care services

Until the mid-1980s, statutory health and social care organisations like the NHS and local authorities were the direct employers of all of their staff. This meant that organisational services like cleaning, catering and security were provided from within the care organisation. However, towards the end of the 1980s financial pressures and a new attitude in government led to care organisations sub-contracting these services to specialist private sector organisations. In practice this meant, for example, that a private sector catering firm was contracted to provide all of the catering services for a care organisation. Similarly, indirect care services, like cleaning and laundry services were gradually sub-contracted, or outsourced, from private companies who competed to obtain these contracts. The purpose of outsourcing was to reduce costs and improve efficiency. Statutory sector care organisations throughout the United Kingdom now outsource many of the indirect care services that they require. As well as catering and cleaning, these services increasingly include large parts of the secretarial, administrative and financial functions as well as security, maintenance and non-emergency transport services.

Informal health care provision

Relatives, friends and neighbours may provide straightforward, usually non-technical health care services to an individual. For example, informal carers often give non-prescription medicines, like cough mixture or paracetamol, for minor ailments and treat small cuts and bruises without going to a doctor or other health care worker. Where a person has a chronic (long-term) health condition, the care team looking after them may instruct or train

Investigate ...

Use the Internet, your local library or other sources of information to identify five examples of private practitioners who offer different types of care service. Produce a leaflet containing a rough map of the area that shows where the practitioners are located and briefly describes the services each offers.

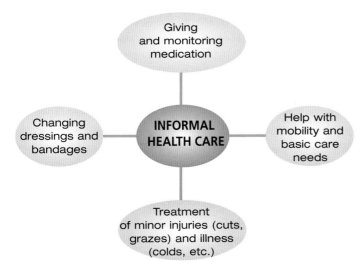

Figure 1.13 Examples of informal health care.

a relative to give more complex health care. For example, giving insulin injections to a diabetic relative or changing the dressing on a healing wound are examples of this. Informal health care provision is generally limited to the kinds of everyday care that people can provide without specialist training.

Knowledge Check

1 Name the two types of health care service provided by statutory health care organisations

2 When did statutory health care services become freely available in the UK?

3 What kinds of events or situations can result in adults needing urgent care or treatment from secondary health care services?

4 What is a primary health care team?

5 What are integrated children's services?

6 Identify three health promotion or prevention services primary health workers offer to clients.

7 Give two examples of specialist care services that are available in the private health care sector.

8 Why do you think some people choose to pay for health care services?

9 Describe two examples of informal health care provision.

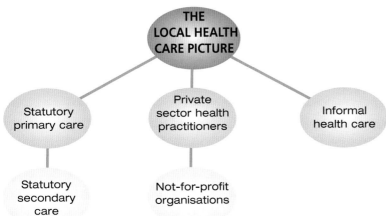

Figure 1.14 The local health care picture.

UNIT 1

Providers of social care services

Social care is a general term used to describe non-medical support and social care services for people who have personal, emotional or financial problems. Service users require social care because they are unable to meet their personal and social needs independently.

National and local social care structures

The **Secretary of State for Health** is the government minister (a politician) who has overall responsibility for making sure that statutory social care services are provided. The **Department of Health**, which includes the **Social Services Inspectorate** (SSI), is the part of government that plans and manages statutory social care services. The government provides the funding for statutory social care services. The SSI also provide guidance to local authorities about social care and monitor and inspect the performance of social services departments.

Level	England	Wales	Scotland	N. Ireland
National (planners and purchasers)	UK Parliament	Welsh Assembly	Scottish Government	Northern Ireland Assembly
	Department of Children, Schools and Families	Health and Social Services Department	Scottish Government Health Directorates	Department of Health, Social Services and Public Safety
				Health and Social Services Boards
Local (providers)	• Local authorities • Voluntary agencies • Private agencies	• Unitary authorities (social services departments) • Voluntary agencies • Private agencies	• Local authorities • Voluntary agencies • Private agencies	• Health and Social Care Trusts • Private agencies • Voluntary agencies

Figure 1.15 National and local social care structures.

Statutory social care services

Local Authorities (local councils) have a long history of providing statutory social care services in local areas throughout the United Kingdom. Local authorities provide social care, housing and education services for people of all ages in their local area.

The **social services departments** of local authorities (local councils) have responsibility for statutory social care services in the UK. The purchasing section of a social services department is involved in buying care services for adult clients whose social care needs have been assessed. The services that are purchased are known as a care package. The provider section of a social services department delivers some of the care services local people need,

Figure 1.16 Examples of statutory social care services.

especially social work services. However, the purchasing section can also pay other voluntary and private sector organisations to provide the care services that their clients need. Even though they are not providing these services directly, this allows them to fulfil their legal responsibilities to provide certain types of care.

Local authorities also provide statutory social care services for children. The Children Act 1989 makes social services departments legally responsible for the welfare of children in need. For example, social services departments must provide child protection services, services for children under five and accommodation for children who are unable to live with their families.

Integrated children's services

Integrated children's services are a source of social care support for vulnerable children and their families. These services are provided through Sure Start Children's Centres, extended schools and specialist children and families teams employed by local authority social services departments.

Investigate ...

Foster care is a form of social care that is provided for children and adolescents. Use the Internet to find out more about what foster care involves. You could start with the Fostering Network site (www.fostering-network.org.uk) and the National Foster Care Association (www.nfca.org.uk).

Over to you!

Find out about services that are provided for children by your local authority. They may provide leaflets or brochure describing the services they offer or have a site on the Internet that you can look at.

Case study

When Jenny was 10 years old, her mum, a lone parent, was admitted to hospital with a serious illness. Jenny, her mum and a social worker decided together that the best option was for Jenny to live with foster carers. Jenny lived with the Wilson family for three months until she returned to live at home with her mum. Jenny said she missed her mum a lot at first and felt like she didn't fit in, but she grew to like the Wilsons. She still receives a birthday card from them.

● Why did Jenny need care at this point in her life?

● What kinds of care and support do you think a foster carer would provide for a child like Jenny?

● When Jenny was missing her Mum, which of her needs were unmet?

Voluntary social care services

There are a large number of voluntary organisations in the United Kingdom. The voluntary sector has its roots in the Victorian era and originated as a way of tackling major social problems such as poverty, unemployment and poor housing. Voluntary social care services are available for all client groups in the United Kingdom. However, unlike statutory social care services, they are not always available in every part of the country. This is because voluntary organisations differ considerably in the size and scope of their work. Some organisations, like the NSPCC or MIND, offer social care services to children and people with mental health problems throughout the country. Other organisations are smaller, focus on specific local issues and have very small budgets. However, when taken as a whole, the voluntary social care sector is a major provider of social care services in the United Kingdom. The services that are provided by organisations in this sector often fill the gaps left by the statutory sector and play a vital part in supporting vulnerable members of all client groups.

 Investigate ...

Find out about the voluntary organisations that provide social care services for people in your local area. Try to identify at least one organisation that works on behalf of children, disabled people and older people. Add a brief summary of your findings to those of your class colleagues to make a directory of services provided by local voluntary organisations.

Figure 1.17 Examples of voluntary social care services.

Private social care services

Compared to the statutory and voluntary sector, the private social care sector is small. There are relatively few social care organisations in the private sector. Those that do exist tend to provide specialised residential care services for older people

Figure 1.18 Examples of private social care services.

Health, Social Care and Early Years Provision

or for disabled people or **domiciliary** (home care) services. People who use private sector social care services either have to pay for the cost of the services themselves or, if they meet the **eligibility criteria**, they may have their fees paid by their local authority social services department.

Informal social care provision

Many people who need social care and support are not catered for by the statutory or voluntary sectors and cannot afford to buy services from the private sector. These people tend to receive informal social care and support from relatives, friends and neighbours. Basic services such as housing, financial assistance and emotional support are often provided this way. In fact, most of the social care provided for sick and vulnerable people in the United Kingdom is delivered in this way. Children, older people and those with long-term care needs receive most informal care services. It's very common for people to provide care for their elderly relatives and children at home.

Informal social care is also provided through support groups in some areas of the United Kingdom. The many thousands of local informal support groups that exist are usually run by informal carers and people who have special health and social care needs themselves. The purpose of informal support groups is to provide practical and emotional support to informal carers and the people they care for. An informal support group might consist, for example, of neighbours who share child care arrangements, people in a local area who all look after a relative alone at home, or a group of people who have got together to raise money to help an individual to finance his or her social care needs.

Over to you!

Find out about the range of private social care services available to people in your local area. Try to identify at least one service each for children, adults and older people.

Figure 1.19 Examples of informal social care provision.

Over to you!

Do you provide informal care for anyone at present? How might this change later in your life?

Health, Social Care and Early Years Provision

Case study

Mrs Bell is 79 years old and lives alone. She has some memory impairment and forgets what time of the day it is, whether she has eaten, and also the names of all but her closest relatives and her neighbour, Mrs Scott. Mrs Bell is unable to walk far due to her arthritis, very rarely goes out alone, and feels frightened of using her bath as she has difficulty getting in and out.

- What forms of informal care would Mrs Bell benefit from?
- Who might be able to provide each form of informal care for Mrs Bell?
- If you were a relative or neighbour of Mrs Bell's, how would you feel about giving up some of your time to offer Mrs Bell informal care and support?

Knowledge Check

1 Identify two examples of social care services.
2 Give two reasons why some people may need social care services.
3 Which government department is responsible for planning statutory social care services?
4 Who are the main providers of statutory social care services?
5 What part does the voluntary sector play in providing social care services in the UK?
6 Give an example of a social care service available in the private sector.
7 Explain what domiciliary care involves.
8 What is an informal support group?

Over to you!

What kinds of informal support groups exist in your local area? Find out by looking for posters and leaflets in places like the local library, sports centre, church halls, mosques or synagogues and in local day centres.

Providers of early years services

Early years organisations and self-employed practitioners like childminders provide education and child care services for children under the age of eight. The aim of these services is to help young children to meet their developmental needs. Play activities that help children to learn and develop their physical, intellectual, emotional and social skills are a common part of all early years services.

There are very few statutory child care services in the UK. This is because child care in the UK is generally seen as the responsibility of parents and other relatives. However, the government and local authority organisations are involved in providing some early years services and there is a lot of voluntary and private sector provision for young children throughout the UK.

Statutory early years services

Local authorities are responsible for purchasing (buying) early years care for children in need in their area. Early years care and education services are usually provided by the social services and education departments of a local authority. However, statutory early years services are only provided for families where a child is 'at risk' or

UK PARLIAMENT

Department of Children, Schools and Families

Private sector services

Local authority children's services

Voluntary sector services

Figure 1.20 Early years structure.

Figure 1.21 Statutory sector early years services.

where family pressures and problems can be reduced by child care support. Children with disabilities and children who have health or developmental problems are also eligible for these statutory services. Examples of early years services for children include playgroups, nurseries, childminders and family centres. Children and families who use these services must have unmet care and development needs that have been identified by a social worker or other early years professional.

The main legal duties that local authorities have for early years services are contained in the Children Acts 1989 and 2004. These laws, for example, make it a requirement that all childminders, and the premises in which they care for children, must be assessed by and registered with the social services department of their local authority.

Integrated Children's Services

Integrated children's services, particularly Sure Start Children's Centres are the main source of statutory early years provision for children and families. Sure Start nurseries offer high quality child care and early learning support for young children who, for a variety of reasons, have fallen behind other children in their language and learning development.

Voluntary early years services

The voluntary early years sector consists of some large national organisations, such as MENCAP, and a larger number of small, local voluntary groups who provide playgroups, nurseries and other support groups for both children under the age of 8 and their parents. The voluntary early years sector is a major provider of early years services. In a very similar way to the voluntary social care sector, these services fill the gaps in statutory and private sector services. Many services and informal support groups are developed and run by parents with children who are not eligible for statutory services and cannot afford or don't wish to pay for private early years care.

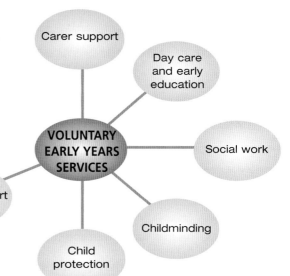

Figure 1.22 Voluntary sector early years services.

Private early years services

Early years services available from the private sector include nursery schools, playgroups, crèches and childminding services. These organisations provide child care and early education services to young children who have needs that are not met by the limited range of statutory sector services. As a child's parents must be able to afford to pay the fees charged, private sector child care services are not available to everyone who might need or benefit from them.

Some child carers also work in their own homes on a self-employed basis. Registered childminders are the largest group of self-employed carers working in this way. Like all self-employed carers, they charge the people who use their services a fee for their time and expertise.

Informal early years provision

The majority of child care is provided by parents and other relatives at home. Caring for children is widely seen as a family responsibility in the UK. Parents who provide informal early years care for their children may also use statutory, voluntary or private services as well to supplement their own child care with additional or specialist input from trained child care and early learning practitioners.

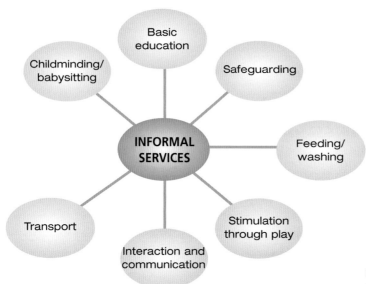

Figure 1.23 Informal early years services.

Partnership and multi-agency working

So far we've looked at how the care system in the UK is organised into four different sectors. We've also considered the types of care services that are provided by local care organisations. This may have given you the impression that practitioners with health, social care or early years backgrounds work separately from each other. You might also be forgiven for thinking that care practitioners work within a particular care sector (statutory, private or voluntary, for example). Both of these situations may have been true in the past. However, there is an increasing emphasis within the health, social care and early years field on care practitioners and care organisations working in multi-disciplinary, multi-agency teams that break down the traditional health, social care and early years boundaries.

As a result of government social policies, health authorities, NHS Trusts and local authority social services departments are now working together to 'modernise' local care services. In some areas this involves developing new Health and Social Care Trust organisations.

It is likely that care practitioners with different professional backgrounds and care organisations from different care sectors are working together to provide services for clients in your local area. Partnership and multi-agency working can be organised in different ways. The three main ways of doing this are:

- multi-agency panels in which practitioners employed by a variety of different care organisations meet regularly as a panel or network to discuss service users with complex needs who would benefit from multi-agency input. Child protection panels are an example of this type of multi-agency service.

- multi-agency teams in which a group of care practitioners with different backgrounds are recruited to form a team that provides assessment, intervention and monitoring for groups of service users with specific needs. Multi-agency disability teams and virtual wards are an example of this type of multi-agency service.

- integrated services in which a range of separate services merge together and work in a collaborative way to meet the broad but closely related needs of a particular client group. Sure Start children's centres and extended schools are an example of this kind of integrated multi-agency service.

The aims of **partnership** and **multi-agency working** are to:

- improve access to services not previously available to service users

- make access to services and care practitioner expertise easier and quicker

- encourage early identification of and intervention in health, social care and developmental problems

- reduce replication of services

- provide better links between service providers

- provide better quality services

- reduce the costs of providing care

- improve the efficiency and effectiveness of local care services.

Knowledge Check

1 Which age group are early years services targeted at?

2 dentify two examples of statutory early years services.

3 Explain why there are relatively few statutory child care services in the United Kingdom.

4 Identify two types of services that voluntary early years organisations provide.

5 Why are private early years services not available to everyone who could benefit from them?

6 Which care sector does a self-employed childminder belong to?

7 Who provides early years care in the informal sector?

8 What does multi-agency working refer to?

9 Describe the main benefits of multi-agency working.

Chapter checklist

The box below summarises the areas covered in chapter 3. Tick the areas that you feel you understand and would be confident about when writing your assignment for this unit. If there are any areas that you don't understand or are not confident about, you will need to return to them before you begin planning or writing your assignment.

Types of service provider
  Statutory providers ❏
  Private providers ❏
  Voluntary providers ❏
  Informal carers ❏

The development of statutory, voluntary, private and informal service provision ❏

Organisation of health care services
  Statutory health care services
  – primary health care ❏
  – secondary health care ❏
  – integrated children's services ❏
  Private health care services ❏
  Informal health care provision ❏

The range of health care services provided for each service user group ❏

Organisation of social care services
  Statutory social care services ❏
  Voluntary social care services ❏
  Private social care services ❏
  Informal social care provision ❏

The range of social care services provided for each service user group ❏

Organisation of early years services
  Statutory early years services ❏
  Voluntary early years services ❏
  Private early years services ❏
  Informal early years provision ❏

The range of early years services provided for children ❏

Organisation of early years services
  Statutory early years services ❏
  Voluntary early years services ❏
  Private early years services ❏
  Informal early years provision ❏

The range of early years services provided for children ❏

Assessment Guide

Your learning in this unit will be assessed through a controlled assessment task. This will be set by the OCR awarding body and marked by your tutor.

The assignment will require you to produce a report based on an investigation into health, social care or early years services in your local community. For example, you could choose to investigate services in the:

- health sector – such as a health centre or hospital (private or NHS)
- social care sector – such as a local authority day centre for older people or a private residential home
- early years sector – such as a nursery, paediatric service or children's centre focusing on the needs of 0-8 year old children.

As part of your investigation you will need to find out about:

- the range of services available in your local community
- whether, and if so how, care organisations work together to meet clients' care needs
- how local care services are organised and how they fit into the larger national framework of care services.

Chapter 3 has covered the structure and organisation of health, social care and early years services for each client group as well as the ways organisations work together. Studying and referring back to chapter 3 should provide you with the background information needed to complete this part of the controlled assessment task.

Chapter 4

The principles of care

> ### Key issue: What values do care workers promote through their work?
>
> Health, social care and early years workers need to understand and use care values in their day-to-day work with service users. Chapter 4 describes and explains the care values which underpin practice with service users. These include:
>
> - Promoting equality and diversity of people who use services
> - Promoting individual rights and beliefs
> - Maintaining confidentiality.
>
> You will need to have an understanding of the background to and the consequences for care organisations and care practitioners of the Every Child Matters agenda. You will also need to understand the balance that services have to achieve between getting involved in people's lives or not, including the risks to both individuals and society associated with both action and inaction. By the end of this chapter you will have a good understanding of how care values play a central part in the way care practitioners approach and interact with service users.

What are care values?

What are 'care values'? This slightly odd sounding phrase really means something quite simple. If you value something, you feel that it is important or worthwhile. For example, you probably expect your friends to be honest with you and to respect your feelings. Why? Because you probably believe that telling the truth and showing respect is the right way to behave, and that telling lies and being disrespectful is wrong. Care values are beliefs about the right ways to treat care service users.

Care values are now seen as an essential part of the work of all care practitioners. Service users, for example, expected to be treated fairly and not to be discriminated against. You would probably expect your GP (family doctor) to say 'I try to treat all people equally, whoever they are'. Similarly, if somebody asked why you were having counselling, you would probably expect your counsellor to say 'It's important to keep the things my client talks to me about confidential'.

Registered care practitioners (such as nurses, physiotherapists and doctors, for example) have a professional responsibility to understand and use care values in their work. For example, they

 Over to you!

Make a list of all the health and social care services you have received. Divide your list into health, social care and early years services.

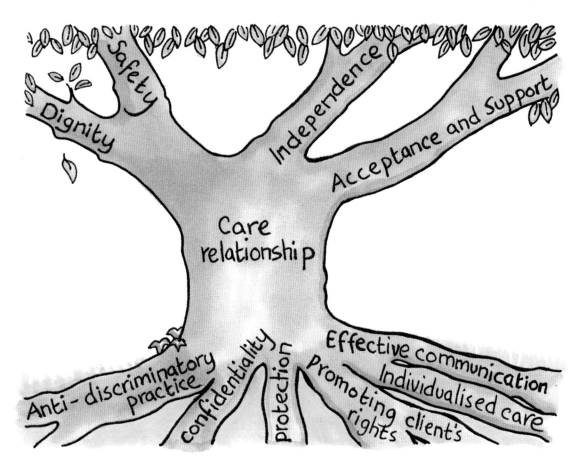

Figure 1.24 **Examples of care values.**

are expected to follow the codes of practice and guidelines about care values that are issued by their professional bodies. Breaking their profession's code of practice or not following guidelines is likely to result in a care practitioner being 'struck off' the professional register. This will prevent them from working in their care profession.

Promoting equality and diversity

Care practitioners in the UK are working in a multicultural society with a socially and ethnically diverse population. It is important for them to recognise that each client is an individual with particular needs and a person who has the right to fair and equal treatment. Unfair discrimination occurs when individuals or groups of people are treated less favourably in comparison to others.

The main cause of unfair discrimination is **prejudice**. When an individual is prejudiced in some way, they hold negative feelings and attitudes towards another person or group of people. These feelings, ideas and attitudes will usually be based on untrue, ill-informed or exaggerated ideas or beliefs. In the United Kingdom, some of the social groups that tend to experience unfair discrimination based on prejudice include:

- minority ethnic groups
- minority religious groups
- women
- lesbians and gay men

Over to you!

It's hard to admit to having prejudices. Often people are not aware of their own prejudices until they are put in a position where they feel threatened by or angry about something. Think about your own views on 'race', religion, sexuality and disability. Do you have any prejudices that may lead you to treating some people unfairly?

- older people
- people with learning or physical disabilities
- people with mental health problems.

Members of these groups may experience unfair discrimination because of their race or colour (racism), gender (sexism), age (ageism), disability (disablism), sexuality (homophobia), religious beliefs or health status. Carers should never unfairly discriminate against service users. Wherever they receive care, all patients and clients are entitled to non-discriminatory treatment. However, anti-discriminatory practice does not just mean treating everybody the same. It also means challenging and reducing any form of unfair discrimination that might be experienced by service users. Care workers who take an **anti-discriminatory approach** are:

- aware of the different forms of unfair discrimination that can occur in care settings
- sensitive to the ethnicity, social background and cultural needs of each individual for whom they provide care
- prepared to actively challenge and try to reduce the unfair discrimination experienced by service users.

Treating one service user differently to another is not the same thing as unfair discrimination. It might be necessary to use a different approach or to offer a different form of care to an individual who has particular needs, wishes or preferences. Automatically treating everyone in exactly the same way won't enable a care worker to acknowledge the diversity of the people they care for. In the end, all individuals should be equally valued and have their individual needs met regardless of their background.

Promoting individual rights and beliefs

Care practitioners should be open-minded and adaptable so that they can meet the health, development and welfare needs of all potential service users. This is a challenge because services have to meet the needs of people of different ages, different genders, different sexual orientations, different ethnic and cultural backgrounds, and people with a broad range of abilities, disabilities, illnesses and impairments. In addition, service users hold a wide range of spiritual and religious beliefs and personal values. These may affect the ways that different individuals want care services to be provided for them. For example, people who have an active faith may have particular worship, dietary and personal care needs that they wish to have met.

A care practitioner who establishes good care relationships will respect a service user's right to have their dignity respected, will ensure service users have choices and can make their own decisions, and will protect each individual's safety and security whilst they are receiving care.

Dignity and privacy

Care settings can be difficult and impersonal places in which to live. However, service users should always have privacy when personal care is being provided. They should not be exposed to the view of others when they are being dressed, undressed,

Health, Social Care and Early Years Provision

taken to the toilet or being helped to wash. Care practitioners need to take simple practical precautions like closing doors, keeping curtains drawn and not leaving individuals partially undressed in situations where other people may walk in or see them. In addition, care practitioners should be respectful of individuals' rights to privacy in their room. Knocking before entering and checking that it is alright to come in is much more respectful than simply throwing the door open, carrying out tasks without asking or sitting on a person's bed or chair without asking permission. Showing respect for each person's dignity and privacy is a very important way of showing the person that you value them as an individual. It also shows that the care practitioner acknowledges the service user's rights whatever their needs, problems or personal difficulties.

Choice

Individuals receiving care need to be encouraged to make their own choices and should be enabled to make decisions on the basis of their own wishes and preferences. Few care workers would dispute the idea that giving individuals choices is a good thing. However, it can be challenging to find ways of putting this into practice on an everyday basis. Ideally, care workers and service users should develop partnerships in which the service user feels equally involved. This kind of relationship is **empowering** because service users are seen as:

- individuals with rights and choices appropriate to their age and needs
- deserving of respect, regardless of their personal or social characteristics.

Care practitioners can also promote and support choice by:

- finding out what each individual's likes and dislikes are.
- developing a unique relationship with each of the people they provide care for.
- adapting their communication style to ensure each individual can communicate as effectively as possible.
- encouraging and supporting each individual to do what they can for themselves. This is known as providing active support.
- offering individuals a choice of activities and choices as to whether and how they participate in them.
- giving people different options on both large and small-scale decisions that affect them.

Some people are unable to make major lifestyle or treatment choices independently. However, every person should be given the opportunity to make the choices and decisions that they are able to make. To support service users in doing this, a care worker needs to be aware of the person's particular wishes and abilities. If a care worker develops an effective relationship with the service users they are caring for, these people will feel more confident about making their wishes and preferences known. If a person is unable to make their needs or preferences known, a care practitioner should always do what is in the service user's best interests, not what is quickest or easiest for the practitioner.

Over to you!

Imagine that you are in hospital, unable to leave your hospital bed because you are recovering from an operation. You are in a mixed sex ward. What would you want the nurses to do to ensure your dignity and privacy were protected?

Protection, health and safety

Working in any setting that contains people, equipment, illness, disease and disability and a lot of work pressures can be risky! One of the golden rules of work in a care setting is that the health and safety of individuals, colleagues and anybody else present should be the main concern. People should not be at risk of injury or harm in a care setting. Care practitioners should, at least, do no harm. As a result, awareness of health and safety issues and safeguarding (protection) principles is a basic competence all care practitioners are expected to have.

Many people who use care services are at a vulnerable point in their life and put a lot of trust in care practitioners to provide them with the protection, help and support that they need. Some groups of service users, including children, older people, disabled people and people with mental health problems are vulnerable to exploitation and abuse by others. Other service users may also find it difficult to follow basic health and safety precautions that protect them from the dangers of everyday life as well as abuse or exploitation by others. This can be a result of the problems that they have, such as learning disabilities or memory problems, or because they are easily influenced by unscrupulous people. As a result, many people who need or who are receiving care face a greater risk of experiencing harm or a form of abuse (physical, emotional or sexual for example).

Protecting service users from harm or potential abuse is something that all care workers should feel is important. Care workers should assess the relationships that their clients have with other people for any signs of abuse and should always act to prevent this occurring or stop it happening when they become aware of it.

A care practitioner should also:

- ensure that their own health and hygiene does not pose a threat to the health and safety of others and that they manage their personal safety at work.

- follow the infection control, moving and handling, accident and waste disposal procedures set out in their employer's health and safety policies.

- make use of any risk assessments that have been carried out to minimise health and safety hazards.

- respond appropriately to security risks in the workplace.

- report health and safety and security issues to relevant people.

Maintaining confidentiality of information

Care service users must be able to trust the people who provide them with care services. If you cannot trust another person with your thoughts, feelings and dignity you are unlikely to develop a strong or deep relationship with them. The care relationship is based on trust and particularly on the need for care practitioners to maintain **confidentiality** whenever possible.

There are times in care work when it is important to keep confidences and information that you have about service users to yourself. For example, if a child at the nursery where you do your

Investigate ...

Find out about the work of the Health and Safety Executive by visiting www.hse.gov.uk. Select Health Care in the 'Your Industry' search for information on health and safety in care services.

work placement swore at you and misbehaved one afternoon, or an elderly resident at a nursing home refused to bathe after wetting herself, you would be breaching confidentiality to reveal these things to your friends. You should not breach confidentiality in situations where service users have a right to privacy or where their comments or behaviour do not cause harm or break the law. Where care workers gossip or talk publicly about events or issues that happen at work they are betraying the trust that service users and colleagues put in them.

However, there are sometimes situations where it is necessary to disclose information about a service user that has been given in confidence. For example, where a service user requests that what they say is kept a secret, this can be overridden if:

- what they reveal involves them breaking the law or planning to do so
- they say that they intend to harm themselves or another person
- they reveal information that can be used to protect another person from harm.

If a service user commits an offence that could have been prevented by a care practitioner disclosing information given to them in confidence, the care practitioner could be brought to court to face charges. As a result care practitioners should never promise service users that what they say will be absolutely confidential. They should explain that there are times when they may have to share information with their colleagues and other authorities.

Over to you!

What kinds of personal information about yourself do you expect your GP to keep confidential?

Over to you!

Read the following confidentiality situations. For each scenario, explain:

1 why confidentiality may be important to the client
2 the dilemma facing the care worker
3 whether you would break confidentiality and why.

- Darren has an appointment with the school nurse for a BCG booster injection. He's worried about it making him ill. He says that he's just taken some ecstasy and pleads with the nurse not to tell anyone.
- Jennifer goes to her GP for contraceptive pills. She asks her GP not to tell her parents. She is 14 years old.
- Eileen has terminal cancer. She tells her district nurse that she's had enough of living and is going to end her own life tomorrow. She says it's her choice and asks the district nurse not to interfere.
- Yasmin tells her new health visitor that her boyfriend is violent and is beating her. She asks the health visitor not to say anything as she is frightened of what might happen. Yasmin and her boyfriend have a three-month-old baby.
- Lee turns up at a hostel for the homeless. He says that he has run away from home because his father has been beating him. He asks the social worker not to contact his family. He is 16 years old.
- A man with a stab wound arrives at the hospital casualty department. He won't give his name and asks the nurse not to phone the police. He says that he will leave if she does. He is bleeding heavily.

Confidentiality is about sharing, transmitting and storing information about individuals in ways that are appropriate to their care needs. It is definitely not about keeping information 'secret'. This means that 'confidential' information can be shared with other care team members who also need to know about and use it. Beyond this, a care practitioner must consult the service users they work with and respect their wishes about who should be informed or given access to information about them.

Investigate ...

How do care service users expect to be treated by care workers? Carry out a brief survey of your friends and family to identify which of the care values we've covered they feel are the most important.

Every Child Matters

With children and young people care practitioners follow the *Every Child Matters* agenda and ensure they:

- keep children safe and maintain a healthy environment
- work in partnership with families and/or parents
- make sure that children are offered a range of experiences and activities that supports all aspects of their development
- value diversity
- promote equal opportunity
- maintain confidentiality
- ensure anti-discriminatory practice
- work with others
- are a reflective practitioner.

The *Every Child Matters* programme resulted from an inquiry into the death of Victoria Climbie, an 8 year old girl who died in hospital in 2000 after suffering 128 different injuries at the hands of her aunt and her aunts boyfriend. A range of care practitioners, including doctors, nurses and social workers, had seen Victoria on a number of occasions prior to her death. These different practitioners were unaware of each others involvement with and concern about Victoria. Because they did not talk to each other and assumed that others would take responsibility for helping her, Victoria was left to suffer from the abuse perpetrated by her aunt and her aunt's boyfriend until she eventually died.

The inquiry into Victoria's death led to a policy called *Every Child Matters: Change for Children*. The aims of the *Every Child Matters* programme (www.everychildmatters.gov.uk) are that all children should:

- be healthy
- stay safe
- enjoy and achieve
- make a positive contribution
- achieve economic wellbeing.

The *Every Child Matters* policy and programme of action led to major reform of children's services in the UK. In particular, services were reorganised so that professionals working with children now have to work closely with each other to jointly address each child's needs. The aim of this is to ensure that every child has the best possible childhood, that professionals become more **accountable** for the decisions they make about children and that the risk of professional missing incidents of abuse or failing to act when abuse is identified are minimised.

Deciding whether to intervene

Care practitioners often face difficult decisions. One of the most difficult decisions is whether or not they should intervene in a situation they are made aware of because of concerns about an individual or family's vulnerability. This type of situation can occur if:

- a child may be at risk of abuse or neglect if they remain living with their family.

- an older person living at home becomes frail and unable to care for themselves but is reluctant to accept help or move into residential care.

- a person develops mental health problems that would benefit from treatment in hospital but refuses to accept that they are unwell.

- an individual with learning disabilities who is trying to live independently requires help with daily living skills but doesn't want care workers involved in their life.

Care practitioners who are in a position to intervene have to balance the risk of not becoming involved in the person's life against the wishes of the individual and the possible negative consequences of doing so. For example, removing a child who is 'at risk' from their family may lead to the child's relationships with family members breaking down or a loss of trust between the care practitioners and the child's parents. Similarly, insisting that an individual receives care in order to protect them from harm removes the person's rights to make their own decisions and to choose how they live their life. Care practitioners who face these situations have to carry out careful risk assessments and must be aware of the benefits and the negative consequences of both intervening and not intervening in an individual's life. The cases of Baby P and Victoria Climbie illustrate what can go wrong when care practitioners decide that, on balance, it is best not to intervene by removing a child from their family.

Case study

Baby P, a 17-month old boy, died in 2007 after suffering more than 50 separate injuries despite being on the 'at risk' register of Haringey Council, North London. Baby P received 60 visits from social workers during his short life. During their involvement with Baby P's family, care practitioners had to decide whether removing him would be in his best interests or not. The decision to leave Baby P in the care of his alleged abusers was strongly criticised by the inquiry into his death. There was a lot of public anger about this case because the death of Victoria Climbie (see above) had also occurred in Haringey, eight years earlier. In both cases Haringey Council apologised for not doing more to protect the children involved. Baby P's mother, her boyfriend and a lodger were convicted of causing Baby P's death and sent to prison.

UNIT 1

Codes of practice, policies and procedures

To help ensure that care workers respect clients' rights, codes of practice, policies and procedures have been developed by professional organisations and employers. Examples of these are now used in all care settings.

Codes of practice

A **code of practice** is a document that outlines an agreed way of working and dealing with specified situations. Codes of practice aim to reflect and set a standard for good practice in care settings. A number of codes of practice have been developed for care workers such as registered nurses, occupational therapists, and physiotherapists, social workers and nursery staff. Codes of practice establish the general principles and standards for care workers and should always refer to equality of opportunity.

Policies and procedures

A **policy** is different to a code of practice in that it tells care workers how they should approach specific issues in a particular care setting. For example, most care homes will have a policy on confidentiality. This will explain in detail how this issue is dealt with in the particular home. Policies should promote equal treatment and equality of opportunity for everyone likely to be affected by them.

A **procedure** describes the way that staff in a particular care setting are expected to deal with an issue or activity that they may be involved in. For example, care homes for older people usually have written procedures that describe how to deal with a situation where a resident goes missing from the home. The procedure will set out in detail all the steps that the staff should take in trying to locate the person and report them missing to the relevant authorities.

Policies and procedures should always incorporate the main values of the care profession. They should ensure that service users' rights are respected and that activities are always carried out in the service users' best interest.

Knowledge Check

1 Identify three important values that are applied by care workers.

2 Explain what a care value is.

3 What is a care value base?

4 Name three groups who often experience unfair discrimination in the UK.

5 What is the main cause of all forms of unfair discrimination?

6 In your own words, explain what care workers do if they take an anti-discriminatory practice approach to their work.

7 What does keeping something confidential mean?

8 Why is confidentiality important in care work?

9 When should a care worker break confidentiality?

10 Do you think that a GP (family doctor) should tell a teenager's parents if she requests to be prescribed the contraceptive pill?

11 Explain why care service users need to be protected from abuse.

12 What is 'individualised' care?

13 What can happen if service users don't receive individualised care?

Chapter checklist

The box below provides a summary of the areas covered in chapter 4. Tick the areas that you feel you understand and would be confident about when writing your assignment. If there are any areas that you don't understand or are not confident about, you will need to return to them before you begin planning or writing your assignment.

Care values
Promoting anti-discriminatory practice ❏
Promoting and supporting individual rights
   to dignity, independence, health and safety ❏
Promoting effective communication
   and relationships ❏
Maintaining confidentiality of information ❏
Acknowledging individual personal beliefs
   and identity ❏

How care values are used in practice
Behaviour ❏
Attitudes ❏
Interactions ❏
Codes of practice, policies and procedures ❏

Assessment Guide

Your learning in this unit will be assessed through a controlled assessment task. This will be set by the OCR awarding body and marked by your tutor.

The assignment will require you to produce a report based on an investigation into health, social care or early years services in your local community. For example, you could choose to investigate services in the:

● health sector – such as a health centre or hospital (private or NHS)

● social care sector – such as a local authority day centre for older people or a private residential home

● early years sector – such as a nursery, paediatric service or children's centre focusing on the needs of 0–8 year old children.

As part of your investigation you will need to find out about:

● the principles of care that are relevant to the services you investigate.

● the ways direct care workers apply care values in their work with clients

● the possible effects on clients if care values are not applied by care workers.

Chapter 4 has covered the range of care principles and care values used in the health, social care and early years sectors. Studying and referring back to chapter 4 should provide you with the background information needed to complete this part of the controlled assessment task.

Chapter 5

Work roles and skills in health, social care and early years

Key issue: What does care work involve and what skills and qualities do care practitioners need to perform their work roles?

There is a wide range of work roles in the health, social care and early years services. Chapter 5 describes the work roles of:

- Primary practitioners – including doctors, nurses, community nurses, health visitors, midwives, health care assistants, portage workers, child development workers, early years practitioners, family support workers, occupational therapists and teachers, for example.

- Secondary practitioners – including practice managers, medical receptionists, school reception staff and catering staff, for example.

You will learn about the day-to-day activities of primary and secondary practitioners who work in health, social care and early years services and develop your knowledge of the skills and qualifications that are needed for different types of care work. By the end of this chapter you will have a good understanding of the main work roles of care practitioners and support staff in health, social care and early years services.

Working in care

Health, social care and early years organisations employ a large number of people. The NHS, for example, employs more people than any other organisation in Europe. As a result, there are a wide range of different work roles in health, social care and early years workplaces.

To simplify the range of care roles it is useful to consider the similarities and differences between:

- health care, social care and early years roles
- direct care workers and indirect care workers.

Health, social care and early years roles

People employed in **health care** roles usually deal with individuals who have physical, medical-related problems such as a disease, injury or acute illness. People employed in **social care** roles usually deal with people who are vulnerable and who have care needs that are mainly social, emotional or financial rather than physical. People working in **early years** roles are usually employed in child care and early education services for children under the age of eight.

Some care service users have a combination of health, social care or early developmental problems. This can mean that a care practitioner has to provide more than one type of care for that person. For example, a community psychiatric nurse who works with people experiencing mental health problems may need to offer their clients both health and social care.

Primary and secondary care practitioners

People who work in health, social care and early years services may have either a direct or an indirect care role. Primary care roles involve directly providing one-to-one, or face-to-face care to service users in a 'hands-on', practical way. Examples of primary care practitioners include:

- nursery nurses
- occupational therapists
- nurses
- dentists.

Secondary care practitioner roles involve providing support services. For example, people who work as receptionists, cleaners and porters have support roles as secondary care practitioners in health organisations. Primary care practitioners such as nurses, doctors, dentists and social workers are the people we are most likely to remember coming into contact with. We are less likely to notice the secondary care practitioners who operate behind the scenes.

Areas of care work

Jobs in health, social care and early can also be grouped into a number of different areas of work. Some of the more familiar work areas are:

Areas of health care work	Areas of social care work	Areas of early years work
Medicine	Social work	Child care – such as childminding
Midwifery	Community social care	Pre-school play and early learning
Nursing – in-patient and community	Residential social care	Early years education
Professions allied to medicine – such as occupational therapy	Family support	Development support – such as speech and language therapy
Managerial and administrative work	Managerial and administrative work	Managerial and administrative work

Within each area of work there are many specialist roles. Care workers tend to become more specialist as their careers progress. For example, within child care a person could begin their career as a nursery assistant, then qualify and work as a nursery nurse and, with further experience and training, go on to become a classroom teacher in primary education, or a nursery manager or early years practitioner for a local authority.

Over to you!

1 Write a sentence that briefly describes what you believe is involved in each of the care roles listed below. You could use careers booklets and the Internet to find out about occupational roles.

2 Reorganise the current list into three new lists headed 'health roles', 'social care roles' and 'early years roles'.

District nurse	Hospital manager
Community psychiatric nurse	Gynaecologist
Care manager	Chiropodist
Social worker	Dentist
Nursery nurse	Childminder
Paramedic	Dental technician
Health visitor	Pharmacist
Residential social worker	Surgeon

 Knowledge Check

1 According to official statistics, which care profession employs more care workers than any other?

2 Name four different areas of care work.

3 Give two examples of indirect care roles in health care.

4 Give two examples of direct care roles in the early years field.

5 Explain the difference between a direct care job and an indirect care job.

Working in health care

Health care is a very broad area that covers a variety of different care professions. These include medicine, nursing, midwifery, health visiting and a variety of professions allied to medicine such as occupational therapy and physiotherapy.

Medicine

People who work in the medical field have some form of direct or indirect care role that involves dealing with individuals who are physically or mentally unwell and in need of diagnosis and treatment. Doctors, working either in hospitals or in general practice (GPs) are perhaps the most well known group of health care practitioners. All doctors of medicine have at least one degree in medicine. Many doctors obtain further qualifications to enable them to work in specialist areas of medicine, such as anaesthetics (pain control), cardiology (heart-related), paediatrics (children's medicine) or psychiatry (mental health) for example. Doctors work in both the NHS and in the private sector. In general, doctors:

● assess and diagnose physical and mental health problems

● carry out physical and psychological investigations and examinations

Case study

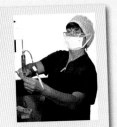

Dr Sandra Saunders has worked as an anaesthetist at St Joseph's Hospital for the last three years. Her job is to anaesthetise patients and then to manage their airway and respiratory system safely while they are being treated or operated on. She works shifts to cover the 24-hour needs of the hospital and its patients. She works in the accident and emergency department and in the hospital's operating theatres. Dr Saunders works closely with other doctors and nursing staff as part of the team on call.

"You have got to be up to date with medical knowledge, careful, alert and confident to do my job"

- prescribe medication and other forms of treatment for health problems
- monitor and support patients who are receiving treatment for health problems.

Doctors who are General Practitioners (GPs) tend to work as part of a primary health care team whilst hospital doctors work as part of multi-disciplinary teams alongside other health care practitioners such as nurses and physiotherapists, for example.

Nursing

Nurses make up the largest group of care staff in the United Kingdom. There are approximately 345,000 qualified nurses working in a range of areas of health care. There are four main branches of nursing - adult (also called general) nursing, children's nursing, learning disability nursing and mental health nursing. There are important differences in the type of training and work that these different groups of nurses do. Qualified nurses can work in in-patient settings (hospitals, clinics) or in community settings (GP surgeries, patient's homes).

Figure 1.25 Different types of nursing in the UK.

Case study

Katie is ward manager in the children's unit of a teaching hospital. After qualifying as a registered general nurse fifteen years ago, she worked her way up to become ward manager. She has also worked in operating theatres and gained her BSc degree in nursing five years ago. Katie's work involves a lot of day-to-day management of the unit. For example, she has to plan the work rota to make sure enough staff are on duty and attend a variety of meetings about the running of the unit, like catering and cleaning. She also spends time supervising the nursing care of the children, meets their parents to provide information and support and talks to a range of other health care practitioners about the needs and treatment of children on her ward.

"I have to be very well organised and need to be able to decide which tasks are a priority every day. Management skills are just as important as nursing skills in my job"

When qualified, a registered nurse generally works as a staff nurse to gain experience and improve their practical skills. The day-to-day work that nurses do depends on the specialist area of care that they work in. For example, mental health nurses spend a lot of time talking with service users and providing emotional support, whereas general nurses working in accident and emergency spend more time treating people's wounds and injuries.

Nurses spend a lot of time in very close contact with patients, providing a wide range of direct care and support. Nursing is often a physically and emotionally tiring job. Caring for people who are sick and dependent can also involves carrying out tasks that may be unpleasant or physically demanding, such as changing soiled beds. As well as carrying out their care role, nurses have to complete administrative work relating to patients and often have a role in training student nurses.

Midwifery

Midwives work with women in all stages of pregnancy, when they are in labour and shortly after they have delivered their baby. Many midwives work in hospital services, especially the delivery suite where babies are born, though an increasing number are also working in the community visiting women at home, at GP practices and at children's centres. It is now necessary to have a degree to become a midwife. Many people now do midwifery degrees though some people take shorter courses in midwifery after they have obtained a degree and some experience in nursing. Once qualified, midwives develop their practical skills, knowledge and experience by working in hospital and community settings. Providing antenatal (pre-birth) and postnatal (following birth) care, support and education and delivering babies are all part of the day-to-day work of a midwife.

Health Visiting

Health visitors work with families, particularly mothers and young children, at home and in community settings. The role of the health visitor is to monitor and promote the health and development of young children. A health visitor will usually visit a mother and newborn baby at home a few days after the birth. They provide advice on a wide range of areas such as feeding,

 ## Over to you!

Find out about the real day-to-day work that nurses do by carrying out an interview with somebody who works as a nurse. You could invite the school or college nurse to talk to your class or arrange to meet and talk with a nurse who works in a local care organisation. Remember to prepare plenty of questions before your interview.

sleep, physical and emotional development and other general child care issues. People who work as health visitors are also qualified nurses or midwives (and often both).

Health care assistant

People who are interested in direct care work can gain some vocational training and experience as a health care assistant or support worker. Many health care assistants take an NVQ (National Vocational Qualification) course and are employed in all areas of health care. They often have a lot of direct patient contact, assisting registered nurses and other staff in providing care.

The role of a health care assistant is different to that of a registered nurse in a number of important ways:

- Health care assistants carry out most of the domestic tasks in a care setting, such as making beds.
- The physical care that health care assistants provide relates to routine procedures such as lifting, bathing and dressing patients.
- Health care assistants carry out care planned by registered nurses.

Like nurses, health care assistants work day and night shifts and may also work at weekends. There is no minimum age requirement for health care assistants. Personal maturity is one of the key factors that employers take into account when recruiting people to these posts.

Over to you!

Which organizations employ health care assistants in your local area?

Investigate ...

Find out more about the work of health care support workers by arranging to talk to a member of staff at a local hospital or nursing home. You might be able to find information by looking at careers websites or by obtaining a job description when a vacancy for this kind of role is advertised in your local newspaper.

Case study

Rob Fitzgerald is 22 years old. He has worked as a health care support worker in a learning disabilities unit for the last five years. He works day and night shifts and provides direct care and support for the ten residents of the bungalow where he works. Rob helps the residents in different ways depending on their individual needs. Some people need help with personal care, such as going to the toilet, washing and dressing, while others need assistance when travelling to college or on social outings. All of the residents benefit from the relationships that they have developed with Rob. He is currently taking an NVQ Level 2 in direct care and plans to go on to develop his care and managerial skills. He hopes to work in day centres and progress to social work training later in his career.

'Most of the time I really like working in the bungalow and going out with the residents. It can be fun and it's practical work, which I like. It's all about the relationships you have with people and the way that you communicate with them really.'

Professions allied to medicine

Physiotherapists and occupational therapists are examples of professions allied to medicine. Both of these professions focus on particular aspects of health and wellbeing, though each has its own specialist training programme and set of professional skills.

Physiotherapists work with people of all ages who have physical problems, particularly movement problems caused by accidents, illness or ageing. Physiotherapists diagnose and treat movement and other physical health problems using specialist physiotherapy techniques, massage and therapeutic exercises. They also provide a lot of health promotion and illness prevention information and guidance. Physiotherapists work in both the NHS and in private sector organizations and as private practitioners. Physiotherapists work in a variety of health care areas, including out-patient departments, intensive care units, women's health (especially labour) units, stroke rehabilitation units, children's services and in a variety of specialist services for people with mental health problems, learning disabilities or physical disabilities. Qualified physiotherapists have a degree in physiotherapy and then gain plenty of 'hands on' experience to improve their knowledge and practical skills. They tend to work in multi-disciplinary teams with other health care workers in both community and hospital settings.

Occupational therapy is a wide-ranging profession. Occupational therapists (OTs) work in hospital, community or specialist educational or care home settings with people of all ages who may have physical or mental health problems or learning disabilities. OTs usually work alongside other practitioners such as doctors, nurses, physiotherapists and social workers as part of a multi-disciplinary care team. Occupational therapists assess people who are having difficulties with some aspect of daily living. They then develop treatment plans that involve the person taking part in forms of purposeful activity that will prevent their problems becoming worse and which will enable them to live as independently as they would like. At the end of a course of occupational therapy the service user and OT will evaluate how effective the treatment has been.

Management, administration and ancillary services

Health care organisations employ a wide range of support staff to carry out the administrative, management and ancillary jobs that are essential for both the organisation and the direct care workers to work efficiently.

Administrative work covers secretarial and clerical jobs such as typing, filing, record-keeping and calculating wages. People who work as receptionists, ward clerks and medical secretaries have roles that provide administrative support for direct care workers and for managers who run health care organisations.

Management work involves taking responsibility for the effective and efficient running of various aspects of a care organisation. People who work as managers may have specialist qualifications in the area in which they are working, such as medical laboratory science, catering or accountancy, for example. Managers have more authority and responsibility than administrative staff and are often responsible for a group of staff and a department.

Case study

Julia Benn is the practice manager at St Joseph's Health Centre. She is responsible for the safe and efficient running of the health centre and for managing the budgets. Julia has day-to-day responsibility for managing the administrative staff, including the secretaries and receptionists at the health centre. She also has overall responsibility for payroll, practice finance and personnel issues and she plays an important role in planning and developing the services of the health centre. Julia doesn't directly manage the health care practitioners at the health centre but she works closely with them to ensure that they are well supported and that they have the resources to provide high quality medical and psychological care to service users.

"My working day is very busy. I have a lot of meetings to attend and need to make sure that I see the support staff regularly. My job requires a range of business and management skills but I think that being a good communicator and problem-solver is the key to it."

Ancillary work covers a broad range of occupations that are required to keep a care organisation running smoothly, such as catering, cleaning and maintenance. Porters who move patients around hospitals, electricians and domestic assistants who clean in-patient areas and change beds are examples of ancillary workers employed in hospitals. People who are employed as ancillary staff may have vocational qualifications appropriate to the area in which they work, such as catering or electrical work. Many obtain their jobs because of their previous experience and the practical skills that they have.

Detailed information on a wide range of health care roles can be found on the NHS Careers website (www.nhscareers.nhs.uk).

Investigate ...

What kinds of care work are you most interested in? Do you know what qualifications and experience are needed for this kind of work? Research the care profession or job role that you are most interested in. Produce a profile of the role that identifies: entry routes and qualifications needed; training; what the work really involves; and ways of developing a career in this area.

Knowledge Check

1 What qualifications are needed to work as a doctor?

2 Name three tasks that doctors perform as part of their work.

3 What name is given to a highly qualified and experienced doctor who specialises in a particular area of hospital medicine?

4 Describe the health care role of a physiotherapist.

5 Which health care professional specialises in the use of purposeful activity?

6 Describe the care role of a midwife.

7 Explain how the work of a health care assistant supports the care role of a registered nurse.

8 What qualifications are needed to train as a registered nurse?

9 Name the four branches of nursing.

10 What kind of skills does a nurse need to work as a ward manager?

11 Name two jobs that involve administrative work.

12 Explain why care organisations need to employ a range of ancillary workers.

13 Explain why a practice manager is an 'indirect' rather than a 'direct' care worker.

UNIT 1

Working in social care

Social care involves providing various forms of non-medical help to people who are vulnerable and in need of support. It can include forms of direct care such as counselling or indirect care such as arranging housing or access to other support services. Social care services are provided by care practitioners who have a variety of different jobs titles, including social workers, youth workers and social care support workers.

Social work

A social worker is a person who has gained a professional social work qualification (normally a diploma or degree in social work) and who has experience of working with people experiencing social, financial and emotional problems. Many of the people who require social work assistance are socially excluded or experiencing some form of life crisis. Social workers work with members of all client groups in a variety of community, hospital, residential home, education and day care settings.

Most qualified social workers are employed as field social workers working directly with service users. This means that they have a caseload of people they work with in community and institutional settings. Some social workers specialise in working with members of particular client groups, such as 'at risk' children, vulnerable older people or adults with mental health problems. However, other social workers work as care co-ordinators or care managers and specialise in assessing clients' needs and purchasing care packages for them. Social workers assess the needs of people referred to them. They then have to decide whether the person is eligible for social care services and, if so, what kinds of help and support they can be offered. Packages of support are then organised and managed to meet the service user's particular needs. It is important that care packages are reviewed regularly to ensure that they are actually meeting the care needs of the person or family they are designed for.

Family support worker

Family support workers are employed by local authorities and voluntary organisations to give emotional and practical support, help and advice to families who are experiencing difficulties. These difficulties may be the result of one or more parent experiencing ill-health, drug or alcohol problems, financial difficulties, disability or mental health problems, for example. The purpose of family support is usually to keep the family together at a time when there is some risk that one or more of the children may be taken into care. Family support workers are often managed by social workers who plan and monitor the kind of support that the family requires. This could involve, for example, demonstrating parenting skills, helping parents to understand and respond to their children's behavioural difficulties or showing them how to promote learning through play. No specific qualifications are needed to become a family support worker. However, maturity and experience of working with children and families in statutory or voluntary services are usually required.

Over to you!

Make a list of reasons why social work is sometimes a difficult and stressful job.

Investigate ...

Find out more about the role of a social worker by looking at the Social Work careers website (www.socialworkcareers.co.uk). This provides information on the role of social workers and training courses. You might also be able to get information by looking at other careers websites, on the Internet, or by obtaining a job description when a vacancy for a social worker is advertised in your local paper.

Work roles and skills in health, social care and early years

Case study

Bhupinder Mann is employed as a family support worker by a local authority. She works with one family at a time, often working a shift system that can include days, nights and weekend work. She has taken an NVQ Level 2 course in Children's Care, Learning and Development, and has also completed food hygiene and counselling courses. Bhupinder works with children and families in their own homes. She has recently helped a family where the parents are physically disabled and needed help washing, dressing and feeding their baby. Bhupinder showed both parents how to do this and helped them reorganise their home to make child care easier. Bhupinder enjoys the practical side of her job and feels that it is important to be well organised and understanding to do her job efficiently.

"My job is quite tiring but I think it's important to help people. I enjoy the practical work and think of my clients as friends as well."

Working in early years

There is a wide range of care roles and career opportunities in the child care and early years field (see figure 1.26). Child care and early years work involves lots of busy, hands-on activities with children. Care workers in this area are responsible for the safety and development of the children they care for and work with. Some early years workers specialise in working with children who have physical or sensory impairments whereas others specialise in working with children who have learning difficulties. Some of the similarities and differences in the roles of different child care and early years workers are described below.

Figure 1.26 Examples of early years roles.

Early years work focuses on learning through play.

Nursery nurses

A qualified nursery nurse has achieved a qualification such as an NNEB, CACHE or BTEC Diploma in Nursery Nursing. Most nursery nurses are employed in private and local authority nurseries, usually providing direct care and education for healthy children under five, though some nursery nurses have specialist roles in hospitals and special education units for sick and disabled children. The main care role of a nursery nurse involves:

- supporting and encouraging children's physical, intellectual, emotional and social development through play
- providing basic physical care for children in the form of feeding, washing and cleaning
- observing children's participation in play, monitoring their progress, identifying any problems and reporting back on this to colleagues and parents
- managing the health and safety of children in the nursery environment.

Portage workers

Portage workers provide home-based services for pre-school children who have physical or learning disabilities or additional development needs. Portage workers work alongside parents, focusing on ways of encouraging a child's learning and development through play and other day-to-day activities. The day-to-day care role of a portage worker might include:

- Observation of children to identity existing skills.
- Identifying a child's development needs.
- Suggesting and planning activities for a child to develop their skills.
- Providing support and motivation for parents to carry out planned activities.
- Visiting children and parents at home to monitor progress or agree new goals.
- Writing reports about children who have been assessed.

Teacher

Early years or nursery teachers work in pre-school, nursery and reception classes with children between 3 and 5 years of age.

Early years teachers promote and develop children's intellectual, social and emotional development. Play and activity-based methods of learning are common ways of doing this. Early years teachers must have a degree in education and experience of working with young children. Good communication skills and the ability to provide and assess learning experiences for children are an essential part of the work role. Early years teachers often have contact with other health and social care practitioners who may also be working with a particular child, especially if they have complex health and development needs.

School reception staff

The people who work in pre-school and early years school receptions have an indirect care role in early years services. Reception staff are the first people that parents and children will meet when they arrive at school. They need to be organised and friendly to welcome people and put them at ease. Reception staff often have to deal with parents and children who become anxious or have worries about where their mum/dad or child is. Reception staff also play a part in managing the health, safety and security of children and teaching staff. Greeting and monitoring visitors and making sure that children don't unexpectedly leave the premises are a part of this. Due to their frequent contact with service users and visitors to their school, reception staff are also an important source of information about children and their families and play a key role in receiving and passing on information about a child's attendance or arrangements to collect them, for example.

Over to you!

Further Education colleges provide a lot of child care and early years courses for full and part-time students. Find out what's available at your local FE college by looking at their website or by obtaining a prospectus of courses.

Knowledge Check

1 What qualifications are needed to train as a social worker?

2 What kinds of care services do domiciliary care workers provide?

3 Name two client groups that domiciliary care workers are most likely to work with.

4 What qualifications do nursery nurses usually have?

5 What skills do you think are needed to work with children under the age of eight?

6 Describe how the work of a nursery nurse is different to that of an early years teacher.

Communication skills and care work

Good care relationships depend on effective communication skills. Carer workers use a range of different communication skills during their working day (or night). These include listening and various types of verbal (talking) skills, as well as touch and forms of 'body language'. A care worker has to use their communication skills when they:

● give or receive information about the care that is being provided for an individual

- provide emotional support to a service user or member of their family
- carry out an assessment of an individual's care needs.

Using communication skills in care work

Care workers use verbal and non-verbal communication skills in a variety of ways. For example, care workers need to have good **observation skills** to learn about their clients. This is important in carrying out assessments of clients' needs and in checking on their progress during or after treatment. Interviewing clients and their relatives is often a part of assessment. This relies on the care worker having the ability to ask questions and listen carefully to what the client says. Effective written skills are also required to write up the assessments so that they can be understood by colleagues.

Care workers have to attend a lot of meetings with colleagues in which they discuss and report on clients' problems and progress. These meetings can occur on a daily basis, where care workers use their verbal and listening skills to update each other on clients' daily progress. Groups of care workers may also meet to hold a case conference or hold another formal meeting to review a client's situation. In both of these types of meetings written notes are often made to provide a record of the meeting and of the client's progress.

Communication is about making contact with others and being understood. It involves sending and receiving 'messages'. We all communicate, or 'send messages', continuously.

Effective communication

People communicate most effectively when they feel relaxed, when they are able to empathise with the other person, and when they experience warmth and genuineness in the relationship:

- **Empathy** involves putting yourself in the place of the other person and trying to appreciate how they 'see' and experience the world. Being empathetic improves a care practitioner's ability to communicate.
- Expressing warmth is important. It makes the person feel accepted, secure and builds trust with them.
- Genuineness involves being yourself and communicating with honesty and integrity. Care practitioners who are genuine will avoid being authoritarian, defensive or emotionally detached. Genuineness also involves making sure that verbal and non-verbal 'messages' match or support each other, being consistent in the way service users are treated and being open and honest with people.

Being sensitive to what other people are saying, thinking and feeling, showing service users respect, and protecting their dignity and rights, are all features of empowering care practice. To be able to do these things, care practitioners need to be sensitive to the spoken and unspoken communication of service users. They also need to be aware of how they themselves think, feel and behave in their interactions with service users.

Over to you!

Observe the way people use their bodies to communicate when you have a chance to watch a group of people talking or socialising together. Try to work out what they are 'saying' non-verbally.

For care workers	For service users
1. Effective communication helps carers to give and receive information that is relevant to an individual's care and wellbeing.	1. Effective communication enables a service user to feel secure and respected as an individual at a time when they may be physically and emotionally vulnerable.
2. Effective communication enables care practitioners to express trust, acceptance, understanding and support.	2. Co-operation, involvement and partnership in a care relationship requires open and supportive communication.
3. Effective communication allows a care practitioner to identify and meet the individual needs of each service user.	3. Effective communication empowers service users by allowing them to express their needs, worries and wishes.
4. Effective communication enables a care practitioner to identify and support service users' abilities and reduces dependency.	4. Service users need to maintain their sense of identity while receiving care. This can only be achieved if they have opportunities to express themselves and to be understood by their carers.

Figure 1.27 The benefits of effective communication

Communicating with diverse service users

People who use health, social care and early years services in the UK come from diverse backgrounds and may need specific communication support in order to make use of the services they need. For example:

- English is not the first language of all service users. Information needs to be provided in the range of languages that are used in a local area, interpreter services and multi-lingual care practitioners may also be required.

- Care practitioners need to be aware of the special communication needs of people with sensory impairments, such as visually and hearing impaired people who may require specialist equipment, environmental adaptations or personal support in order to communicate effectively.

- Individuals who have developmental or mental health problems may not be able to communicate as effectively as adults or children who are well and may need support and a bit more time to understand care practitioners and to make their needs known.

- Care practitioners working with children should be aware that a child's age and stage of development affects their language skills. Using complex words or simply talking too much may prevent a child from understanding or communicating effectively.

Knowledge Check

1 Name the two main types of communication.

2 What are the two things that people have to do during verbal communication?

3 Describe two ways that care workers might use their communication skills in a care setting.

4 Describe two benefits of effective communication for service users.

5 Explain how the diverse backgrounds and needs of service users may have an impact on the strategies care practitioners use to communicate with service users.

Chapter checklist

The box below provides a summary of the areas covered in chapter 5. Tick the areas that you feel you understand and would be confident about when writing your assignment. If there are any areas that you don't understand or are not confident about, you will need to return to them before you begin planning or writing your assignment.

Types of care role
  Health care roles ❏
  Social care roles ❏
  Early years roles ❏
  Direct care roles ❏
  Indirect care roles ❏

Work roles in health care
  Doctor / Medical Practitioner ❏
  Nurse ❏
  Midwife ❏
  Health visitor ❏
  Health care assistant ❏
  Physiotherapist ❏
  Occupational therapist ❏
  Manager / administrator ❏

Work roles in social care
  Social worker ❏
  Social care worker ❏
  Family support worker ❏

Work roles in the early years sector
  Nursery nurse ❏
  Portage worker ❏
  Teacher ❏
  School reception staff ❏

Communication skills ❏

Assessment Guide

Your learning in this unit will be assessed through a controlled assessment task. This will be set by the OCR awarding body and marked by your tutor.

The assessment task will require you to produce a report based on an investigation into health, social care or early years services in your local community. Your could, for example, choose to investigate services in the:

- health sector – such as a health centre or hospital (private or NHS)
- social care sector – such as a local authority day centre for older people or a private residential home
- early years sector – such as a nursery, paediatric service or children's centre focusing on the needs of 0-8 year old children.

As part of your investigation you will need to find out about:

- the role of a direct care worker in meeting the needs of service users
- the qualification pathways that can lead to this direct care role
- the different skills and qualities required to perform this direct care role.

Chapter 5 has covered the range of work roles in the health, social care and early years sectors and the qualifications, skills and qualities needed to perform them. Studying and referring back to chapter 5 should provide you with the background information needed to complete this part of the controlled assessment task.

Unit 2

Understanding Personal Development and Relationships

Introduction

This unit is about personal development and relationships across the life span. You will learn about:

- The way people grow and develop during each stage of life.

- The factors that influence the way people grow and develop as they get older.

- How people develop a self-concept and personal relationships throughout life.

- The types of relationship that are important to personal development.

- The life events and changes that can affect personal development during each stage of life.

Health, social care and early years workers help people of all ages and backgrounds. Knowing about expected patterns of human growth and development can be important when people experience health problems or have care needs. Knowing what kinds of physical and language skills a two year old child normally has would help a children's nurse to assess a child in hospital or allow a playworker to plan suitable activities at a nursery, for example. This unit will give you a better understanding of human growth and development.

Chapter 6

Human growth and development

Key issue: How do individuals grow and develop during each life stage?

How does a person grow and develop throughout the course of their life? People experience physical, intellectual, emotional and social development in each life stage. A **life stage** is a defined period of growth and development. This topic will focus on the patterns and processes of human growth and development that occur in the following six life stages:

- Infancy (0–2 years)
- Childhood (3–8 years)
- Adolescence (9–18 years)
- Early adulthood (19-45 years)
- Middle adulthood (46-65 years)
- Later adulthood (over 65 years).

Chapter 6 will also focus on how the self-concept develops and changes across the life stages and the factors that affect this.

What are growth and development?

The term growth refers to an increase in size. Typically, a person will experience a gradual increase in their weight and height as they move from infancy through childhood and into adolescence and adulthood. Development is different to growth. **Development** happens when a person gains new skills, abilities and emotions. Typically, our skills, abilities and emotions become more sophisticated and complex as we progress from childhood through adolescence and into adulthood.

Developmental norms

Human growth and development tends to follow a pattern. Growth and **developmental norms**, sometimes also called 'milestones', refer to the points in a person's life where particular changes are expected to happen. For example, the point in infancy when you were first able to sit up unaided, when you took your first steps and when you said your first words will be relatively similar to the point at which other people of your age first did these

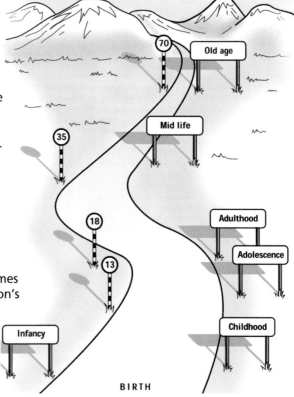

things too. Though human growth and development follows a relatively predictable pattern it is important not to think of this as an exact timetable that 'normal' people follow. An infant, child, teenager or adult is not abnormal if he or she reaches growth or developmental milestones at slightly different times to the expected pattern. A person's growth and development can be different to the 'norm' for a variety of reasons.

Figure 2.1 Examples of developmental norms.

Age	Developmental changes
3–4 months	Infants start on solid foods, develop better head control, can roll from side to side, reach for objects
6–9 months	Teething begins, learns to sit unaided, lift their heads and look around, use thumb and index finger to grasp objects
9–12 months	Infants can crawl, chew food, use their hands to explore, can walk holding on to parent or furniture ('cruising'), may say a few words, know their name and start to understand their parents words
12–18 months	Toddlers learn to feed themselves, walk unaided, can understand simple requests – 'give it to me' – develop better memory and concentration
18–24 months	Toddlers can run, turn pages of a book, use simple sentences, have temper outbursts and know their own name
10 years (girls)	Puberty begins
12 years (boys)	
45–55 years	Menopause occurs

Investigate

Before you begin studying the five main life stages of human growth and development, go to **www.babycenter.com/pregnancy-fetal-development-index**. This website explains how development occurs in the womb during pregnancy. In small groups choose one trimester of pregnancy and investigate what is happening to both the mother and the baby. Summarise your findings in the form of a poster or leaflet.

Using the PIES approach

Human growth and development has been studied in great detail by scientists and health and social care specialists for centuries. In the twenty first century we now have a detailed understanding of what happens to human beings in each life stage. One clear way of explaining the complex process of human growth and development is to identify four types of growth and development. This is known as the PIES approach. **PIES** stands for physical, intellectual, emotional and social development.

Physical growth and development

Physical growth and development refer to the way in which a person's body changes throughout their life. A person will experience most of their physical growth (in height and weight) during infancy, childhood and adolescence. Physical growth is very rapid during infancy, slower but continuous during childhood and then very rapid again during adolescence when a final growth spurt occurs. A person generally reaches their

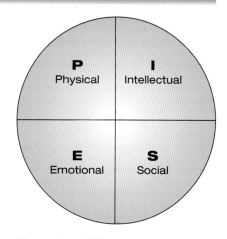

Figure 2.2 PIES.

Understanding Personal Development and Relationships

maximum height during adolescence and will not get any taller during adulthood. Unfortunately, the same can't be said for weight! A person can gain and lose weight throughout adulthood and later life. However, most of our natural body-building processes are completed in early adulthood.

Physical development, like growth, is a continuous process. Human beings begin developing physical skills from birth. We experience a peak in our physical abilities during adulthood. A slow and gradual decline in physical ability then occurs as we move into later adulthood.

The sequence of physical changes that happen in each life stage is known as **maturation**. This process is thought to be controlled by a biological 'programme' built into our genes. Though we all change physically as we grow older, the rate, or speed, at which people age varies. For example, some very old people remain physically active and mentally alert right up until the end of their lives. Other people lose their physical skills and mental abilities at a much earlier point in their life because they have aged more quickly. The rate at which a person ages is influenced by factors such as:

- whether the person inherits 'long life' genes from their parents
- the person's attitude to life
- the person's health and fitness routines
- the extent to which the person lives a stressful life.

Intellectual development

Intellectual development is concerned with thinking, memory and language skills and occurs in every life stage. This is sometimes also referred to as '**cognitive development**'. People used to believe that a child was born with a mind like an empty book. It was thought that the 'book' gradually filled up with knowledge as the child experienced the world around it. However, scientific research has shown that babies start learning in the womb and already have some basic abilities and lots of potential at the moment of their birth. Jean Piaget (1896 – 1980) a Swiss psychologist, first put forward the theory that we are born with basic intellectual abilities that improve as we experience different stages of intellectual development during infancy, childhood and adolescence.

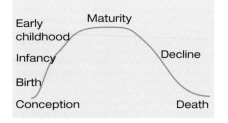

Figure 2.3 Development is a continuous process.

Over to you!

Have a look through your family photographs and identify the ways in which you and your family have changed as a result of 'maturation'.

Emotional development

Emotional development is concerned with a person's feelings. People experience emotional development in each life stage. We develop and express emotions, such as love, happiness, disappointment and anger, through the various relationships and social situations we experience. As we grow older we learn to recognise, understand and take into account other people's feelings too. The very early relationships we have with parents and close relatives, such as brothers, sisters and grandparents, play a vital role in our emotional development. Feeling loved, secure and cared for during infancy provides an important foundation for later emotional development. As we grow older the way that others treat us also has an effect on our emotional development. Emotional development involves:

- becoming aware of your '**self**'
- developing feelings about your 'self'
- working out your feelings towards other people
- developing a self-image and personal identity.

Social development

Social development is concerned with the relationships we create with others, the social skills we develop and learning the culture (or way of life) of society. Parents and teachers have a key role in our early social development. They teach us:

- the acceptable ways of behaving
- how to relate to others in everyday situations
- the importance of making and keeping good relationships with others.

This process of helping a person to develop socially is known as **socialisation**. Friends and work colleagues also become important sources of socialisation during adolescence and adulthood. Friends are particularly important during later adolescence when we are trying to create our own individual identity.

Knowledge Check

1 What does the term 'growth' refer to?
2 What is meant by development?
3 What are developmental norms?
4 Which four aspects of growth and development are referred to as PIES?
5 What does the term 'maturation' refer to?
6 What kinds of skills and abilities improve as a result of intellectual development?
7 What is emotional development?
8 What role do parents and other family members play during early socialisation?

UNIT 2

Infancy (0–3 years)

Infancy is the first human life stage that begins at birth and continues until about 2 years of age. A newborn baby will experience a huge amount of physical growth as well as physical, intellectual, emotional and social development during infancy.

Physical growth and development

Physical growth happens very quickly during infancy. A baby is born with a number of primitive reflexes but is largely helpless and dependent on others during the first year of life. **Reflexes** are automatic physical movements that a baby makes without intending to (see figure 2.4). As a result of rapid physical growth and development children quickly change from being small, very dependent babies into much larger, stronger and more capable 'toddlers' in the second year of their life.

Physical change in very young infants occurs from the head downwards and from the middle of the body outwards (see figure 1.5). As a result, a child is first able to hold their head up without help before they are able to use their body to sit up. Following this children are able to use their legs to crawl. A child's bones gradually grow and harden and their muscles get stronger in this same head-downwards, middle-outwards pattern during infancy. This allows the child to carry out new sorts of movement as their body undergoes physical development and change.

During their first 18 months infants gradually develop **gross motor skills**. These are whole body movements, such as sitting up, crawling and walking that depend on being able to control the large muscles in their arms and legs. By the end of infancy, most children also have some **fine motor skills**. These are manipulative movements that we make with our fingers which rely on control over smaller muscles and fine movement. The physical changes that infants experience transform their appearance as well as their movement abilities. They also provide the foundation for other forms of intellectual, social and emotional development to occur.

Placing

stimulus: brushing the top of foot against table top

response: the baby lifts its foot and places it on a hard surface

Walking

stimulus: held standing, feet touching a hard surface

response: the baby moves its legs forward alternately and walks

Sucking

stimulus: placing nipple or teat into the mouth

response: the baby sucks

Rooting

stimulus: brushing the cheek with a finger or nipple

response: the baby turns to the side of stimulus

Moro (startle)

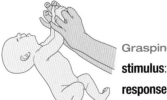

stimulus: insecure handling or sudden noise

response: the baby throws its head back, fingers fan out, arms return to embrace position and the baby cries

Grasping

stimulus: placing object in the baby's palm

response: fingers close tightly round the object

Figure 2.4 Reflexes of new babies.

Measuring physical change

A child's physical growth is usually measured by a health visitor during infancy. After weighing and measuring a child, the health visitor will record their details on a percentile chart (see figure 2.6). **Percentile charts** of weight and height have been compiled after studying and recording the growth patterns of thousands of children to work out average and expected patterns. There are different charts for girls and boys. When they are completed for a specific child, a percentile chart provides clear, visual information about their growth.

The bold line on the chart in figure 2.6 shows the average trend in weight gain expected in boys during the first 12 months of their life. This means that if a 4-month-old boy weighs 7 kg, on average 50 per cent of boys of the same age will weigh less than him and 50 per cent of boys of the same age will weigh more than him. If a boy weighs 13 kg at 11 months, then the graph says that 97 per cent of boys of the same age will weigh less than he does and 3 per cent will, on average, weigh more. Care practitioners, such as health visitors and GPs, use percentile charts to monitor progress and note whether a child's growth is following an expected pattern.

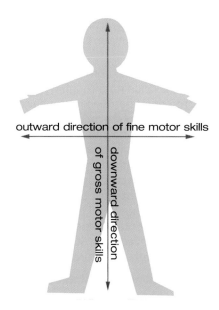

Figure 2.5 Direction of motor development.

Intellectual development

Intellectual development refers to the development of thinking and understanding. It involves changes in a person's ability to make sense of situations, remember and recall things and use language. Intellectual development begins in the womb and never really ends until the person dies. A great deal of basic intellectual development happens during infancy.

The Swiss psychologist Jean Piaget identified a number of stages of intellectual development. He saw infancy as the period when children went through the **sensorimotor stage**. During this stage, infants learn about themselves and the world through their senses (touch, hearing, sight, smell, and taste – hence *sensori*) and through physical activity (also known as *motor* activity). As well as handling, listening to and looking at new things, infants often put objects into their mouths as a way of investigating and trying to understand them.

One very important lesson that children learn during this stage is that objects and people in the world continue to exist even when they can't be seen. This might seem obvious to you now, but it's not to a young baby. A child of 8 months or less won't usually search for an object that has been hidden or which they drop out of sight because, to the child, it no longer seems to exist. A child will search for 'hidden' objects in later infancy because they develop what is known as **object permanence**. This means that they learn that objects do still exist even though they can't see them.

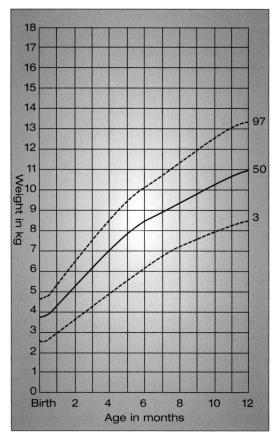

Figure 2.6 Boys percentile chart.

Language development

Learning to speak is a key feature of intellectual development during infancy. People who are responsible for young children have an important role to play in helping them to communicate well and to use language in a wide variety of ways. While children do not actually use their first proper words until they are about one year old, babies begin developing communication skills almost straight from birth.

A baby is, in fact, born with the ability to communicate in a range of ways, including through crying, babbling and using facial expressions. Infants acquire a better understanding of the world around them quite quickly as they begin to explore their surroundings and interact with their main carers. By the time they are 2 years old most children will point at and name familiar objects when they see them ('dog' or 'bus' for example) and be able to join a few simple words together ('go park' or 'shoes on', for example). However, whilst most children don't begin asking questions or using longer sentences until early childhood, the environment in which an infant lives can influence the speed and extent to which they develop intellectually. Stimulation, support and encouragement are all important features of this early learning.

Emotional and social development

Emotional and social development during infancy is extremely important. It is thought that a person's earliest relationships set the pattern for other relationships that they will go on to develop in each life stage. Ideally children should develop feelings of trust and security during infancy. This happens when a child establishes an **attachment relationship** with their parents or main caregivers in the first year of life. The parental response to this emotional linking is known as **bonding**. Attachment and bonding are needed for a first relationship to occur. The quality of the relationship between a baby and parent is influenced by:

- how sensitively the parent understands and responds to the baby's needs
- the personality of the parent or carer
- the consistency of the care that the baby receives
- the baby's own temperament.

We gradually expand our social circle during infancy by making relationships with brothers, sisters, other relatives and perhaps neighbours' children. These relationships are strongly influenced by the infant's emerging **communication skills**. A child is increasingly able to look at the world from the point of view of other people, becoming less **egocentric**, as they progress through infancy. This is demonstrated by the gradual changes that occur in the way in which children in this age group play.

Knowledge Check

1 What kinds of reflexes do newborn babies have?

2 What physical changes need to happen before a child can crawl?

3 Explain what gross motor skills are, giving examples.

4 Using examples, explain what fine motor skills are.

5 What is a percentile chart used for?

6 How do children learn during the sensorimotor stage of development?

7 What is an attachment relationship?

8 What factors help children to develop successful social relationships?

Investigate ...

Ask your parents about your own early growth and development. Try to find out whether you followed the expected pattern of development, when you reached different 'milestones' and what their memories are of you as a baby and infant.

0 – 1 year: solo play

It's difficult for me to think of people other than myself so I like to play on my own. I learn through exploring everything around me.

2 – 3 years: parallel play

I'm still mainly interested in myself and I can't see the sense of sharing yet. I am interested in other people so I like to be near them. I learn by imitating other people.

Figure 2.7 Early stages of play.

Case study

Luke is 18 months old. His mum, Cheryl, spends most time with Luke looking after him at home whilst his dad, Simon, is out at work. Cheryl has recently started taking Luke to a playgroup one day a week. Luke really enjoys this, running around, using the toys and playing alongside other children. Luke likes toys that he can pick up and hold, like teddies and small building blocks, as well as toys that he can push and move about, like toy cars and trains. Luke also likes dogs a lot. He will point and say 'dog' whenever he sees a dog on the television or whilst he is outside at the park or in his pram.

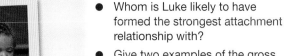

- Whom is Luke likely to have formed the strongest attachment relationship with?
- Give two examples of the gross motor skills Luke has developed.
- How does Luke use fine motor skills at the playgroup?
- What types of play does Luke take part in when he is at playgroup?
- Is Luke's language development appropriate for his age? Give reasons for your answer.

Early childhood (4–10 years)

Compared to infancy, childhood is quite a long life stage. Growth and development during childhood isn't as rapid as in infancy. However, a person will change a great deal in all of the PIES areas during their childhood.

Physical growth and development

If you go to a primary school you will see that learning activities in the reception and lower infant classes are often directed towards refining and expanding co-ordination and fine motor skills. Young children begin to gain greater control over their bodies and develop a range of complex physical skills during childhood. A child will improve their balance control and coordination early in childhood. This will allow them to develop more complex physical skills, such as skipping, catching a ball and riding a bicycle. A child's body changes noticeably in early childhood as they lose their baby shape and gradually develop the proportions of a small adult. Most children will experience a **growth spurt** in the middle part of childhood, though their rate of growth is slower in childhood than it was during infancy.

Intellectual development

According to Jean Piaget (see page 83), the second stage of intellectual development occurs in early childhood between the ages of 2 and 7 years. This is known as the **pre-operational stage**. In this stage children become less reliant on physical learning (seeing, touching and holding things) because they develop the ability to think about objects and **concepts** that are not actually there in front of them. Children need to understand concepts like numbers, letters of the alphabet and colours to be able to learn to read, write and tell the time. Intellectual development during childhood results in huge improvements in a child's thinking and language abilities and in their communication skills. In early childhood, children ask lots of questions in an attempt to understand more about their environment and the society in which they live. By the end of childhood a child will be able to use adult speech easily and will have vastly improved their knowledge and thinking skills.

Moral development

An important change occurs in a child's sense of values and in the way that they think about 'right' and 'wrong' and 'good' and 'bad' during early childhood. This is because a child's **conscience** is said to develop during this life stage.

During childhood children learn to base their judgements about right and wrong and good and bad on rules that they have been taught by people who have authority in their lives, such as parents and teachers. Children will generally obey rules if this means that they will avoid being punished or that they will receive rewards. The standards of morality that are taught or demonstrated by parents tend to have a big influence on young children who wish to be a 'good boy' or 'good girl'. This lasts until late childhood or early adolescence, when making a moral judgement becomes a more sophisticated process.

Emotional development

Children begin to learn to cope with their emotions and the feelings that others express towards them during early childhood. Controlling anger, jealousy and frustration and dealing with disapproval and criticism of their behaviour are part of emotional development during this life stage. A child's parents, siblings, teachers and friends all play a part in this process and also nurture a child's emotional development by offering love, acceptance and respect too. A child who feels encouraged and supported and who has good role models will develop self-confidence and a sense of independence more easily than a child who is criticised, discouraged and over-protected during early childhood.

Most children gradually increase their self-confidence, make friendships and become a little more independent at primary school. However, some children also find their first days at school emotionally difficult and distressing. Children are able to cooperate, appreciate the viewpoints and feelings of others in ways that infants cannot. This enables children to play together and to join in groups and team games. Friendships become very important and can also be emotionally intense during childhood.

Social development

Children need to make relationships with people from outside of their own family during early childhood. They have to learn to co-operate, communicate and spend time with new people. Going to nursery and then primary school are two important ways in which children do this. Children's play changes from the **solo** and **parallel play** of infancy to **associative** and **cooperative play** during this life stage (see figure 2.8). Children are now able to choose their own friends and want their peers to like and approve of them. Successful social relationships among children are helped by:

- secure attachment in their early years
- mixing with other children, especially where this involves activities that require co-operation

Over to you!

What could a parent do to encourage a child to have a positive, happy attitude towards life?

- the personality of the child: friendly, supportive and optimistic children make friends more easily than children who are negative and aggressive.

Most children develop a preference for same-sex friends and become very aware of and sensitive to differences between boys and girls.

3 years old: associative play

Over 3 years old: cooperative play

I can see that it's more important to share and help other children. I realise that if I cooperate with the other children we have more fun and do more interesting things.

I'm beginning to understand how they feel and to be sympathetic, so that makes it easier to play with other children. I learn a lot by imitating and pretending to be people who are important to me.

▲ Figure 2.8 Later types of play.

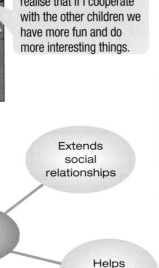

Develops imagination

Extends social relationships

Encourages interest in others

PLAY

Helps cooperation

Promotes interaction

Figure 2.9 How play helps.

Case study

Hanif, aged 5, has recently started primary school. He was anxious at first but now he loves to go. He likes playing with other children, painting and listening to the stories that his teacher reads to the class. Hanif's teacher encourages him to take part in a range of practical activities and always praises him for doing his best and working with other children. Hanif is learning to name colours, write his name and count to ten. Hanif's teacher has noticed that he has made two friends in the class whom he likes to sit by and play with. Hanif and his two friends often chase each other around the playground and play imaginary games together.

- Which stage of intellectual development is Hanif in?
- What kinds of concepts will Hanif need to understand to be able to write a story and do basic arithmetic?
- How will the development of Hanif's conscience affect his behaviour during this life stage?
- What evidence is there that Hanif has developed socially since starting primary school?
- What kind of play does Hanif now take part in with his friends?

Knowledge Check

1 What kinds of physical skills do children develop during childhood?

2 How does a child's thinking change develop during childhood?

3 What does the term moral development refer to?

4 How can going to school influence a child's social development?

5 How can a child's self-confidence and independence be developed?

6 What does the term 'egocentric' mean?

7 What is co-operative play?

Adolescence (11–18 years)

Adolescence can begin from the age of 9 and typically ends at about 18 years of age. The process of maturation that happens in this life stage is called **puberty**. It is a process that results in a lot of physical growth and change as well as considerable intellectual, emotional and social development.

Physical growth and change

The growth spurt and physical changes that occur in puberty are caused by an increase in hormonal activity. **Hormones** are chemical secretions that pass directly into the blood from the endocrine glands. The thyroid gland and the pituitary gland are the two main glands that secrete growth and development hormones. Several different hormones are secreted by each of these glands (see figure 2.10).

The pituitary gland controls the production of hormones that affect growth and development. The pituitary gland is located at the base of the brain and is only the size of a pea. The thyroid gland is located in the neck. It influences our general growth rate, bone and muscle development and the functioning of our reproductive organs. During puberty the testes in boys produce the hormone testosterone and the ovaries in girls produce oestrogen and progesterone. These hormones control the development and function of the reproductive organs.

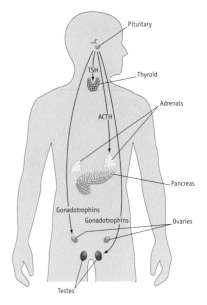

Figure 2.10 Hormones are released from endocrine glands.

Physical changes in boys	Physical changes in girls
Grow taller and heavier	Grow taller and heavier
Grow pubic, facial and underarm hair	Menstruation (periods) start
Penis and testes grow larger	Develop breasts
Shoulders and chest broaden and muscles develop	Hips broaden and shape changes
Voice 'breaks' or deepens	Grow pubic and underarm hair

During puberty boys and girls develop the secondary sexual characteristics that enable them to produce children and which give them their adult body shape.

Intellectual development

The emergence of **abstract thinking** skills is the key feature of intellectual development during adolescence. A person who can think abstractly can think about things in a theoretical or hypothetical way. For example, mathematical equations involve abstract thinking as does thinking about what you would like to do in the future. Children do not have abstract thinking skills so they can't plan ahead in the same way as adolescents. Piaget called this the **formal operational** stage of intellectual development. It enables the person to use logic to think through and solve the problems they face in everyday life. Abstract thinking is considered to be the final stage of thought development. However, a person's intellectual development is not completed in adolescence because we gain and use experience during early, middle and later adulthood to improve our thinking, understanding and decision-making.

Emotional development

Adolescence can be an emotionally difficult but eventful time. The hormonal changes of puberty can cause mood swings and intense emotions that may at times be difficult for the adolescent, as well as their family and friends, to cope with. Developing a clear personal identity, making friendships and experiencing emotional support from peers and family members are all important concerns in this phase.

Adolescents often experiment with intimate personal relationships with members of the opposite sex, and sometimes the same sex, as they explore their sexuality and the positive and negative emotions that result from close relationships. This experimentation can include making decisions about whether or not to engage in sexual activity as part of a boyfriend / girlfriend relationship. In this phase of emotional development, individuals tend to gain greater understanding of their own emotions as well as the thoughts, feelings and motives of others.

Social development

Adolescents strive to achieve a personal identity that is distinctive and separate from that of their parents. As a result social relationships with people outside of the person's immediate family become more important. For example, peer groups and close friends become important influences and sources of advice and guidance in the quest for a new sense of 'who' the adolescent is. The questioning and sometimes rejection of parent's values and opinions that is often a part of this process can lead to conflict. Adolescents may also experiment with their clothes, appearance and behaviour to both try and find an identity for themselves and to fit in with others of the same age and background. Wearing the right clothes, listening to the right music and being seen in the right places with the right people become important issues for many adolescents. Because of their need to fit in and achieve a sense of belonging to a peer group, some adolescents experiment with alcohol, drugs and sexual relationships. **Peer group pressure** can lead some adolescents into

Emotions and relationships can feel intense and be difficult for many adolescents to manage

Figure 2.11 Peer groups affect various aspects of development.

activities and situations that they find difficult to resist or challenge despite them knowing that they shouldn't participate.

Moral development

During adolescence the way that people think about moral issues - such as the difference between 'right' and 'wrong' - changes. Adolescents typically base their judgements about what is 'right' and 'wrong' on the rules, or norms, of the social groups to which they belong. Family, friendship and peer groups and any churches or clubs to which we belong influence our moral judgements. In contrast to childhood when we believe that good behaviour is what pleases the important individuals in our lives, we tend to be guided by the more abstract laws and rules of society during adolescence. Adolescents are more likely to be guided by a sense of duty to conform to the general rules of the social groups to which they belong rather than obeying the specific things that their parents tell them. Being law abiding and a good citizen or accepted as one of the gang is now more important than being a 'good boy' or a 'good girl'.

Over to you!

How have you developed since you left primary school? Using the headings 'Physical development', 'Intellectual development', 'Emotional development' and 'Social development' list the ways in which you have changed and developed since this time.

Knowledge Check

1 What is the process of maturation that happens in adolescence called?

2 Describe three physical changes that girls experience during puberty.

3 Describe three physical changes that boys experience during puberty.

4 How do hormones influence growth and development during adolescence?

5 Which new type of thinking skill develops during adolescence?

6 How is a person's way of judging moral issues likely to change during adolescence?

7 What does the term 'peer group' mean?

8 Explain why conflict with parents is often a feature of adolescence.

Case study

Maddie is 14 years of age. She currently has a poor relationship with her mum who she says is 'too mean and always picking on me'. Maddie believes that she is 'grown up enough' to meet her friends from school in town on Saturday. Maddie's parents agreed until one of their neighbours told them that Maddie had been seen smoking and drinking alcohol with her friends and some older boys in the garden of a local pub. Maddie's parents were very annoyed about this and have since stopped her from going out at weekends unless they are with her. Maddie is equally annoyed with her parents. She claims their reaction is 'embarrassing' her and that they are ruining her friendships. Maddie refuses to accept that she has done anything wrong because 'no one got hurt, did they?' She becomes very angry when her mum says that she will 'get a reputation' if she carries on behaving like this. Maddie argues that as 'everyone else treats me like an adult, you should too'.

- What is the process of maturation that Maddie is currently experiencing called?
- Describe the main physical effects that Maddie's hormones will be having on her body.
- Explain why teenagers like Maddie often come into conflict with their parents.
- Are Maddie's parents right to be concerned about her behaviour or is this 'normal' for someone in her life stage?
- Do you think Maddie's social development is likely to be helped or hindered by close involvement with her peer group?
- Why do you think Maddie is unable to accept her parents view that her behaviour is wrong?

Adulthood (19–65 years)

Early adulthood is when people commonly think of themselves as being 'grown up'. It is, in some ways, the high point of human development. Early adulthood is the developmental stage in which people achieve their maximum physical size and capacity and the stage at which a person's intellectual abilities are at their peak. Overall, adulthood is the longest human life stage though there are significant differences between early, middle and late adulthood.

Physical growth and development

Physical changes in adulthood are not like the changes that occur in childhood and adolescence, as they are not always about growth. Physical growth is largely complete by the end of adolescence. However, a lot of physical development does occur in early adulthood as people apply their physical potential and abilities. For example, most people are capable of achieving their maximum physical performance during early adulthood. You may have noticed that athletes and sports professionals tend to achieve their best performances while they are young adults. Early adulthood is also the life stage in which men and women usually produce their children.

Physical change is occurring gradually throughout early adulthood. A person's physique, their fitness and their physical abilities are all slowly declining as the person ages. For example, in the second half of early adulthood, from about 30 years to 45 years, the amount of fatty tissue in a person's body increases, they move more slowly and take longer to recover from their efforts. By the end of early adulthood, many people have begun to lose their hair or go grey and will begin to see wrinkles developing around their eyes as their skin becomes less supple.

Most women have their children during early adulthood.

Case study

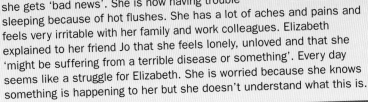

Elizabeth is 50 years of age. Recently she has been feeling as if she is both mentally and physically unwell. She has tried to explain this to her husband but can't properly express how she feels or explain how bad it can get some days. Elizabeth's husband said she should see her GP (family doctor) to get some help. Elizabeth is reluctant to do this in case she gets 'bad news'. She is now having trouble sleeping because of hot flushes. She has a lot of aches and pains and feels very irritable with her family and work colleagues. Elizabeth explained to her friend Jo that she feels lonely, unloved and that she 'might be suffering from a terrible disease or something'. Every day seems like a struggle for Elizabeth. She is worried because she knows something is happening to her but she doesn't understand what this is.

- What is the name of the physical change that is affecting Elizabeth?
- Explain why Elizabeth is experiencing this physical change.
- How might Elizabeth's emotional development be affected by this experience?
- What could Jo do or say that might be supportive for Elizabeth?

Physical change becomes more obvious during middle adulthood when many people experience a reduction in their physical abilities and a decline in their physical performance compared to earlier stages of their life. These physical changes are often referred to as **ageing**. During middle age, from about 45 to 65 years of age, a person is likely to experience some or all of the following physical changes:

- increasing and more obvious hair loss
- slower movement and reduced stamina
- reduced hand-eye coordination
- less muscle power
- deteriorating eyesight
- appearance of wrinkles as the skin loses elasticity
- decline in fertility as sperm production diminishes (men)
- loss of natural fertility following the onset of menopause (women)
- an increase in weight.

Physical fitness helps to maintain health in middle age.

The role of hormones

Both men and women lose some or all of their ability to reproduce during middle adulthood. In men a gradual reduction in fertility occurs as their levels of testosterone decline throughout adulthood. A better-known physical change is the one which affects women. **Menopause**, or the ending of menstruation and the natural ability to produce children, occurs because a woman's ovaries produce less and less of the hormones oestrogen and progesterone until a point is reached at which the ovaries stop producing eggs.

Intellectual development

Adults are generally capable of abstract thought, have memories functioning at their peak and can think very quickly. Adults often improve their intellectual skills and abilities through education and training and by using them to solve problems at work and in everyday life situations. Acquiring new knowledge and skills is necessary during adulthood to cope with the changes that frequently occur in a person's personal life – such as having children – or at work or in the job they do. People who seek to progress in their jobs or gain promotion will need to undertake some additional learning to achieve their goals. Compared to older people, however, younger adults lack experience. As a result, they may not always make good decisions or have the same depth of knowledge.

The highest position that a person achieves in their job or career is often reached during middle age. This is the point in life where people are able to combine intellectual abilities developed during adolescence and early adulthood with the experience they have gained throughout their working life. Many people in this life stage also seek intellectual stimulation through their hobbies and social life or by extending their education through evening classes or other part-time courses. It is also not unusual for people to retrain for new careers or to pursue new directions in their personal life during their middle age. These kinds of changes often require the person to acquire further knowledge and learn new skills.

Emotional development

It is difficult to generalise about emotional development in early adulthood because people have such a broad range of experiences. Achieving a stable and fulfilling relationship, perhaps also having children, is a life goal for many young adults. However, other young adults choose to live their life without a partner and may not wish to have children either. Adults are expected to be emotionally mature and to have more self-control and self-awareness than adolescents.

People can experience a number of transitions that have important emotional consequences during early adulthood. Marriage and divorce, parenthood and increasing work responsibility, and the loss of elderly parents for example, are life events that may be experienced during early adulthood and which influence emotional development.

Figure 2.12 Factors influencing adult emotional development.

The nature of emotional development during middle age is often determined by the emotional foundations laid by the person earlier in life. For some people, middle age is a period of contentment and satisfaction. For others, it is a period of crisis. People who experience good health, financial stability and already have caring and supportive family and friends are more likely to enjoy their middle age than those who fear growing old, have health problems and lack support from others.

Moral development

Many people find that they need to revise their ways of judging right and wrong and how they make other moral judgements during adulthood. This happens where people discover that the complexities of adult life mean the simple, clear-cut moral rules they used in adolescence are no longer helpful. As a result some adults develop what is known as **principled morality**. This means that they tend to make judgements on self-chosen principles. They discover situations where they feel that rules and laws need to be ignored or changed and try to use universal principles like truth, equality and social justice to make their decisions. This way of thinking about moral issues is clearly very different to that of children who apply simple rules to gain the approval of parents and other people.

Social development

People typically leave home to live independently of their family in early adulthood. Greater independence requires new relationships. Often young adults make new friendships through work and social life, focus quite strongly on finding a partner and sustaining an intimate relationship. New responsibilities and an extension of the person's social circle may also result from marriage or cohabitation. Much of adulthood is concerned with trying to find a balance between the competing demands of work, family and friends. Each of these types of relationship contributes to social development by giving the person a sense of connection and belonging to others.

Social development during middle age tends to revolve around people trying to achieve their position in society, their ambitions in life and adjustments to some of their existing relationships.

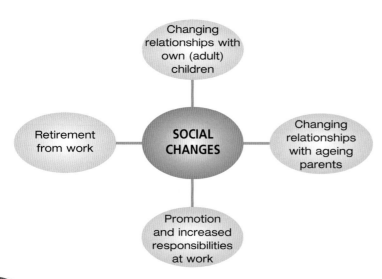

Figure 2.13 Social changes during middle age.

During middle age people often find that they need to review and adjust their social relationships as children leave home (the 'empty-nest syndrome'), parents become unwell or infirm and retirement from work becomes a reality. For many people, these changes in social relationships have a significant impact and result in changes to their self-concept. Adjusting to the 'empty-nest syndrome', retiring from work and finding a new role and purpose in life are social challenges faced by many people in this life stage.

Over to you!

What skills, qualities or abilities do you want to develop by the time you reach middle age? Make some lists using *skills*, *qualities* and *abilities* as headings to organise your ideas.

Case study

Richard Masters is 41 years of age. As an ambitious deputy head teacher, Richard has recently attended a course to prepare him for a headship. He is hoping to apply for jobs in the near future. However, other parts of Richard's life are less successful. Richard feels very disappointed that his 18-year marriage has failed. His wife and 11-year-old daughter Katy have moved away and he is missing them. Richard feels that he still has a responsibility to support Katy financially and wants to maintain his close parental relationship with her. Richard's mother Belinda, who is 82 years of age, recently moved to live in a residential home as she is no longer able to live on her own. Belinda now relies on Richard for practical and emotional support. She looks forward to visits from Richard and Katy as they usually have lots of news to tell her. Richard hasn't told his mum about his marital problems and he is feeling very stressed by this.

- Which aspect of Richard's development has been affected by his attendance at the recent headship training course?
- How would you expect Richard's body to have changed during the life stage he is currently in?
- Identify three experiences Richard has had during early adulthood that will have influenced his emotional development.
- How might Richard's personal development be affected by the failure of his marriage?
- In what ways might Richard's personal development be affected by his changing relationship with his mother?
- What could Richard do to improve his social development as he enters middle age?

Knowledge Check

1 Why are most athletics records set by people in early adulthood?

2 What kinds of physical changes happen in early adulthood?

3 Describe three physical changes that affect people during middle age.

4 What does the term 'menopause' refer to?

5 Why do women experience the menopause?

6 Explain why intellectual development is important during early adulthood.

7 What can people do to promote their intellectual development during middle age?

8 What kind of events can affect emotional development during early adulthood?

9 Describe how the 'empty-nest' syndrome might affect an individual's personal development during middle age.

10 What does the term 'principled morality' mean?

11 Describe the kinds of factors that influence social development during early adulthood.

Understanding Personal Development and Relationships

Later adulthood (65+ years)

The process of physical ageing quickens for all people from about the age of 55 years. By the age of 75 years the physical effects of ageing are clearly evident. However, despite the reality of physical decline in later adulthood older people don't suddenly or always become unwell, infirm or need extra care. Many older people are physically healthy, robust and active enough to continue living without any special support in their own homes. While the stereotypes of older people are quite negative, the gradual decline in abilities that occur in later adulthood doesn't necessarily mean that older people have a poor quality of life or are unhappy.

Physical development

During later adulthood people experience a gradual physical decline in both the structure and functioning of their body. These changes are part of the normal ageing process and include:

- Reduced heart and lung function.
- Reduced mobility, often resulting from muscle wastage, brittle bones and stiff joints.
- Loss of elasticity in the skin and the development of wrinkles.
- Changes in hair colour (grey then white) and texture (finer and thinner). Many men, and a smaller proportion of women, lose hair from the top of the head.
- Changes to the nervous system may impair the person's sense of taste and smell and can mean that they are less sensitive to the cold. This increases the risk of hypothermia.
- Hearing tends to deteriorate slowly as people age. Quiet and high-pitched sounds (and voices!) become more difficult to hear.
- Sight is affected because the lens in the eye loses its elasticity. The result is that older people find it harder to focus on close objects.
- Weakening of bones, also known as **osteoporosis**, also affects some people in later adulthood. Calcium and protein are lost from the bones and older people can become physically frail and experience fractures as a result.
- Many people become shorter in later adulthood as their intervertebral discs in the spine become thinner and their posture becomes bent.

Intellectual development

Older people maintain and use their intellectual abilities in much the same ways as adults and middle-aged people. Both the young-old (60–75 years) and the old-old (75 years and over) need and enjoy intellectually stimulating activities in their lives. The speed at which older people are able to think and respond is generally reduced, but mental capacity and intelligence are not lost. Older people do not become any less intelligent as a result of ageing!

There are many negative ideas about older people's intellectual abilities. While it is true that a minority of older people do

Older people are often physically active.

Ageing doesn't necessarily reduce intellectual ability

develop dementia-related illnesses and have memory problems, the majority of older people do not. People who develop **dementia-related illnesses** tend to have memory problems, especially in recalling recent information, and become confused more easily. These types of illnesses also result in sufferers gradually losing speech and other abilities that are controlled by the brain.

Emotional and social development

Social and emotional development takes on a new importance in the later stages of the life span. Many older people reflect on their achievements and past experiences as a way of making sense of their life. This may involve coming to terms with the changes that occur in their relationships as children move into early and middle adulthood, partners and friends may die and a range of previous life roles (work and personal) may end. However, older people do continue to develop and change emotionally as they experience new life events and transitions, such as becoming grandparents and retiring from work. They may also have more leisure time in which to build relationships with friends and family members. Despite this many older people also experience insecurity and loneliness if their social contacts are reduced and they become isolated.

Grandchildren can promote emotional development.

 ## Case study

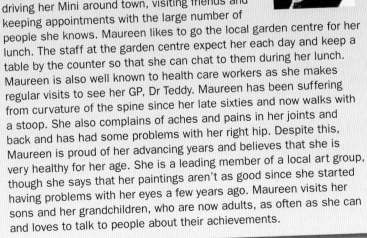

Maureen Walker is 83 years of age, and very proud of it! She has one son who is now in his early sixties. Maureen's husband Gerald died ten years ago. Her only sister Stella died earlier this year. Maureen is still grieving for the loss of her sister. However, Maureen is very sociable and keen to make the most of each day. She enjoys driving her Mini around town, visiting friends and keeping appointments with the large number of people she knows. Maureen likes to go the local garden centre for her lunch. The staff at the garden centre expect her each day and keep a table by the counter so that she can chat to them during her lunch. Maureen is also well known to health care workers as she makes regular visits to see her GP, Dr Teddy. Maureen has been suffering from curvature of the spine since her late sixties and now walks with a stoop. She also complains of aches and pains in her joints and back and has had some problems with her right hip. Despite this, Maureen is proud of her advancing years and believes that she is very healthy for her age. She is a leading member of a local art group, though she says that her paintings aren't as good since she started having problems with her eyes a few years ago. Maureen visits her sons and her grandchildren, who are now adults, as often as she can and loves to talk to people about their achievements.

- Which aspects of Maureen's physical health may be the result of normal ageing?
- Which aspects of Maureen's life are likely to influence her intellectual development and wellbeing?
- Which events in Maureen's life may have had a significant effect on her emotional development?
- How might Maureen's relationships with others contribute to her social development and wellbeing?
- What effect might normal ageing have had on Maureen's intellectual abilities?

Investigate ...

Use your knowledge of human growth and development to produce a set of questions that you could use to interview an adult or older person about their pattern and experiences of growth and development. You will need to ensure that your interviewee is a willing volunteer and is happy for you to write about the things they tell you. Produce a timeline and a profile describing the key features of and influences on the person's growth and development.

Knowledge Check

1 Is it true that some people get shorter in old age?

2 Explain why people develop wrinkles as they grow older.

3 What does the term 'osteoporosis' mean and why does it occur?

4 Do all people over the age of 70 suffer from dementia-type illnesses?

5 What kinds of events can affect a person's emotional and social development during later adulthood?

Chapter checklist

The box below provides a summary of the areas covered in chapter 6. Tick the areas that you feel you understand and would be confident answering exam questions about. If there are any areas that you don't understand or are not confident about, you will need to return to them before you begin your exam revision.

Life stages ❏	Emotional development ❏
Developmental norms ❏	Social development ❏
Infancy	
Physical growth ❏	**Adulthood** ❏
Physical development ❏	Physical growth ❏
Emotional development ❏	Physical development ❏
Social development ❏	Intellectual development ❏
	Emotional development ❏
Childhood ❏	Social development ❏
Physical growth ❏	
Physical development ❏	**Later adulthood** ❏
Intellectual development ❏	Physical growth ❏
Emotional development ❏	Physical development ❏
Social development ❏	Intellectual development ❏
	Emotional development ❏
Adolescence ❏	Social development ❏
Physical growth ❏	
Physical development ❏	**Self-concept** ❏
Intellectual development ❏	Factors affecting self-concept ❏

Assessment Guide

Your learning in this unit will be assessed through a one hour written examination.

The examination will consist of short and longer answer questions covering all aspects of this unit. You will need to show that you understand:

● the stages and patterns of human growth and development

● the different factors that can affect human growth and development

● factors affecting the development of self-concept.

Chapter 6 provides full coverage of all of the topics you may be asked about in the examination.

Chapter 7

Factors affecting human growth and development

> ### Key issue: What factors affect human growth and development and how can they influence an individual's health, wellbeing and life opportunities?

What factors cause human beings to grow and develop? Human growth and development is a complex process that follows some predictable patterns and processes but which also results in people who are unique and individually different. Chapter 7 focuses on the different types of factors that affect human growth and development, including:

- *physical factors*, such as **genetic inheritance**, diet, amount and type of physical activity, sexual health and experience of illness or disease

- *social and emotional factors*, such as gender, family relationships, friendships, educational experiences, employment / unemployment, ethnicity and religion and life experiences such as birth, marriage, death and divorce

- *economic factors*, including income and **material possessions**

- *environmental factors*, such as housing conditions, pollution and access to health and welfare services

- *abuse and neglect* and their impact on personal development.

This chapter focuses on how these factors can influence an individual's pattern of growth and development and their self-concept.

Physical factors
e.g. genetic inheritance, diet, exercise

Social and emotional factors
e.g. gender, family, friends, education, ethnicity, culture, religion, employment/ unemployment

- **Growth**
- **Health**
- **Wellbeing**
- **Life opportunities**

Environmental factors
e.g. pollution, housing conditions

Economic factors
e.g. income/wealth, material possessions, property, social class

Figure 2.14 Factors affecting growth and development.

Physical factors

The genes we inherit, our diet, the amount and type of exercise we undertake, whether we smoke or consume alcohol to excess and the illnesses and diseases we experience are all examples of physical factors that can affect our growth and development.

Genetic inheritance

The genes that we inherit from our parents play a very important role in controlling our physical growth, appearance and the abilities we develop. Each cell in the human body contains two sets of 23 chromosomes – one set from each parent.

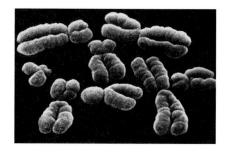

Human chromosomes magnified.

Each **chromosome** can contain up to 4,000 different genes. These are the 'instructions' or codes that tell our body's cells how to grow. The genes that control how we grow are a unique combination of our biological parents' genes. One consequence of this is that we can do very little to change the physical features and growth potential that we have. If both of your biological parents are over 6 feet tall, have large feet and are fast runners, you are also likely to grow tall, have large feet and be able to run fast! It also follows that if your parents aren't tall, you are very unlikely to grow tall. Because of your genetic inheritance, you will grow and develop to look like one or both of your parents as your body responds to the 'instructions' in your genes.

Genes also carry a lot of information that affects growth and development throughout life. A person's genes are often responsible for the illnesses and diseases that they develop during their lifetime. This is because the risk of getting conditions like heart disease, cancers and **strokes** can be inherited. A person born into a family with a history of heart disease is at greater risk of developing this condition if they have inherited 'heart disease genes'. Whether this person goes on to develop heart disease or not will depend on many non-genetic factors too. Lifestyle, for example, will be a key issue for a person in this position.

Diet

Food is essential for life and a balanced diet is the basis of good physical health. This is true in all life stages. However, the amount and types of food that a person requires to meet their physical needs will depend on factors such as their age, physical build and gender as well as how physically active they are.

An infant less than six months old can gain all the nutrients they require from breast milk or infant formula (specially made powdered milk). However, as they become more active they need to be weaned on to a balanced range of solid foods in order to grow and develop appropriately.

Children also need a balanced diet to maintain their physical growth and development and provide 'fuel' for their increasingly active lives and growing bodies. When a child consumes too much food, or an excessive amount of sugary or fatty food, they are likely to become overweight or even **obese**. This can harm the child's physical development as it may reduce their opportunities to exercise, limit mobility and hinder muscle

Investigate ...

Use the Internet to research the following genetic conditions: PKU, cystic fibrosis, sickle cell anaemia and Friedrich's ataxia. Identify:

- What each condition is
- The main effects on the health and development needs of individuals who have the condition
- How the condition is treated.

development. Being overweight or obese can also lead to social and emotional problems for children. Being teased or bullied for being 'fat' may have a negative effect on a child's emotional development because it can lead to low self-esteem. An obese or overweight child may develop a negative self-image that also inhibits their self-confidence and their ability to make and maintain relationships with other children.

The onset of puberty during adolescence results in a physical growth spurt that has to be 'fuelled' by a diet of nutritionally balanced and regular meals. However, at the same time as needing to feed a growing and rapidly changing body, adolescents (particularly girls) become more conscious of how they look and may be less conscientious about eating either balanced or regular meals. In some instances this can result in the development of eating disorders such as **anorexia nervosa** and **bulimia nervosa**. Both of these conditions tend to develop in response to a fear of 'being fat'. However, whilst most sufferers have a distorted rather than a realistic body image, the consequences of starving themselves or making themselves sick can be serious and may cause long-term physical damage.

An adult's dietary needs will depend on how much energy they require for their work and everyday life. People who have very physically demanding jobs have high energy needs. They can safely consume more food than people who have much less physically demanding jobs or lifestyles. However, an adult's dietary needs may change if they become unwell, if they are pregnant or breastfeeding or if they raise or reduce their level of physical activity for some other reason. A person who does not have a balanced diet may develop health problems because they lack vital nutrients, such as vitamins and minerals, or may become obese, develop heart disease or even diabetes if they consume too much fatty or sugary food and are not active enough to burn off the calories in their diet.

Physical activity

Undertaking an appropriate amount and type of exercise is important for physical growth and development in every life stage. Activity that exercises the different parts of the body is important in infancy and childhood because it builds up strength,

Over to you!

- Athletes often consume a diet that contains a large amount of carbohydrates. Why do you think this might be?
- What factors affect the choices you make about what you eat? Make a list of the range of factors that influence what you regularly consume.

Investigate ...

Dietary deficiencies can lead to the development of health problems. Investigate one or more of the following conditions and identify which nutrient deficiency is linked to it:

- Tooth decay
- Rickets
- Beri beri.

Figure 2.15 The benefits of exercise.

stamina, suppleness and co-ordination. Failing to exercise may result in a person becoming unfit, overweight and even obese during any life stage. Lack of physical fitness, stiff joints, heart disease, **osteoporosis**, constipation and strokes may all be experienced by adults and older people who have not looked after their bodies well enough by taking regular physical exercise.

Exercise isn't just about physical health and development though. It can also be a good way of meeting a person's emotional and social needs. For example, exercise is a good way of managing and reducing stress, can be a good way of meeting people and making friendships and generally has a positive effect on a person's self-esteem and mood.

Sexual health

Everybody has sexual needs. People have sex for a variety of reasons. These include having babies, having orgasms and expressing sexual needs and feelings. Sexual health is about having a positive and respectful approach to sexuality and sexual relationships. People who achieve sexual health have consenting, pleasurable and safe sexual experiences. Sex isn't terrible, dirty or dangerous. However, choosing to be sexually active does have consequences and can lead to physical ill-health and problems with emotional wellbeing. The main health risk of sexual activity is from **sexually transmitted diseases**.

Illness and disease

Many of the illnesses that we experience are short-term and treatable. Coughs, colds and even broken limbs can all be cured with the right medicine and treatment and don't have any lasting impact on growth or development. However, some illnesses and diseases can have much more serious consequences. Genetic diseases, such as haemophilia, Down's syndrome and cystic fibrosis, are all lifelong conditions that cannot be cured and which have an impact on a person's growth and development. Infectious diseases, such as tuberculosis, meningitis and HIV, can

Case study

Victor O'Brien is 72 years old. He was diagnosed with Alzheimer's disease three years ago. Victor first noticed problems with his memory when he was out shopping with his wife. He often had difficulty recalling what he wanted to buy and relied on his wife remembering where they had parked the car. Victor gave up driving when his memory problems and bouts of confusion increased. Victor's GP finally sent him to see a consultant psychiatrist at the local district general hospital when Victor got lost after popping out to get a newspaper from his local shop. Victor walked over 10 miles looking for his home and was eventually found, crying and frightened by the police. Victor still lives at home with his wife. She now helps him to wash, dress and eat. Victor says less and less but does like to sit listening to the radio. He has lost the ability to read and write though his wife believes that Victor does still recognise her and is able to understand most of what she says to him.

- How has Alzheimer's disease affected Victor's mental health?

- What impact has Victor's condition had on his intellectual development and wellbeing?

- What kind of care needs does Victor have as a result of having Alzheimer's disease?

- What could Victor's wife do to ensure that Victor is as physically healthy as he can be?

also cause significant and permanent damage to a person's health and development and may prove fatal if left untreated. Degenerative conditions, such as Alzheimer's disease, multiple sclerosis and arthritis, tend to affect people's health and development opportunities in adulthood or later adulthood. As well as having a severe physical impact, degenerative conditions such as these can also have a major impact on a person's social relationships, result in emotional distress and destroy their intellectual abilities.

Abuse and neglect

Children and young people, vulnerable adults, older people and people with disabilities who do not receive protection and safeguarding may experience abuse, neglect and ill-treatment that damages their personal development. Abuse and neglect are most commonly perpetrated by parents on children, by one partner on another and by carers on vulnerable people who are unwell, frail or who have developmental problems. The different forms of abuse that members of vulnerable groups experience include:

- physical abuse
- sexual abuse
- emotional and psychological abuse
- financial exploitation
- neglect.

Abuse and neglect can damage personal development in a number of ways (see figure 2.16) but are particularly damaging to an individual's social and emotional development.

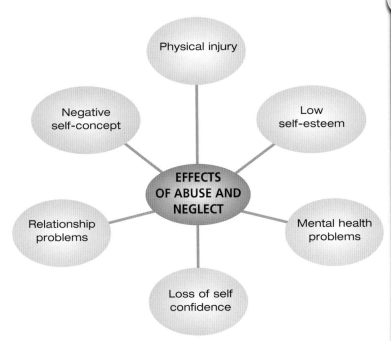

Figure 2.16 How abuse and neglect can affect people.

Knowledge Check

1 What does the term 'genetic inheritance' mean?

2 What effect can genes have on physical growth and development?

3 Describe the impact that Alzheimer's disease can have on personal development.

4 What effects might being obese have on an adolescent's personal development?

5 How can exercise have a positive effect on personal development?

6 What effects can unprotected sex have on a person's health and development?

7 How can a person achieve sexual health?

8 Name three sexually transmitted diseases beginning with 'c'.

9 Describe two ways of minimising the risk of catching a sexually transmitted disease.

Social and emotional factors

Social and emotional factors are those things that influence our relationships with, attachments to and feelings about ourselves and other people in our life.

Figure 2.17 Social and emotional factors influencing development.

Gender

A person's sex refers to whether they are biologically male or female. **Gender** on the other hand refers to the behaviour society expects from men and women. In Western societies girls are taught, or **socialised**, to express 'feminine' qualities such as being kind, caring and gentle. In contrast, boys are socialised to express 'masculine' characteristics such as being boisterous, aggressive and tough. Parents, schools, friends and the media all play a part in gender socialisation.

The gender expectations that we experience influence how we think about ourselves and how we relate to others. The idea that boys and men should experience better opportunities – especially in education and in employment – than girls and women because they are the 'superior sex' has a long history that is now being challenged. Gender is still an important issue that affects personal development but it isn't as powerful as it once was. Girls and boys now have the same educational opportunities and there are similar numbers of men and women in employment. However, on average men still earn more than women and still occupy more of the higher paid and most powerful jobs. Girls on the other hand currently get better results than boys in public examinations, like GCSEs, and may change this situation in the future.

Family relationships

Most people live as part of a family at some time in their life. The family is often seen as the foundation of society because of the key role it plays in human development. The family is said to carry out primary **socialisation**. This means that family members, especially parents, teach children the values, beliefs and skills that will prepare them for later life. The relationships we have with parents, brothers and sisters ensure that we are provided for, supported and protected as we grow and develop.

Figure 2.18 The functions of the family.

Providing	Supporting	Protecting
The family provides informal education and socialisation for children. This teaches children attitudes, values and how to behave. The family also provides the physical resources needed for growth and intellectual development, such as food, toys and other stimulation.	Families give emotional support from infancy through to adulthood. Early attachment and bonding are important sources of the stability and security we all need.	Family members protect the health and wellbeing of other members by giving informal care, advice and guidance. Family relationships are often very deep and have a lifelong influence on human development.

Whether we live in an extended family, a nuclear family, a lone parent family or a blended family our physical, intellectual, emotional and social development will be strongly influenced by other family members.

Friendships

Friendships play an important role in our social and emotional development. We first learn how to behave and relate to others through family relationships during infancy. As we move into early childhood, we begin meeting other children and increase our range of friendships. Friendships can feel especially important during adolescence when young people are trying to forge an identity separate from their parents and in adulthood where friendships form the basis of our social lives outside of the family. Friendships in later adulthood can be a vital source of companionship and connection to a person's past.

Throughout life, a person's personality, social skills and emotional development are all shaped by their friendships. Friendships play a role in helping people to feel they belong, are wanted and liked by others and that there are people they can turn to for support. However, the other side of childhood and adolescent relationships, such as bullying and rejection by peers, can have a negative effect on an individual's self-esteem and identity.

Educational experiences

In the United Kingdom most children go to school between the ages of 5 and 16 years to receive their formal education. People in the United Kingdom now have to spend a minimum of twelve years in primary and secondary education. Education promotes intellectual development because it is about learning. Intellectual development happens when a person increases their knowledge and thinking skills. However, education also has a powerful effect on a person's social and emotional development. Educational experiences are part of what is known as **secondary socialisation**. In this situation, friends, **peers** (people of the same age and social group) and teachers influence the attitudes, values and ways in

Over to you!

Make a list of all the current and past friendships that have influenced your personal development. Try to identify how each friend has influenced you. Who, out of all of your friends, would you say has been most influential?

which we behave. This builds on the primary socialisation that has already occurred within the family.

Some people learn a lot at school, succeed at exams and see education as a positive influence on their personal development. Educational success is very good for the self-esteem and self-image of these people. However, not everybody enjoys school and not everybody succeeds. Failure and bad experiences at school can lead some people to develop a negative self-image and low self-esteem.

Employment and unemployment

Employment also contributes to secondary socialisation because a person's values, beliefs and attitudes are often influenced by employers and work colleagues. Work is also an opportunity to develop new skills and extend physical, intellectual and social abilities. People often develop strong friendships at work, especially if they stay in the same job for a long time. As well as learning the social skills of co-operating with and supporting others, work-based relationships can lead to emotional development where colleagues care about each other and have a shared sense of belonging to a friendship group.

Being unemployed can also affect an individual's development because it is a stressful experience. People who become unemployed may feel angry about what they have lost, anxious about their future and can suffer a sense of rejection that affects their self-esteem and self-concept. The loss of income that unemployment brings may also mean that an unemployed individual is no longer able to participate in social and leisure

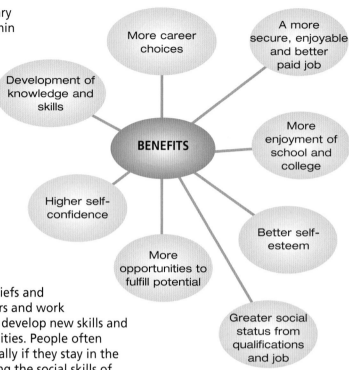

Figure 2.19 The benefits of a good education.

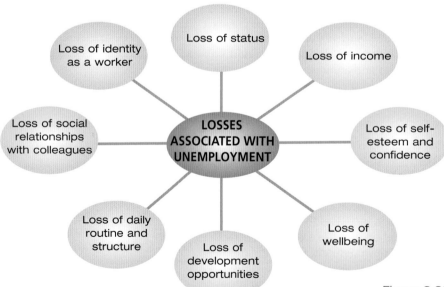

Figure 2.20 The possible impact of unemployment.

Case study

Ken Brown, aged 56, has been employed in Bennett's Department Store since he left school at 16 years of age. Forty years and many promotions later, Ken is now operations manager for the whole store. Ken is very proud of his achievements and believes that he has played an important part in the success of Bennett's over the years. Recent financial problems, largely resulting from growing unemployment in the area, have led to a crisis situation at Bennett's. Ken and the rest of the employees have been told that the company is in a lot of difficulty and may go out of business if sales don't improve in the run-up to Christmas. This has come as a huge shock to Ken. He sees Bennett's as an extended family, a place where his colleagues are also his friends and where he has grown up. Ken met his wife, another employee, at Bennett's and still sees his job as a central part of his everyday life. He claims that he has learnt more during his time at Bennett's than he ever did at school or could have learnt at college. Ken feels very emotional when he looks around the store and talks to his colleagues about the prospect of Bennett's closing down.

- How has employment at Bennett's contributed to Ken's intellectual and social development?
- Identify how working at Bennett's has influenced Ken's emotional development.
- Which aspect(s) of Ken's development are likely to be affected if Bennett's closes down?
- What impact might unemployment have on Ken's self-concept?

activities with friends, such as going to the cinema, the pub or on holiday together. Over time this could affect social relationships and may even exclude the unemployed person from a friendship group. Long-term unemployment can reduce a person's self-esteem and limit their ability to use and develop their social skills and to provide a good quality of life for themselves and their family.

Ethnicity and religion

People who have the same **ethnicity** have a shared way of life or **culture**, a common geographical origin, a particular skin colour or a common language or religion. Ethnicity can be an important feature of a person's identity, particularly where religion plays a part. It may affect personal development because it leads the individual to seek out and take part in particular activities or social groups. It may also be a label (e.g. 'Asian', 'Black', 'Welsh', 'Muslim' or 'Jewish') that influences how other people treat and respond to the person. This in itself can have a powerful effect on personal development.

Ethnicity and religion often overlap or combine to affect an individual's personal development. People who are religious generally have a set of beliefs and take part in forms of worship that focus on the existence and importance of God. Religious beliefs of one sort or another are present in all societies. Many different religions are now practiced in the United Kingdom, including Christianity, Islam, Hinduism, Sikhism and Buddhism amongst others. People who are religious often develop particular moral beliefs (about right and wrong, good and bad) and behave in ways that are expected of members of their faith. For example, drinking alcohol, cohabiting with a partner and eating meat are all practices that followers of some religions would avoid. As a result religion can have a strong influence on an individual's intellectual, social and emotional development.

Ethnicity, culture and religion often combine in special festivals.

Religious beliefs tend to have a positive effect on a person's mental health because they raise self-esteem and give an individual the sense of belonging to a larger community of people and of having a relationship with God. However, people who are not religious sometimes argue that religious beliefs limit a person's development because they impose rules and restrictions on how an individual ought to live. As a result, non-believers may see religion as restricting the range of social relationships an individual might develop and as being the cause of low self-esteem in those people who lose their faith or who cannot live up to or break the rules of their religion.

Life experiences

Life experiences are major events, both expected and unexpected, which have a profound effect on the direction of a person's life or personal development. People in middle and old age are often able to look back on their lives and identify key events or experiences that caused their lives and personal development to go in a particular direction. This is much harder to do in adolescence and early adulthood as there isn't so much to look back on!

Life events and experiences such as the birth of children, marriage, the death of loved ones and divorce, have a powerful effect on an individual's social and emotional development. Life events often cause people to think hard about themselves, what they want from life and how they relate to other people. As a result they can often trigger important phases of personal development as a person adjusts or comes to terms with the life event.

Knowledge Check

1 Explain how a person's gender can affect their personal development.

2 What does primary socialisation involve?

3 How can an infant's family influence their growth and development?

4 What does secondary socialisation involve?

5 How can friendships influence a person's development?

6 How can a person's sexual orientation affect their personal development?

7 Which aspects of personal development are promoted by involvement in local community activities?

8 What does the term 'ethnicity' refer to?

9 Describe how a major life event, such as as divorce, could affect a person's social and emotional development.

Case study

Matthew is sitting in a solicitor's office, explaining that he no longer loves his wife, Sarah. He has come to the conclusion that he is a very different person now compared to when he married Sarah 10 years ago. Matthew has told the solicitor about the regular arguments he and Sarah have about money and about how they should bring up their three-year-old son. He believes that Sarah is incapable of listening to his point of view and is unwilling to accept that their son has behaviour problems. Matthew explains that he is now taking anti-depressants and sleeping tablets because of the stress that his marital problems are causing him. He believes that his relationship with Sarah has broken down and is seeking legal advice on the best way to bring it to an end.

- Which aspects of Matthew's personal development are likely to be affected by the breakdown of his relationship with Sarah?

- How has Matthew's health and wellbeing been affected by the current situation?

- What impact might divorce have on Matthew's self-concept and self-esteem?

- What effect might a divorce have on the personal development of Matthew and Sarah's son?

Economic factors

Personal development can be affected by a number of money-related or **economic factors**. Economic factors have a strong influence on the kinds of opportunities that a person is able to enjoy in each life stage.

Income

Income refers to the money that a household or individual receives. People receive money through working, pension payments, welfare benefits and other sources such as investments. The amount of income that an individual and their family have, and the things they spend it on, can have a big impact on their personal development because it affects the quality of life available to them. People with plenty of income are likely to have better educational and leisure opportunities and will live in better circumstances than people who have little income and who may be in poverty. Having better opportunities and little or no money-related stress puts some individuals and families in a position to make the most of their abilities and potential. The reverse is the case for poorer people.

Homeless people usually live in poverty.

Material possessions and poverty

People who have a very low income and **fewer material** possessions are likely to be living in **poverty**. They are also more likely to suffer ill-health and have their opportunities for personal development restricted. The following quotation explains this:

"Poverty means staying at home, often being bored, not seeing friends, not going to the cinema, not going out for a drink and not being able to take the children out for a trip or a treat or a holiday. It means coping with the stresses of managing on very little money, often for months or even years. It means having to withstand the onslaught of society's pressure to consume … Above all, poverty takes away the building blocks to create the tools for the future – your 'life chances'. It steals away the opportunity to have a life unmarked by sickness, a decent education, a secure home and a long retirement. It stops people being able to plan ahead. It stops people being able to take control of their lives." (C. Oppenheim and L. Harker (1996) *Poverty: The Facts*, 3rd edn, Child Poverty Action Group)

Because of the existence of welfare benefits it is rare for people in the UK not to have enough income for essential food, clothing and housing. Despite this, there are still situations in which some people fall through the welfare benefits 'safety net' and live for periods of time in **absolute poverty**. This means that they find themselves without the basic means to pay for essential items like food, clothing and housing.

Far more people in the UK live in **relative poverty**. This means that a person is poor when compared to most other people in society. People living in relative poverty often don't have access to the same services and can't afford the same material possessions as others in their local community. As a result many people living in poverty are said to experience

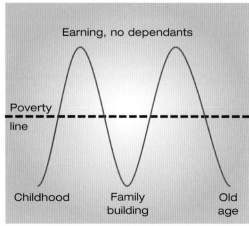

Figure 2.21 A poverty cycle.

social exclusion. Children who are born into families experiencing poverty may find this difficult to escape from. Poverty and social exclusion have such a powerful effect on personal development and life chances that people are often held back by the disadvantages and lack of opportunities that result from social exclusion.

Environmental factors

A person's physical growth as well as other aspects of their personal development can be directly and indirectly affected by the physical conditions, or environment, in which they live. Important features of the physical environment that affect growth and development include the quality of a person's housing, pollution and their access to health and welfare services.

Housing conditions

The quality of a person's housing is important because it can affect their physical health and development. Overcrowded and neglected properties provide the kinds of conditions that lead to respiratory disorders and infectious diseases, such as bronchitis and tuberculosis. Overcrowded and cramped housing can also have a damaging effect on the growth and physical development of babies, children and young people who need enough space to play and be active. The type and standard of housing that people live in is related to their income. People with low incomes are less able to afford a good standard of housing and are less able to maintain it and heat it adequately.

Pollution

Physical growth and development can be directly affected by the presence of pollution in the atmosphere. Carbon monoxide and other harmful gas emissions from vehicles, ships and factories are particularly damaging to a person's respiratory system. Babies and children can have their growth potential restricted, though people at all stages of life can have their physical health

Aircraft are a source of noise and air pollution.

Over to you!

What is good housing? Identify the features that you feel are important in making a person's housing conditions 'healthy'. Alternatively, if you were looking for somewhere to live, what kind of conditions would put you off renting or buying a house or flat?

damaged by the effects of poor air quality. Noise pollution from vehicles, aircraft and busy crowded environments can damage a person's hearing and their psychological wellbeing. Unwanted noise is also associated with high stress levels, sleep disturbances and high blood pressure. Noise pollution is worst in built-up, urban environments.

Access to health and welfare services

Good access to health and welfare services is likely to improve a person's life chances as they will be able to obtain services that meet their needs. This may be particularly important for people who have chronic health problems, for women when they are pregnant and for older people who make more use of health and welfare services as they age. However, the **'postcode lottery'** faced by some people, particularly those living in rural areas, means that some people may not have an equal and fair chance of receiving health and welfare services when they require them. Specialist care for children or for people with cancer, for example, is not equally available throughout the UK. People living in remoter rural areas may also find they have to travel long distances to access both general health care and more specialist services.

Over to you!

How does the place where you live affect your ability to access health and welfare services? Are most services available locally or do you have to travel some distance to see health care workers? How far away from where you live are the specialist services, such as a children's hospital, that provide care for a whole region?

Knowledge Check

1 What does the term 'income' refer to?

2 How might a family's income affect the personal development of its members?

3 What does the term 'material possessions' refer to?

4 Describe two forms of poverty and their impact on personal development.

5 Describe two sources of air pollution.

6 What effect might air pollution have on the health of a developing child?

7 How can a person's housing conditions affect their health and development?

8 Describe how living in a rural environment may affect an individual's ability to access health and welfare services.

9 Explain the term 'postcode lottery'.

Chapter checklist

The box below provides a summary of the areas covered in chapter 7. Tick the areas that you feel you understand and would be confident answering exam questions about. If there are any areas that you don't understand or are not confident about, you will need to return to them before you begin your exam revision.

Physical factors
- Genetic inheritance ☐
- Diet ☐
- Exercise ☐
- Sexual health ☐
- Illness and disease ☐

Social and emotional factors
- Gender ☐
- Family relationships ☐
- Friendships ☐
- Educational experiences ☐
- Employment / unemployment ☐
- Ethnicity and religion ☐
- Life experiences ☐

Economic factors
- Income ☐
- Poverty and material possessions ☐

Environmental factors
- Housing conditions ☐
- Pollution ☐
- Access to health and welfare services ☐

Assessment Guide

Your learning in this unit will be assessed through a one hour written examination.

The examination will consist of a series of short and longer answer questions covering all aspects of this unit. You will need to show that you understand:

● the different factors that can affect human growth and development.

Chapter 7 provides full coverage of the range of factors that you could be asked about in the examination.

Chapter 8

Self-concept and different types of relationships

Key issue: What factors influence the development of a person's self-concept and what effect do relationships have on an individual's personal development?

Self-concept

A person's **self-concept** is their view of 'who' they are. Self-concept is a combination of **self-image** and **self-esteem**. An individual's self-concept is continually developing during each life stage and is closely linked to emotional and social development. It expresses what we think and feel about ourselves as individuals and gives us our sense of identity.

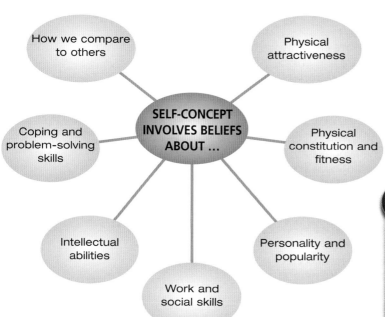

Figure 2.22 Aspects of self-concept.

Self-esteem refers to the way a person values themselves. Self-esteem often results from the way we compare ourselves to other people. People who compare themselves negatively to others, thinking they are not as good, not as attractive or not as capable are more likely to have low self-esteem.

Over to you!

Think about your main features and characteristics. For example, consider:
● your height
● your gender
● your eye colour
● where you live
● your personality.

Using both words and pictures, produce a self-portrait that describes your self-image. How would you sum up your view of the 'essential you' at this point in your life?

Over to you!

How do you feel about yourself as a person at the moment? Write some comments about the things that you:
- like about yourself
- would like to change if you could
- are good at
- feel weaker or no good at.

Figure 2.23 Factors affecting self-concept across the lifespan.

People who are confident but not arrogant, who accept that they have both strengths and weaknesses, and who feel encouraged, loved and wanted, tend not to undervalue themselves so much. Their self-esteem is generally higher as a result.

Having a clear, positive picture of who we are and how we feel about ourselves helps to make us feel secure and affects the way that we relate to other people. A number of factors influence the way an individual's self-concept develops and changes.

Age

The image that you have of yourself today will not be the same self-image that you reflect on when you are 40, 60 or 80 years old. The physical, intellectual, emotional and social changes that occur as you age and mature will affect your self-concept over time. For example, a person's self-image can be linked to the view that they have of their physical capabilities. Your physical capabilities will change as you experience health, fitness, illness and disability at different points in your life. The value that society attaches to you as an individual will also alter as you grow older. In Western societies old age is generally viewed negatively and older people seem to be less valued than younger people. This is sometimes different for members of minority ethnic groups who may value old age more. The way that people of different ages are portrayed in the media confirms this and inevitably affects the self-concepts of many older people.

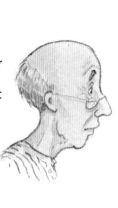

Appearance

A person's physical features, their clothes and their non-verbal behaviour, all influence and express aspects of their self-concept. How we present ourselves and how we believe others see us are particularly important influences on self-concept when we are adolescents and young adults. As we get older, physical appearance and the way that we present ourselves tend to have a smaller impact on our self-concept.

Gender

Gender refers to the way ideas about masculinity and femininity are applied to men and women in our society. Wider social attitudes towards gender can shape a person's self-concept. In Western societies there are a number of gender stereotypes associated with male and female roles and behaviour. The images of men and women presented in the media express these stereotypes and the general social expectations of men and women.

Even though gender stereotypes do not reflect the reality of most people's lives in British society they can still shape self-image and self-esteem in a positive way, especially where an individual is able and wishes to conform to the roles and ways of looking and behaving that the stereotypes suggest. Gender stereotypes can also have a negative effect on self-concept. They can induce guilt, a sense of inadequacy and lack of self-confidence, especially where the person is unable or unwilling to match up to the stereotype of men or women in a particular situation.

Culture

Ethnicity affects self-concept by influencing people's feelings of belonging and ideas about membership of different social groups. Culture and ethnic identity can, for example, give people a sense of shared values. However, it can also lead to people being treated differently, perhaps in an unfair and discriminatory way, and thereby affects their sense of self-worth and self-esteem.

Emotional maturity

An individual will generally become more emotionally mature as they age. Growing maturity allows a person to become more reflective and accepting of themselves. This can mean that as people age they come to recognize both their personal strengths and limitations. Emotional maturity and self-knowledge play an important part in an individual's ability to establish and maintain close personal relationships as well as working relationships with others.

Education

Educational experiences can have a major impact on a person's self-concept. The things that teachers and fellow students say, and the way that they treat us, can affect our self-image and self-esteem during childhood and adolescence. We are very open to suggestions about who and what we are during these life stages. For some people, educational success helps to form a positive self-image and promotes high self-esteem. For others, school can be a more negative experience that leaves them feeling less capable than others, or with a negative view of themselves, their skills and their self-worth.

Investigate ...

Use your knowledge and understanding of the influences on self-concept to write some survey questions about the way male and female teenagers think about themselves and develop their self-concepts. Conduct your survey by asking the questions to an equal number of boys and girls. Write a brief summary of your findings.

Understanding Personal Development and Relationships

Case study

Rachel Stein is 25 years old. She has been doing a lot of thinking about herself and her life recently. Rachel has worked in the same nursery since leaving school at 18. This is something Rachel now regrets. In particular, she felt left out and a bit of a failure when her friends all went off to university. Despite enjoying her job as a nursery team leader, Rachel feels she could – and should – have achieved more in life. Because she works long work hours, Rachel doesn't meet up with her friends very often. In fact, she rarely sees people outside of work. Many of Rachel's friends have also got married over the last few years. Rachel regrets not having found a partner but can't see why anyone would be attracted to her. Rachel thinks she looks 'plain and a bit overweight'. She has started to think that her life is not as good as that of other people her age. Rachel looks at herself in the mirror each morning, wondering how she got into this situation, wishing she could change the way that she feels about herself and her life.

- What image does Rachel have of herself?
- How would you describe Rachel's self-esteem?
- Using the information provided in the example, summarise Rachel's self-concept.
- What factors do you think have influenced the way Rachel's self-concept has developed?
- Explain why Rachel's self-concept is likely to change as she moves through adulthood.

Relationships with others

The relationships that an individual has, especially within their family, during education and at work, will have a powerful effect on their self-concept. Family relationships play a critical role in shaping our self-concept. Early relationships are built on effective attachments to parents and close family members. The sense of security and feelings of being loved that can develop from these bonds are key ingredients in a positive self-concept. Poor family relationships, however, can do lasting damage to a person's self-concept.

We go through a number of phases of emotional and sexual development during adolescence and adulthood as we experience new friendships and more intimate relationships with non-family members. These experiences affect our self-concept. Simply because we grow older and become more emotionally mature, we also tend to adapt our outlook and behaviour

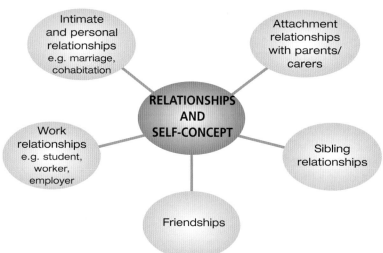

Figure 2.24 Relationships affecting self-concept.

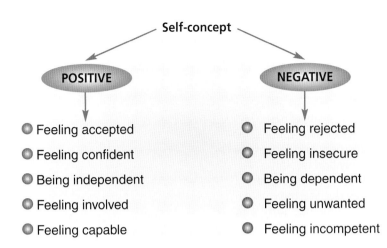

Figure 2.25 Effects of positive and negative concepts.

towards others to take account of the thoughts and feelings that other people have. For example, a couple who may both have had a strong image of themselves as young, free and single individuals learn new things about themselves and have to adapt their self-concepts when they form an intimate, long-term partnership or get married.

Sexual orientation

A person's sexual orientation refers to their preference for either a same-sex or opposite sex partner. Whilst some people identify themselves as heterosexual (attracted to the opposite sex), others identify themselves as lesbian, gay (attracted to the same sex) or bisexual (attracted to either sex). We tend to first become aware of our sexual orientation in adolescence though many people remain uncertain about, experiment with or change their sexual orientation during adulthood. A person's sexual orientation will have a significant impact on their self-concept and on their social and emotional development.

 Over to you!

Identify one way in which the following individuals have influenced your personal development:

- Your mum or dad
- Your brother(s) or sister(s)
- Another relative in your family
- A teacher
- A friend
- Neighbours.

Analyse which aspects of your development each person influenced and then explain who has had the most significant effect on the development of your self-concept.

 Case study

Angelo and Charisa are Year 12 pupils and best friends. They go out to parties and clubs together at weekends but have other partners. Angelo has a boyfriend who he has been seeing for 6 months. Charisa doesn't have a girlfriend at the moment but has had short relationships with older girls in the past. Both Angelo and Charisa are open about their sexuality to close friends and members of their family. However, they are very concerned about other people, particularly other pupils at school, finding out about their sexual orientation. This is because they have seen how other pupils and teachers have been taunted and bullied for 'being gay'. Angelo has also been chased by a group of local teenagers on his way home from school. This frightened him a great deal so he now makes sure he doesn't walk home on his own or take shortcuts across the park. Charisa has recently reported two girls in her years at school who have been calling her 'sick' and who sent her threatening and pornographic text messages.

- Which aspects of personal development are likely to be affected by a person's sexual orientation?

- How might a person's development be affected if they were unable to express their preferred sexual orientation?

- How does sexual orientation affect Angelo and Charisa's relationships with members of their peer group?

- What impact might bullying have on Angelo and Charisa's self-concept?

Understanding Personal Development and Relationships

Male homosexuality was illegal in the United Kingdom until 1967. Lesbian relationships have never been illegal in the UK though social disapproval and unfair discrimination against people who had same-sex partners, whether male or female, was widespread until the late twentieth century. However, social attitudes have changed significantly so that a person's sexual orientation is now much less of an issue in most situations. This does not mean that prejudice and social disapproval about same-sex relationships has disappeared and many people still struggle to 'come out' about their homosexuality. Gay and lesbian adolescents and young people are particularly vulnerable to bullying and intimidation from peers if they declare their sexual orientation. Therefore many choose not to 'come out' until they are older and able to find support from a group or community of people who understand their interests, needs and concerns.

Knowledge Check

1 What does the term 'self-concept' mean?

2 Why might a person have low self-esteem?

3 What are the characteristics of high self-esteem?

4 How can a person's educational experiences affect their self-concept?

5 What impact can family relationships have on an individual's self-concept?

6 During which life stage does physical appearance seem to have a strong influence on an individual's self-concept?

7 Explain how a person's ethnicity may have a positive effect on their self-concept.

8 Explain how being uncomfortable with your gender may affect a person's self-concept.

9 Describe how a person's self-concept changes as they get older.

The effect of relationships on personal growth and development

People form different types of relationship at different stages of their life. Family relationships tend to be most important during infancy and childhood. There is a then a gradual shift in adolescence as friendships become more important, though emotional support from within family is also essential for adolescent development. A whole range of new personal and working relationships are formed as the individual progresses into adulthood.

Family relationships

You will know from previous learning that there are many different types of family structure. Whatever type of family structure a person lives in, their relationship with their parent(s) will play a big part in their personal development. Relationships with siblings (brothers and sisters in the family) are also important family relationships. An individual's feelings about

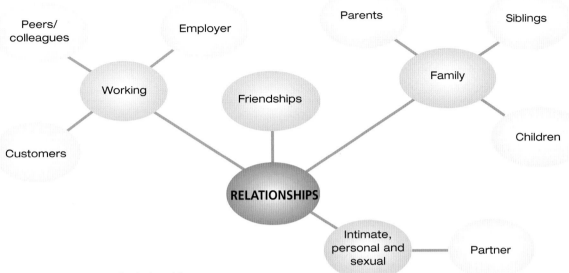

Figure 2.26 Types of relationship.

their family and the skills they develop (or don't develop) in relating to others within the family will play an important part in the wider relationships they develop outside of the family during each life stage.

An individual's family relationships develop and change as they move through different life stages. Family relationships are usually seen as 'special' because of the biological connections and often very close emotional bonds between family members. However, whilst family relationships can be a source of love, protection and mutual support, negative family relationships that involve abuse, neglect or violence can also result in people being physically hurt or psychologically and emotionally damaged. Family relationships are often complex and many people have both good experiences of family relationships that support their personal development and some difficult times within their family relationships that they struggle to deal with.

Over to you!

Use sociology textbooks or the Internet to find out about the differences between the different types of families in figure 2.27. Which type(s) of family have you been a member of?

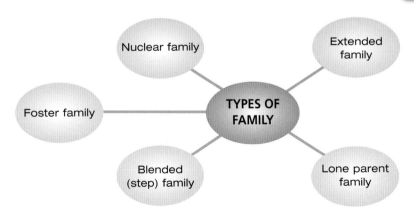

Figure 2.27 Types of family.

Infancy

An infant generally forms their first relationship with one or both of their parents. Close physical contact, the provision of food and regular, reassuring care and communication between the child and their parents should result in an **attachment**

relationship developing. This will provide the child with a sense of emotional security and basic self-confidence if they feel loved and learn to trust their parents. An infant's relationships with their **siblings** will vary depending on how close in age they are and whether their brother(s) or sister(s) were jealous about their arrival in the family. A new baby may cause jealousy and a hostile reaction if the older child feels they are no longer important or less loved by their parents. However, siblings can also provide role models for younger children and may also be very caring and interested in their infant brother or sister. Infants do show interest in other children of the same age when they meet them but are not able to form friendships until they have a clearer sense of their own identity. This tends to develop in early childhood.

Childhood

A child's parents continue to play an important role in their development as they get older and move into childhood. Parents become role models, socialising the child, providing care and support and helping them to learn how they should behave towards others. During this stage of life parents have a strong influence on their child's self-concept and self-esteem. Siblings can form strong, supportive and very close friendships during childhood although there are often ups and downs in these relationships as brothers and sisters argue, fight and make up again.

Adolescence

By the time they reach adolescence, an individual is likely to have a much broader and more complicated network of personal relationships than when they were a child. Family relationships, particularly with parents, are still a vital part of this network. However, when a person moves into adolescence their relationship with their parents tends to change. In particular, there is less focus on socialisation and providing physical support and more focus on emotional support. Despite the growing desire for independence and the strains and tensions that this can bring to family relationships, an adolescent still needs affection, trust and approval from their parents. Adolescents who have a trusting, supportive and affectionate relationship with their parents will tend to have better self-esteem and be better equipped for the transition to adulthood than adolescents who lack this. Adolescents are often less confident about themselves and more uncertain in their relationships with other people than they let on. To support social and emotional development, parents need to remain open and approachable to their adolescent children during this life stage without being too controlling, judgemental or directive.

The pattern of sibling relationships in a family is often set within childhood. Teenage siblings may argue and fight whilst also being very caring and supportive of each other. It is important for parents to avoid favouring one sibling over others as the less favoured sibling may feel hurt or undervalued and may direct their upset or anger about this at the favoured sibling. Disagreements and arguments between siblings can seem quite serious during adolescence. Even where there appears to be a fundamental dislike and breakdown of the relationship, it is often the case that siblings will resolve their differences and form

Over to you!

Can you remember your childhood friends? Did you have a 'best friend' during early childhood? Did any of your early friendships affect your self-image and self-confidence?

Case study

Sharon McDonagh is 23 years old. She returned to live with her parents when she left the Royal Navy 6 months ago. Sharon is now keen to move into a flat with her boyfriend, Gareth. Sharon's parents have quite strong views about marriage and cohabitation. They believe that Sharon and Gareth should get married before they begin living together. Sharon and Gareth disagree and have explained that they don't wish to get married as they have only known each other for a year. Sharon feels torn between living her life in the way she wants to and keeping her parents happy. She feels that although she still loves her parents a great deal, her relationship with them is changing. She has tried to explain this to her mum who has complained that 'Gareth seems to mean more to you than we do'.

- Which aspects of Sharon's personal development are currently undergoing change?

- What is happening to Sharon's relationship with her parents?

- How might Sharon's personal development be affected if she continued to live with her parents throughout early adulthood?

good relationships again as they mature and become more self-confident during adulthood.

Adulthood

A person's family relationships may change significantly during adulthood. The majority of people leave home and begin new relationships with people outside of their birth family, perhaps getting married or living with a partner and starting a family of their own. As a result adults tend to readjust the relationship they have with their parents. Whilst still being their parent's child, an adult is also now independent, able to manage their own life and committed to relationships in their new family. Despite this parents can still play an important part in an adult's emotional life and may still be consulted about important decisions or issues that the person faces. Good relationships with parents and siblings can also cushion the impact of negative life events, such as divorce, **redundancy** or serious illness that may affect an individual during their adult life.

As people enter later adulthood their role within the family often changes. Their decision-making role is likely to change as their children become independent adults. They may take on the new role of grandparent as their children have children of their own. This new role enables many people to provide a useful range of practical help and emotional support and gives them a valued role within the family. Existing family relationships can also be the main source of support for people in later adulthood. However, the care and daily living needs of older people can become increasingly difficult for family members to meet. This is partly because caring for an older parent or other relative requires a change in a person's usual role and relationships within the family. Providing personal, intimate care, for example, may be something that both the older person and their adult relative is deeply uncomfortable with. The loss of work status, changing family roles and an increasing need for support can put pressure on the family relationships of older people. Whilst an older person may need more support they may be reluctant to acknowledge or accept this. Family relationships in later

Case study

Heather Davis gave up work at the age of 23 to have children. At the time she was very happy to be 'just a housewife'. She has spent the last twenty years bringing up her two daughters and supporting her husband who has a busy life as the managing director of a local furniture company. Heather's daughters have now left home. Her husband is busier than ever. Heather has started to think about her own future. She is looking forward to becoming a grandmother in a few months time and has now come to terms with the death of her own mother last year. Heather has recently begun an art class, attends a book group and goes to Pilates once a week. She is also thinking about volunteering at the local hospice shop to give herself a work focus. Heather's husband is very supportive of her efforts to find new things to do with her time and has also promised to throw himself into the role of grandfather in a few months time.

- Which aspects of Heather's personal development may have been affected when her daughter's left home?

- In what ways might becoming a grandparent affect Heather's self-concept?

- What effect might Heather's new leisure and work activities have on her personal development?

adulthood can make a positive contribution to an individual's social and emotional development, particularly their self-concept, where the person feels valued and supported. Where this isn't the case, difficulties in family relationships can lead to low self-esteem and poor emotional wellbeing.

Knowledge Check

1 Identify two different types of family relationship that affect personal development during infancy and childhood.

2 Explain why good family relationships are important for emotional development during infancy.

3 Briefly explain what the term 'sibling' means.

4 Explain how family relationships change during adolescence.

5 How can parenthood affect an individual's emotional and social development?

Friendships

Friends are people whom we generally see as likeable, dependable and whom we can communicate easily with. People form friendships for a variety of reasons. Common attitudes, values and interests, a need for emotional support and companionship are a few of these reasons. Friendships tend to boost a person's self-esteem, self-confidence and help people to develop social skills. Overall, friendships make an important contribution to an individual's emotional and social development and the formation of their self-concept.

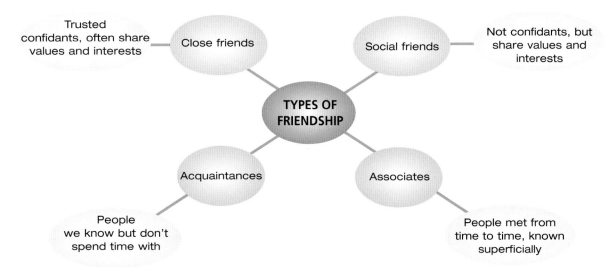

Figure 2.28 Types of friendship.

Early friendships

Friendships start to affect an individual's development during childhood. Initially friendships are quite superficial and involve playing with other, familiar children. It is only at the end of childhood as the individual is preparing to move into adolescence that friendships come to be seen as a supportive two-way relationships. Throughout childhood, friendships play an important part in developing and supporting a child's self-esteem. Being liked and accepted by other children is very important for self-confidence and self-image. By contrast, children who struggle to make friends or who are rejected or bullied by other children are likely to suffer low self-confidence and have lower self-esteem because they become aware of this lack of social acceptance. This can damage the child's long-term social and emotional development if they develop a negative self-concept as a result.

Friendships become increasingly important, and are often more intense, during adolescence. Boys and girls now begin to form opposite sex friendships in contrast to childhood where friendships are mainly with members of the same sex. Girls tend to want to belong to smaller friendship groups and have more emotionally involving and intense friendship relationships whereas boys tend to form larger friendship groups in which members share common practical or sporting interests. Belonging to a friendship group provides an adolescent with an important sense of belonging and social acceptance outside their family. Some adolescents who lack social skills or who have significantly different values to their peers or who are physically different in some way can be ostracised or left out of friendship groups. This can be damaging to self-esteem and social and emotional development generally. Similarly, adolescents who lack self-confidence and self-esteem may find themselves vulnerable to **peer group pressure** within friendship groups. This can lead them to take part in activities, such as drinking, petty crime, drug use or sex, that they are not comfortable with but which they go along with to remain a member of the group.

Case study

Ffion, Nia and Eleri are all 32 years of age. They have known each other since they started primary school together when they were 5 years old. The three women are all now married, have two children each and live in different parts of the UK. Living hundreds of miles from each other hasn't got in the way of their friendship. All three communicate regularly, sending text messages a couple of times a week and speaking quite frequently on the phone. Ffion still lives in the part of Wales where the three friends grew up. When Nia and Eleri visit their families at Christmas and in the summer, they also arrange to go out for a meal or have a barbeque at Ffion's house. Ffion, Nia and Eleri discuss quite personal feelings and seek advice from each other when they have personal or practical problems to deal with. Each trusts the other a great deal and believe they have an honest, supportive and genuine friendship that they can rely on whatever else is happening in their lives.

- Which aspects of their personal development is likely to have been affected by the friendship between Ffion, Nia and Eleri?

- Explain why the friendship between these three women is likely to have had a positive effect on each individual's self-concept.

- Using the information provided, identify possible reasons why the friendship between the three women has been so long-lasting and successful.

Adult friendships

Adult friendships tend to be carefully chosen and based on shared interests and values. Friendships in adulthood tend to be longer lasting than earlier friendships if both parties meet each other's emotional needs for support, loyalty and honesty in the relationship. Adult friends can be especially important for social and emotional development as they provide the basis for a supportive social network. They are particularly important when an individual experiences life events, such as divorce, unexpected illness or stress, which has a significant impact on them and requires people who will listen and offer emotional support. Adults can also experience emotional difficulties when they lose friends as a result of retirement from work, ill-health or death. The loss of friends can lead to loneliness, isolation and feelings of insecurity.

Intimate, personal and sexual relationships

People generally start to become interested in more personal relationships in their early teens. Adolescents tend to fall in and out of love quite frequently as they experience 'crushes' or infatuations during puberty. This can be emotionally painful but most teenagers use these experiences to learn more about the emotional aspects of relationships and to extend their understanding of their own needs and preferences. Girls tend to seek and engage in romantic, intimate and, to a lesser extent sexual, relationships at a younger age than boys. For many teenagers their first intimate relationship is an intense emotional experience rather than a sexual one.

Intimate relationships do develop out of sexual attraction although sexual intercourse is not necessarily a part of teenagers' intimate relationships. Kissing, hand-holding and other forms of physical contact are more frequently used to express physical and emotional attraction during this life stage. Intimate personal relationships tend to be short-lived during early adolescence but become longer and are more emotionally and physically involved in later adolescence. These longer term relationships are based on greater emotional maturity and a stronger sense of personal identity. They also help to prepare young people for future relationships with the partners they meet as adults.

Sexual relationships are a normal part of intimate personal relationships during all phases of adulthood. Engaging in sexual activity with a partner expresses both a physical and emotional need for most adults. Sexuality often becomes a feature of an individual's self-concept during adulthood. During adulthood people typically search for a partner and develop emotionally and physically intimate relationships with one or more individuals before they form a longer term, usually monogamous, relationship. Whilst some people avoid sexual relationships outside of marriage, many other people form intimate relationships before, or without, getting married. The physical and emotional intimacy of a close personal and sexual relationship contributes to an individual's social and emotional development. Unprotected sex, promiscuity and extramarital affairs may damage an individual's existing relationship and personal development because of the risk of unwanted pregnancy, sexually transmitted disease, and the emotional distress that this can cause to existing partners. Adults who find themselves in sexually abusive relationships may also experience significant emotional distress, physical injury, or low self-esteem until they find a way of ending the relationship or stopping the abuse.

Working relationships

Working relationships are different to other forms of relationship because the relationship serves a particular, non-personal purpose – it is about work or getting a particular job done. Most working relationships are also formed between individuals who are not of equal status. One person usually has more power or authority in the relationship than the other. Relationships between students and teachers, between employers and employees and between work mates are examples of working relationships.

Effective work relationships tend to be based on good communication, trust and respect between the people involved. Figure 2.29 identifies some other qualities of good working relationships.

Effective, positive working relationships contribute to social, emotional and intellectual development because they can lead to:

- higher self-esteem
- positive self-image
- development of new skills and understanding
- a positive sense of self-worth
- a clear sense of personal identity.

Over to you!

Think about a working relationship of your own (with a teacher or employer perhaps) that has had a positive effect on you. Did any of the relationship features listed in figure 2.29 play a part in the success of this relationship? Try to identify reasons why the relationship had a positive effect on you.

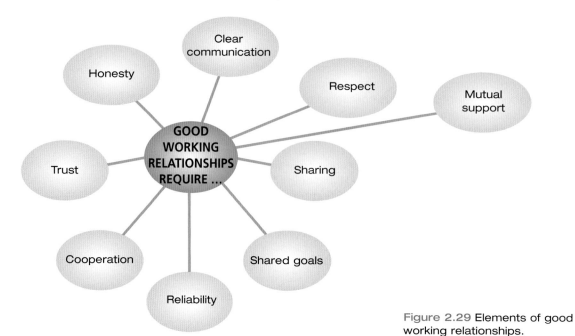

Figure 2.29 Elements of good working relationships.

Student/teacher relationships

Learning is the specific focus of student-teacher relationships at any age. Children typically begin attending primary school at 5 years of age in the UK, though many attend nurseries and other pre-school day care provision before this age. Relationships with class teachers and nursery workers become important in children's lives from this point. A child needs to trust their teacher or nursery worker to establish the kind of relationship that enables them to develop their communication skills, self-confidence and self-esteem. A lack of trust or a negative, unsupportive relationship is likely to hamper the child's social, emotional and intellectual development.

Relationships with teachers are vital for intellectual development during adolescence. The relationship between a student and teacher becomes more of a partnership during adolescence. Both parties have an interest in promoting and experiencing learning and general intellectual development. The teacher may still have more authority in the relationship but learning cannot occur without the student's willing and active participation. A good working relationship between student and teacher is likely to contribute positively to the self-esteem, self-confidence and self-concept of both individuals and provides the basis for the student's intellectual development.

Employer/employee relationships

Relationships between employers and employees can be an important influence on personal – especially social and intellectual – development. The employer-employee relationship is an example of a **formal relationship**. This means it is based on a set of rules and expectations about how people should relate to each other because of their employment relationship. The employer has the most power and authority to direct the activities of the employee in these situations. Employment relationships can affect an individual's self-image, their social

Knowledge Check

1 Identify three reasons why people form friendships.

2 Which aspects of personal development are promoted by relationships with friends?

3 What effects can a lack of friendships have on an individual's development?

4 How do relationships with friends tend to change during adolescence?

5 Explain why friendships become more important for personal development during adolescence.

6 Identify two distinctive characteristics of an intimate relationship.

7 How can an intimate sexual relationship have a positive effect on an adult's personal development?

8 What impact might an abusive sexual relationship have on an individual's emotional development?

9 Identify three types of working relationship.

10 Using examples, explain how effective working relationships can contribute to personal development.

skills and their intellectual development – depending on the type of work they do and the development opportunities they are given. A person's relationship with their employers may also influence their attitudes, values and behaviour as well as their self-concept.

Peers and work mates

Some work colleagues are peers. That is, they are people of equal status and similar background. People involved in these types of working relationships may also be friends and tend to have equal status within the relationship. Effective relationships with peers and work mates are important because people often need to learn to cooperate and work together in work situations. Being liked and valued by work mates also increases an individual's self-confidence and self-esteem.

Chapter checklist

The box below provides a summary of the areas covered in chapter 8. Tick the areas that you feel you understand and would be confident answering exam questions about. If there are any areas that you don't understand or are not confident about, you will need to return to them before you begin your exam revision.

Factors affecting self-concept

- Age ❑
- Appearance ❑
- Gender ❑
- Culture ❑
- Emotional maturity ❑
- Education ❑
- Relationships with others ❑
- Sexual orientation ❑

Types of relationship

- Family relationships ❑
- Friendships ❑
- Intimate, personal and sexual relationships ❑
- Working relationships ❑

Assessment Guide

Your learning in this unit will be assessed through a one hour written examination.

The examination will consist of a series of short and longer answer questions covering all aspects of this unit. You will need to show that you understand:

● The development of self-concept

● Types of relationships

● The effects of relationships on personal development.

Chapter 8 provides full coverage of the range of factors that you could be asked about in the examination.

Chapter 9

Major life changes and sources of support

Key issue: How can life events affect an individual's personal development and what support is available to them during these times?

The events that a person experiences in their life will influence how they develop and change in each life stage. Having different life experiences is part of the reason for individual differences between people. The important life events that people experience include:

- relationship changes – such as marriage, divorce, living with a partner, birth of a sibling or own child, or the death of a friend or relative (**bereavement**)
- physical changes – such as puberty, menopause, accidents or injury
- changes in life circumstances, such as moving house, starting school, college or a job, retirement, redundancy or unemployment.

This chapter will enable you to identify and describe different types of life event and the positive and negative effects that they can have on personal development. You will also learn how people use sources of support to cope with the effects of life events. These sources of support include:

- partners, family and friends
- professional carers and services
- voluntary (third sector) and faith-based services.

Life events and change

A **life event** is an experience that changes the direction of a person's life and affects their personal development. Every person's life changes as a result of the significant events that happen and the experiences they have at each stage of their life.

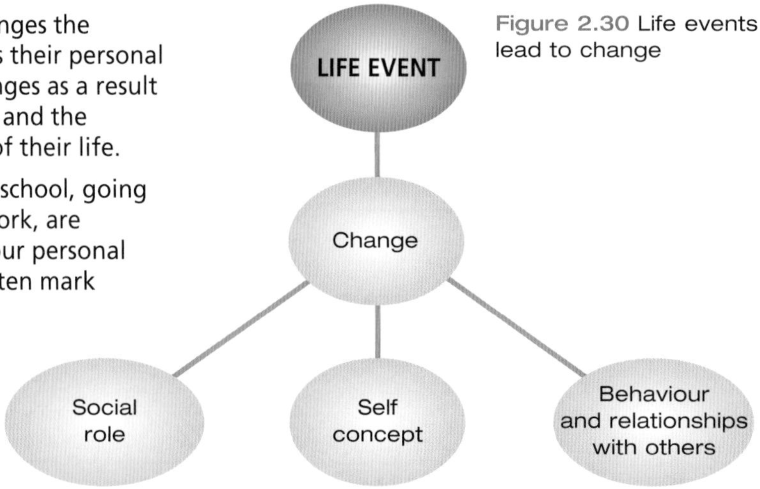

Expected life events, such as starting school, going through puberty and retiring from work, are predictable and act as milestones in our personal development. Expected life events often mark a transition from one stage of life or status to another. **Unexpected life events**, such as sudden illness or injury, redundancy and the death of a friend or relative, occur in an unpredictable

Figure 2.30 Life events lead to change

LIFE EVENT

Change

Social role

Self concept

Behaviour and relationships with others

way and are often associated with loss. However, unexpected life events can sometimes result in positive changes occurring in a person's life. For example, illness or disability may force someone to give up a certain kind of work which might allow them to move into a new career, have more time for a hobby or interest, or even return to education or training again.

Changes in relationships

People have different types of relationship in each of the main life stages. These include family relationships with parents, **siblings** (brothers and sisters) and other relatives, friendships, work relationships and intimate and sexual relationships with partners in late adolescence, adulthood and old age. Changes in our relationships can occur for many reasons. They often have a big impact on our emotional and social development.

Marriage

Marriage is a life event that is generally viewed positively and which is celebrated by hundreds of thousands of people each year (see figure 2.31). It can involve a major adaptation in personal relationships and behaviour for both the couple involved and their close relatives and friends. Ideally, the couple will establish a deeper emotional and psychological commitment to each other. Marriages also alter family relationships. The roles of family members change and new members are introduced into family groups. For example, in-laws become part of a wider family network and relationships between original family members may weaken because of the practicalities of a son or daughter moving away to live with their new partner. This can cause a sense of loss for the parents of the new couple and for the couple themselves as they move away from their birth family to begin a family of their own.

Investigate ...

Interview an adult or older person about significant events in their life. Draw a timeline highlighting:

● Expected life events that have happened to them

● Unexpected life events that have happened to them.

Using the information you obtain, and being careful about confidentiality, describe the impact of these life events on the person's personal development, particularly their self-concept.

Over to you!

What does the graph tell you about the general trend in marriages? In which year (approximately) was marriage most popular? How many people got remarried in 2007?

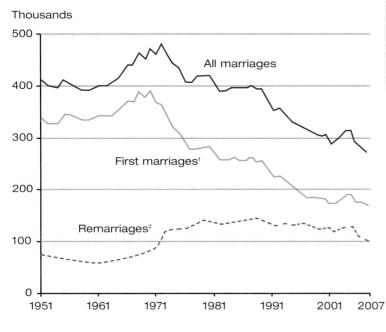

Thousands

Figure 2.31 Marriages, United Kingdom, 1951–2007, ONS

1 For both partners   2 For one or both partners

Divorce

People do not marry intending to get divorced, but divorce is now relatively common in the UK. One in three marriages are likely to end in divorce. Despite being relatively common, divorce is an unexpected life event that often has a major emotional impact on the couple involved and on those who are part of any family that has resulted from the couple's marriage. Marriage breakdown and the process of going through a divorce usually have major financial and practical consequences too. Separation will probably mean having to find different accommodation and independent sources of income. Where the couple has children, the impact of their divorce will be felt by the children because of new living arrangements, changing relationships and sometimes the need to adapt to step-parents. Though divorce can have a negative impact on the lives of those affected, it may still be preferable to being in a stressful and unsatisfactory relationship.

Living with a partner

Cohabitation or 'living together' is increasingly common in the UK. Many people live with a partner before getting married or forming a civil partnership. Between 1996 and 2006 the proportion of cohabiting couple families increased from 9 per cent to 14 per cent. Younger adults are most likely to cohabit with 33 per cent of men aged 25 to 29 years of age and 29 per cent of women aged 25 to 29 years of age cohabiting. People may choose to live together because they do not wish to marry or because they have been married and don't wish to risk getting divorced again.

Living with a partner may be an alternative to marriage but often involves the couple having to make a very similar commitment to share financial resources and provide emotional and practical support for each other as happens in a marriage. The partners in a cohabiting relationship are also likely to experience the same distress and feelings of loss that a married couple will feel if their relationship breaks down. Practical and emotional issues relating to any children and other relatives closely involved in the cohabiting couple's life will also need to be taken into account if the couple separate.

Birth of a sibling or own child

The birth of a child is a significant life event for every member of the family into which the child is born. New relationships are formed and existing relationships, with parents and other brothers and sisters, have to be adapted and change as a result of the addition of a new baby. Children can have mixed feelings about the arrival of a new brother or sister. Whilst a new arrival provides an opportunity to form new relationships and develops a child's self-concept as an older brother or sister, some children also resent the loss of attention from their parents and feel a need to compete with their brother or sister for their parent's affection.

Becoming a parent is a very significant event in life. It is usually seen as a positive change in a person's life although it can also be seen as a point at which an individual 'lost' their individual freedom and sense of identity. New parents are faced with a challenging situation because they have to adapt their own roles

Case study

Sameena and her husband Raj spent 10 years trying to produce their first child. Following a referral by her GP to the fertility clinic at her local General Hospital, both Sameena and Raj underwent several fertility investigations. The couple then had a course of invitro-fertilisation (IVF) in which two embryos were implanted in Sameena's womb. Nine months later Taleem and Younis were born. Sameena is now a devoted mother and very proud parent of 18-month-old twins. She finds caring for Taleem and Younis very tiring but also sees it as the best thing that has happened to her. Raj does his best to provide practical help when he is at home. He is also very proud of his new role as a dad but says that his relationship with Sameena is sometimes strained by the pressures of caring for their children. Sameena and Raj spend almost all their time with their children and now see a lot less of their friends and family. Raj hopes that this will change as their children get older as he misses spending time with his friends. Sameena says that she finds it hard to remember what her life was like before she had children. Sometimes she worries that she will get stuck being 'just a mum'.

- Which aspects of Raj and Sameena's personal development have been affected by them becoming parents?

- In what ways has parenthood affected Raj and Sameena's self-concepts?

- What concerns do Raj and Sameena have about the effects parenthood might be having on their personal development or relationships?

and relationship to cope with the needs of a dependant child without any prior training or experience. This can feel overwhelming for some people, particularly where they have limited experience of young children. Many people cope by drawing on their own experiences of childhood and by relying on their parents and other relatives to provide practical and emotional support.

Parenthood can also be a major test of the new parents' relationship as both find themselves under increasing pressure. Some people are able to offer their partner the practical and emotional support needed and strengthen their partnership when they become parents. Other people find that they are unable or unwilling to do this and experience relationship difficulties and even the breakdown of their marriage or partnership as a result. Parenthood tends to result in a shift in a person's self-concept as they adapt to their new 'mum' or dad' role.

For many the birth of a child is a positive emotional milestone that results in them changing their lifestyle and life goals in order to be the best possible parent they can be. However, for others, parenthood can be an unwelcome burden that triggers personal mental health difficulties or leads them to neglect or abuse their child because they cannot cope with the pressures and demands that parenthood places on them.

Death of a partner, relative or friend

Bereavement is the term given to the deep feelings of loss that people experience when someone to whom they are emotionally attached, such as a partner, relative or friend, dies. Bereavement can cause a major change in a person's life, affecting their social and emotional development as well as impacting on their self-concept. Sometimes a person's death may be anticipated and prepared for because of old age or because they have a terminal illness. In other cases, however, a person's death can be sudden and unexpected. Even when a person's death is anticipated because of illness, the sense of loss that follows can be very hard to accept and the powerful emotions of disbelief, sadness, anger and guilt that can follow the death of someone close may be very difficult to deal with. Bereavement can be even more traumatic and psychologically difficult when a person's death occurs suddenly or dramatically because of an accident, serious injury or suicide, for example. A sense of bereavement can cause both short-term and long-term problems in accepting and adjusting to the loss of the person concerned.

Case study

Eric, the drummer in Positive Peace, a reggae band, was 25 years old when he developed leukaemia. Eric's fellow band members and close friends were all shocked when he told them his diagnosis and that he would be having chemotherapy. Eric's friends and family were all very hopeful that the doctors who were treating Eric would be proved right and that he would survive the leukaemia. Eric was in hospital for several weeks, receiving treatment and being monitored. Robbie, Eric's closest friend in the band, was present with Eric's family when he died after an unexpected deterioration in his condition. Robbie was deeply affected by the loss of his friend and by being present when he passed away. He said he felt numb for weeks and cried a lot when he was on his own. Robbie now thinks about how long he might have left to live and says it taught him that nobody lives forever. A year later he still can't believe that Eric has gone. Robbie has now lost interest in playing music and says that he still finds it hard to listen to his reggae albums because it brings back the feelings he had when Eric died.

- Which aspects of Robbie's experiences following the death of his friend suggest he has suffered a bereavement?

- Explain how Eric's death has affected Robbie's emotional wellbeing.

- What impact might Eric's death have on the development of Robbie's self-concept?

Knowledge Check

1 What is a life event?

2 Describe a life event that can be expected to occur during early adulthood.

3 How can marriage influence personal development?

4 Explain why an unexpected life event like divorce can have a negative effect on a person's social development

5 What impact can the birth of a sibling have on a child's personal development?

6 How might becoming a parent for the first time impact on an adult's self-concept and relationships with others?

7 How might the death of a partner affect a person's emotional development?

Physical changes

Physical changes related to human growth, development and ageing, as well as the experience of illness, can also have a major effect on the way we develop in each life stage. Puberty and the menopause are two of the most notable physical changes that occur in adolescence and middle adulthood. Accidents and illnesses can occur in any life stage.

Puberty

Puberty is a physical process that occurs during a person's adolescent or teenage years. Puberty is a major life event because of the major physical changes that occur but also because of the emotional impact that it can have. The physical changes that occur in puberty involve growth and the development of sexual or reproductive capability. These physical changes, and the way that other people relate to the person who experiences them, can affect the development of self-image and self-concept. For example, adolescents often become concerned about their appearance and their attractiveness to others during puberty. A person's beliefs about these issues will contribute to the development of their self-concept. Boys and girls who experience puberty either later or earlier than average may experience particular difficulties. This can happen if the person feels uncomfortable and self-conscious about the onset or absence of changes to their body or if their peers respond to this by teasing, bullying or harassing them.

Accidents and injury

Accidents and illness can affect a person's development at any stage of their life. Where an accident or illness is serious it may cause either a temporary problem that the person can recover fully from or have a permanent effect on the person. For example, accidents and some types of illness can result in a disability, such as the loss of a person's sight or hearing or the loss of a limb. A person who acquires a disability in this way will need to adapt their skills and lifestyle to cope with the everyday situations that they face. For example, a disability can cause practical problems, such as not being able to move, pick up and hold things or manage personal hygiene and toilet needs without assistance. It may also result in psychological stress, change a person's self-concept and affect their personal relationships. Friends, family and colleagues will need to adjust their relationship with the person to take account of the disabled person's new situation.

Serious illness can be a major but unexpected event in an individual's life. It can result in massive changes to the person's whole lifestyle as he or she tries to cope with the effects of the illness. People who experience serious illnesses, such as heart attacks, multiple sclerosis or cancer, may find they are no longer able to carry out their usual daily routines, and they may lose their independence. They can also find that their relationships with others change because of their illness. This might be because they need additional practical help or emotional support from close relatives or their friends. For partners and close relatives, the person's illness may be the central factor around which they now have to organize their own time, lifestyle and relationship with the person.

Understanding Personal Development and Relationships

Case study

Valerie Fitzharris, aged 66 years, had two operations on her spine last year. Her problems started with a nagging pain in her lower back. Despite painkillers and massage, these pains just got worse until she began experiencing intensely painful stabs of sharp pain that left her unable to move and often in tears. Valerie's GP referred her to a specialist centre for spinal injuries. After several scans they diagnosed that one of the discs in Valerie's spine was crumbling and a piece of it was sticking into her spinal cord. They decided to operate straight away. The operation was successful and Valerie quickly regained her mobility.

Valerie was very keen to get back to her old routines and activities following the operation. In fact, she made the mistake of going on a five-day coach trip to France with some friends a month after her operation. When she returned, she knew something was wrong. The pain in her back gradually returned and Valerie had to have a second operation to remove another piece of the broken disc. Valerie is now much more careful about not overstretching herself each day. She says the experience has made her think differently about her needs and abilities. As someone who had never really been unwell before, this episode has changed the way she thinks about herself and her future. She also said that she found out who her real friends were as they gave her a lot of practical and emotional support when she was at her lowest point.

- Which aspects of Valerie's personal development and wellbeing have been affected by her recent health problems?

- How might long-term spinal problems affect the way that Valerie is able to live her life?

- What impact might Valerie's experiences of illness have had on her self-concept?

Menopause

Menopause is a naturally occurring physical change that affects women in early middle age, typically between 45 and 55 years of age. It is the time when a woman stops menstruating and loses the ability to conceive children. Menopause is a major life event because of the sometimes unpleasant physical changes that occur and because of the psychological impact that the loss of reproductive ability can have on some women. The menopause is seen by some women as a signal that they are moving from young adulthood into middle age and that their (re)productive years are over. This in turn can cause some women to reflect deeply on their past experiences, their role in life as well as on their future. Hormone Replacement Therapy (HRT) is used by some women to control the physical symptoms of the menopause.

Changes in life circumstances

A change in a person's life circumstances will usually involve some kind of **social transition**. Some of these transitions, like starting work, are expected; others, like redundancy, are unexpected. A change in life circumstances can have a big impact on a person's development because it affects the opportunities open to them or disrupts the way they currently live their life or their future plans.

Knowledge Check

1 Why is puberty a significant life event for an adolescent?

2 How can puberty affect a person's self-concept?

3 Explain the impact that the menopause can have on a woman's development and wellbeing during middle age.

4 Describe the ways in which being involved in a serious car accident might affect a child's PIES development.

5 How can acquiring a physical disability as a result of accident or illness affect a person's close relationships?

Moving house

Moving home is recognised as a stressful life event for many people. Home is usually a place that people associate with safety, security and stability in their lives. Moving home means a break with the past and perhaps with friends, neighbours and the security of familiar surroundings. The practical demands of organising the removal of possessions, arranging finance to cover the cost of moving, and perhaps buying a house or flat, add to the emotional strain associated with this life event.

A person may relocate their life from one place to another for a variety of reasons. For some people, moving house is a positive choice. An adult may choose to move from one part of the UK to another to be nearer to relatives, to live with their partner or to take up work or educational opportunities. A great deal of this kind of internal migration occurs within the UK each year. In these cases people frequently make choices that have a positive effect on their personal development.

Where a person experiences bereavement, redundancy or is unable for some reason to stay in the place they would like to live, relocation may be a forced choice and may have a disruptive and negative effect on their personal development. This can be the case for children and adolescents who are required to move house, leaving friends and school mates behind, when their parents decide to relocate. Social relationships and emotional attachments may be lost as a result of relocation and the individual may feel isolated and unsupported in their new location. This can also happen when an older person moves, perhaps reluctantly, from living in their own home to living in a care home. A fundamental change in self-concept can occur in this situation as the older person loses their independence and their social and emotional connections with friends, neighbours and the community more generally.

Moving home can be a stressful life event.

Starting school

Going to school for the first time is a big event for most children. Families and schools often try hard to prepare children for this

---

Case study

Michelle is 11 years old. She lives in a small village with her parents and two younger brothers: Tim, aged 8, and David, aged 6. Her grandparents live 10 miles away and are regular visitors. Michelle is about to finish at primary school and move to a secondary school in September. She knows everyone at her primary school. All the children come from the same village and the same teachers have worked at the school since she started. Michelle doesn't want to leave her primary school and admits to being scared of going to secondary school 8 miles away. Michelle's best friend at school is Natalie. They go to swimming club together and belong to the same church group. Michelle is upset that Natalie will be going to a different school in September.

- How might moving from primary to secondary school affect Michelle's development and wellbeing in the next few months?

- What type of help and support might Michelle need as she experiences this change in her life?

- If you were one of Michelle's parents, what would you tell her about the possible impact of changing schools on her friendship with Natalie?

life transition. Talking about what happens at school, going for short visits and then for morning or afternoon play sessions can all help a child get used to the idea of starting school. However, even the most well prepared child may still feel frightened and reluctant to be left at school by their parents on their first day. Teachers and other school staff who are used to this situation can usually provide enough support and reassurance to help young children settle at school.

Starting secondary school can also have a significant impact on a child's personal development. The case study about Michelle illustrates some of the issues that children face when making this transition.

Starting college

The transition from secondary school to a further education college or sixth form is an expected event that most people look forward to. The increase in freedom that college students enjoy and the more relaxed, less formal atmosphere (no school uniform, jewellery and make-up allowed!) means that students are treated more like adults. However, with this change come new responsibilities to organise and motivate yourself and cope with less guidance and direction from teachers. Some young people take this in their stride whilst others struggle to adjust.

Beginning work

Starting work is a predictable life event for most people. In the United Kingdom, schooling is compulsory up to the age of 16 years, though a majority of young people don't leave school until they are older than this. Nevertheless, everybody finishes school and studying at some point in their life. Starting work places different responsibilities and expectations on people. It is a point at which young people, as workers, are required to behave more independently, without the support of parents and teachers.

Retirement

Retirement is the point at which people end their working career. For many people this happens between the ages of 60 and 65 years. Recent changes in legislation and the date at which people will become eligible for a state pension mean that people will have to work longer and will retire at a later age in future. At the same time, it is also not unusual for people who have the financial resources to take early retirement before they reach the point at which they can receive a state pension. Whenever it happens, retirement is a major predictable change that requires an adjustment in an individual's daily routine. It also means an alteration in status and has an impact on people's social relationships and financial situation. Retirement can have both positive and negative effects on development and wellbeing.

For people who have been very committed to their work, and whose work provided their social life, retirement can result in too much time to fill and the loss of contact with work friends. Retirement can also cause financial problems. State and occupational pensions usually provide less money than a salary. For many older people retirement can be the beginning of financial hardship. For other people who have planned for their retirement and who have other interests and friendships, retirement can offer new opportunities, provide more time to enjoy hobbies and more time to enjoy the company of friends and family. For these people retirement is welcomed as a positive life event.

Redundancy

Redundancy happens when an employer decides that a job is no longer required and ends the contract of employment of the person who does that job. It is different to dismissal or sacking, as people who are made redundant lose their jobs through no fault of their own. However, being made 'redundant' can have a significant effect on a person's self-esteem and emotional wellbeing.

Because of rapid changes in the way that businesses are run and recent economic recessions, redundancy has become a much more common experience. Sometimes workers are unaware of the financial problems that their employer is facing so redundancy is unexpected and may happen suddenly. Even when redundancy is anticipated, it can still be upsetting or unwelcome. Redundancy can have a major impact on a person's wellbeing and lifestyle as the loss of salary can lead to financial problems and emotional insecurity. Redundancy can also break up firm friendships and leave people feeling as though they have no clear or valued role in life. This can affect a person's self-esteem and self-concept.

 Case study

Jimmy Davis is 49 years of age. He was made redundant from his job in a car factory nine months ago. He has applied for over a hundred jobs since then but still hasn't been able to get work. Jimmy has recently started to feel depressed, thinking that he will never get another job and that he is 'no good' because he can't find work. He has started an Open University course, which he enjoys, in order to fill his time whilst he looks for work. However, Jimmy's wife has started to worry about the way he is feeling and has suggested that he should go to see his GP to talk about it. Jimmy says he'd be too embarrassed to talk about 'being a failure'.

- Which aspects of Jimmy's personal development are likely to be affected by his redundancy?
- Using the information in the case study, identify some of the effects that redundancy has had on Jimmy's self-concept.
- Suggest reasons why Jimmy's experience of redundancy might actually have a positive impact on his personal development in the long-term.

 Knowledge Check

1 Identify how moving house can be both a positive and a negative life event.

2 What type of life event is starting primary school?

3 How might a person's development benefit from starting further education?

4 What is the difference between retirement and redundancy?

5 What impact can retirement from work have on personal development and wellbeing?

6 Which PIES areas of development are likely to be affected by the experience of redundancy?

There can be a positive outcome to redundancy for some people. The loss of a job may motivate them to learn new skills, to start a small business or to change their lifestyle in a way that leads to them feeling happier and more satisfied in the long term.

Over to you!

Which of the following life events are expected and which are unexpected? Make a list of each type of life event.

- Becoming a parent
- Starting school
- Getting married
- Getting your first job
- Being promoted
- Moving to a new house
- Leaving home
- Getting divorced
- Retiring from work
- Going bankrupt
- Taking exams
- The death of a loved one
- Losing your job
- Learning to read
- Going into care
- Winning the Lottery
- Getting a nursing qualification.

Investigate ...

Produce a checklist of 10 expected and 10 unexpected life events. Use your checklist to conduct a survey of 10 people in your school or college or who you know outside of school. Ask each person to identify in order of importance (1=most impact) the five life events that they feel would have the most impact on their personal development if they experienced it. Summarise your findings and compare them with those of your class colleagues.

Sources of support

Support from other people can help us to cope with the unsettling effects of major life events such as going to school, starting work, marriage, divorce and bereavement. Different sources of support, including partners, family and friends, professional carers and services and voluntary and faith-based services can be used to obtain help.

Partners, family and friends

Family support is often the first form of help that people seek when they experience a major life event. Partners, relatives and close friends may be able to provide practical and emotional support in times of stress, change or crisis. Providing a person with somewhere to stay, transport or a shoulder to cry on can help them to overcome problems that they face. People need support from their partner and family at different stages in their lives. For example, marriage and the birth of children are major life events in which adults are often supported emotionally, financially and practically by their partners, relatives and close friends. Similarly, divorce, bereavement and redundancy are life events that may require family members to support each other emotionally and financially.

Professional carers and services

In some situations people who need support do not have a partner, family or friends whom they can ask for help. In other situations the problems a person faces are too involved or too time-consuming for partners, family and friends to deal with. For example, a woman whose partner has died unexpectedly may need help with child care, financial assistance and considerable

Over to you!

Can you think of any times or events when your family or friends were an important source of support, advice or help to you?

emotional support to cope with everyday life. When a person faces difficulties like this they can draw on the support of professional carers and services. Health, social care and early years workers are trained and qualified to deal with the complex difficulties that families and friends are unable to help with. Where people need financial help and advice, support is available from professionally qualified advisers, banks, building societies and government departments such as the *Department of Work and Pensions*. General Practitioners, the *Citizens Advice Bureau* (CAB) and Local Authorities (Councils) are the main sources of information on where to obtain health, social care and welfare support.

Voluntary and faith-based services

Voluntary services are provided by charities and local groups of people who wish to offer support to people experiencing particular problems. For example, *MIND* provides services for individuals and families affected by mental illness, *MENCAP* provides services for people affected by learning disability and *Relate* provides support and counselling services to couples who need marriage guidance. Faith-based organisations, such as Churches, Mosques, Synagogues and other religious groups, also provide support to members of their local community who are experiencing social and emotional problems. The services of voluntary and faith-based groups are usually free or low-cost. The services offered are wide-ranging and include advice and guidance, information-giving, counselling as well as a range of practical help to meet specific needs.

 Case study

Julie is a member of Christ the King Pentecostal Church. Together with a couple of friends she runs a playgroup for under-fives on a Monday morning. The playgroup is quite informal, offering a range of play activities and a mid-morning snack for young children. Julie also ensures that tea, coffee and cakes are available for the parents who bring their children along to the group. Many of the parents who bring their children to the group come because it offers them a chance to meet other parents and to have a break from providing child care at home. The children who use the group enjoy playing with the various dolls, toys and pieces of play equipment. Most will also sit in small groups when Julie or one of the parents reads a story or provides them with a 'picnic snack' midway through the two-hour playgroup session.

- What kind of organisation provides the playgroup described in the case study?
- What kinds of services are provided by the playgroup?
- How might going to the playgroup affect the personal development of the children who attend?
- How might going to the playgroup be beneficial for the personal development of the parents who attend?

Understanding Personal Development and Relationships

Over to you!

How we react to a change in life circumstances is important as it can affect our health, wellbeing and development. Identify ways of coping with the changes that may result from each of the major life events listed below. Write down examples of the types of support that you think would help a person to cope with each situation.

- The break up of a marriage or long-term relationship.
- Leaving school or college with no job to go to.
- Moving to a new area of the country with your family.
- Being involved in a car crash.
- Losing your sight.
- Being promoted to a very responsible position at work.
- Leaving home to go to university or to live with friends.
- The birth of your first child.
- Being made redundant.
- Failing to get the exam grades that are needed for a job.
- The death of a close relative or friend.
- Being diagnosed with a serious illness.
- The onset of puberty.
- Winning the National Lottery jackpot.
- Being sent to prison.
- Starting employment.
- Moving from primary to secondary school.
- Getting married.
- Getting into serious debt.
- One of your parents developing Alzheimer's disease.
- Retiring from work after forty years in the same job.

Discuss your ideas with a class colleague, explaining the reasons for your decisions.

Knowledge Check

1 Describe a life event or problem for which the support of family, friends or partners would be the most suitable.

2 When is it appropriate to seek support from professional carers and services?

3 Which organisation offers support to people who are experiencing marital or relationship problems?

4 What kinds of problems do faith-based organisations provide support for?

5 What kinds of help do faith-based organisations offer?

Chapter checklist

The box below provides a summary of the areas covered in chapter 9. Tick the areas that you feel you understand and would be confident answering exam questions about. If there are any areas that you don't understand or are not confident about, you will need to return to them before you begin your exam revision.

Expected and unexpected life events ❏

Relationship changes
Marriage ❏
Divorce ❏
Living with a partner ❏
Birth of children ❏
Death (of partner, relative or friend) ❏

Physical changes
Puberty ❏
Accidents and injury ❏
Menopause ❏

Changes in life circumstances
Moving house ❏
Starting school ❏
Starting college ❏
Beginning work ❏
Retirement ❏
Redundancy ❏

Sources of support
Partners, family and friends ❏
Professional carers and services ❏
Voluntary and faith-based services ❏

Assessment Guide

Your learning in this unit will be assessed through a one hour written examination.

The examination will consist of a series of short and longer answer questions covering all aspects of this unit. You will need to show that you understand:

● expected and unexpected life events

● how different types of life events can affect personal development

● sources of support that can help people to cope with the impact of life events.

Chapter 9 provides full coverage of the range of factors that you could be asked about in the examination.

Promoting Health and Wellbeing

Introduction

This unit is about the different ways that people think about and try to achieve personal health and wellbeing. You will learn about:

- Definitions of health and wellbeing.

- Common factors affecting health and wellbeing and the different effects they can have across the human life span.

- Methods used to measure an individual's physical health.

- Ways of promoting and supporting health improvement for an individual or for a small group.

As a care student, and possibly a future care practitioner, health and wellbeing are concepts that you should understand. It is important that you are able to identify what good physical health involves and that you have an understanding of some of the measures of health used by care practitioners. You should be able to explain the effects of a range of factors on an individual's health and wellbeing. Learning about the positive and negative effects that a range of factors can have on health and wellbeing will be of benefit if you choose to work with people in care situations. Knowledge and understanding of how health and wellbeing can be promoted and improved will also be helpful to you in your personal as well as your professional working life.

Chapter 10

Defining health and wellbeing

Key issue: What is health and wellbeing?

Health and wellbeing are important concepts that all care practitioners need to understand. This might seem obvious but it is also important to know about and understand the different methods used by care practitioners to define health and wellbeing. These include:

- **Holistic** definitions of health, based on a combination of PIES factors
- Positive definitions of health, based on achieving and maintaining things like physical fitness and mental stability
- Negative definitions of health, based on the absence or lack of physical illness, disease and mental distress.

Chapter 10 will introduce and explain these different types of definitions. It will also cover how ideas about health and wellbeing change over time, differ between cultures and vary according to a person's life stage. By the end of the chapter you will understand that the terms health and wellbeing can be defined and used in different ways by care practitioners and service users.

Defining health and wellbeing

What is health? Is it something you're born with, something to do with your body and the way that it works? Or is it more than this? 'Health' is a word that people use all the time but what does it mean?

The ideas you have about health are those that other people in your society and culture use and have probably taught you. We tend to take these ideas for granted and generally assume there is only one way of thinking about 'health'. In fact, there are many different ways of understanding health and wellbeing. Chinese and Indian cultures, for example, adopt very different approaches to the Western **biomedical approach** that is generally used by health care practitioners to understand health and ill-health in the United Kingdom.

The biomedical approach

In Western societies, health professionals use a biomedical approach to define health and wellbeing. This approach includes several different terms that identify when a person's health is lacking or poor. For example, the terms disease, illness and ill-health are commonly used to describe an unhealthy state. **Disease** is a term used by doctors and other health care workers to refer to a physical change in the body's correct structure or

Over to you!

List as many words as you can which describe being or feeling 'unhealthy'. Identify the main words that you use when talking about health with your friends and family. Are these different to the words you use when talking to your GP or other health care workers?

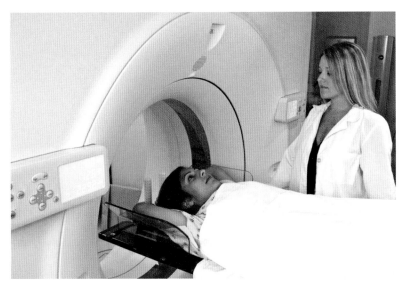

Scanning machines can show disease inside the body.

way of working. Health professionals use the term 'disease' only when they can measure, see or picture (using X-rays or scans perhaps) some type of abnormality. A disease is diagnosed when the health care practitioner can observe signs of abnormal physical change in the individual's body or the way that it is functioning.

The term illness, on the other hand, is generally used to describe a mental or physical state that is causing the person pain, distress or is affecting their ability to function in some way. Health care practitioners use the term 'illness' more broadly to describe ill-health that is identified from the symptoms that the person complains about, such as aches, pains and feeling sick. These symptoms can't always be directly seen or observed by others. This doesn't mean that the person is making up their symptoms or that there is nothing wrong with them! It means that they don't feel in good health and that physically, emotionally or mentally they're not at their best. Illnesses are usually seen as less serious or a more temporary threat to health than diseases. Even so, Western doctors and other health professionals see a lot of people each day who feel ill and want their help to get over their temporary health problems.

It is also important to note that a person can have a disease (a change in their body) without feeling ill or noticing that anything is wrong. This is one of the reasons for having **screening programmes**. Cervical smears, breast screening after the age of 50, childhood blood tests and chest X-rays are all carried out to identify diseases that, in their early stages, often don't cause people to feel ill.

Positive and negative definitions

The Western biomedical approach to defining health and wellbeing is based on the idea that a person is healthy if they don't have any illnesses, injuries or diseases or if they simply feel 'okay'. This is known as a negative view of health because being healthy is defined as not being or feeling unwell! A health care practitioner who uses this approach would assess whether an individual is experiencing any physical illness, disease or mental distress. If they are not, the care practitioner would say the

Over to you!

Can you think of an example of a disease and an illness? Use the explanation above to guide your choices.

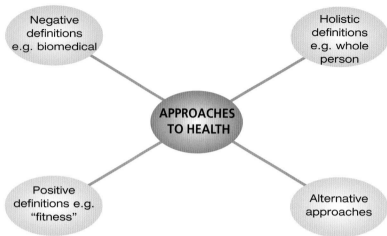

Figure 3.1 Different approaches to health.

person is 'healthy'. This type of definition is widely used by hospital doctors and GPs who look for evidence of illness and disease when they examine patients.

An alternative, positive view of health that is also used in Western societies involves identifying the qualities and abilities that a person ought to have in order to be healthy. For example, being physically fit, the correct weight for their height and feeling happy might be seen as evidence that a person is healthy. A care practitioner who uses this approach would assess whether an individual is physically fit and mentally stable. If the person met these criteria, they would be seen as 'healthy'.

Holistic definitions

There is a third approach to health that takes a broader view than either the positive or negative approaches described so far. The holistic approach to health suggests we should take all aspects of a person's life into account when we're looking at their health. This approach is concerned with the 'whole person' and includes an individual's:

- physical (bodily) health and wellbeing
- intellectual (thinking and learning) wellbeing
- social (relationship) wellbeing
- emotional (feelings) wellbeing.

The term 'wellbeing' is linked to, but also different from, health. **Wellbeing** is used in Western societies to refer to the way people feel about themselves. If people feel 'good' (positive) about themselves and are happy with life they will have a high level of wellbeing, and vice versa. As individuals, we are the best judges of our personal sense of wellbeing.

Over to you!

How do you think about health? Is your approach closer to the negative or positive view? Or do you use another approach to assessing your 'health'? Describe what 'being healthy' involves for you and compare your ideas to the definitions of health that are provided above.

The World Health Organisation takes a positive and a holistic view when it defines health as:

'a state of complete physical, mental and social wellbeing, not merely the absence of disease or infirmity'

(WHO, 1946).

Life stage differences

The way in which we think about and judge whether or not a person is 'healthy' is affected by the person's life stage. Being able to walk ten miles may be a sign of good physical health (or fitness at least) in an 18-year-old, but it isn't something you would expect a 90-year-old person to do even if they were very healthy for their age. That last bit, 'for their age', is the important point. The way we think about health should take into account a person's age-related needs and abilities. So, we could say that a physically active 90-year-old man might be just as physically healthy, considering his age, as his 18-year-old great grandson.

A person can be healthy (or unhealthy) at any age

The social construction of health and wellbeing

Health and wellbeing can be seen as **socially constructed** ideas. This means that the ways in which people think about health and wellbeing are not fixed but change over time and make sense within a particular society at a certain period in its history. People have defined health and wellbeing differently in the past and members of other, non-Western cultures also have alternative ways of thinking about health and wellbeing to those we have discussed so far.

Health in the past

People have thought about health and wellbeing in a variety of different ways for thousands of years. Many of these ideas seem unusual to us by present day standards. Ideas about health have changed over time, but many present-day thoughts and theories about what it means to be healthy have also been developed from these earlier ideas.

Whatever historical period they've lived in, people have always needed to know how to avoid disease and illness, how to deal with sickness and how to remain 'healthy'. It is hard to get evidence from prehistoric times (around 17,000 years ago). However, a possible source of evidence about health ideas is found in the skulls discovered by archaeologists that belong to this period. Some of these skulls had holes drilled in them. One theory is that prehistoric people did this to release the 'spirit' of a person who had died. However, many of the skulls show evidence that the person survived this operation and was therefore alive when it happened! Was this procedure, known as **trepanning**, part of the health beliefs and treatment approach of prehistoric people?

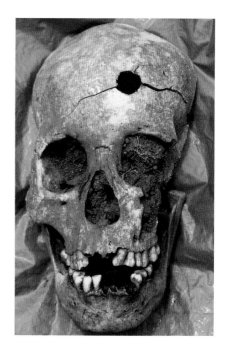

A trepanned skull.

More recent evidence from nomadic and non-industrialised societies shows that in the not too distant past some more modern cultures also based their beliefs about health and the causes of illness on the existence and work of spirits and gods. In some of these cultures, good and bad spirits were seen to affect everyday life and to cause a person to suffer from illness, or even die, by entering their body. The cure for this was to rid the body of the evil spirit. A religious leader or traditional healer would be called on to banish the spirit from the person and return them to health. These ideas are very different from those of present-day Western societies.

It's important to remain open minded about the various ways of thinking about health and the causes and best ways of treating ill-health. Even though they don't fit in with present day medical views, many of the apparently old and unusual ideas about health from earlier times and different cultures continue to be used in the UK and throughout the world. This is often because they work by helping people to get over health problems and by making them feel better. Ongoing research into traditional cures and treatments also shows that the ideas of the past were sometimes based on good sense and played an important part in improving people's lives at the time. For example, modern scientists are now finding that the plants and herbs that were used by ancient civilizations as painkillers and sedatives provide very effective forms of 'natural' treatment. In fact, many modern day medicines are produced from plants and herbs - aspirin, for example, comes from willow bark.

Ideas about health and ill-health in the United Kingdom changed with the development of scientific thinking in the eighteenth century. People began to move away from the belief that magic, evil spirits or a disapproving God controlled health and illness. The development of microscopes, knowledge about human anatomy and growing understanding of body chemistry resulted in medical and scientific approaches to health and new ways of dealing with ill-health. Based on theories and observations of how the human body works, these ideas about health and ill-health are those that we currently recognise and use as 'true'. Instead of having religious leaders and traditional healers to banish evil spirits, we now have doctors and other health professionals to put these biomedical ideas about health into practice.

Health in other cultures

Western ideas about health and wellbeing are different from those of some other cultures. For example, Chinese herbal medicine is based on ideas about health that are 2000 years old. **Chinese herbal medicine** deals with both physical and mental health problems. It also provides ways of strengthening a person's recovery power, their immunity and capacity for wellbeing. Chinese herbal medicine is growing in popularity and is being used by an increasing number of people in western countries.

Chinese herbal medicine practitioners try to diagnose the 'patterns of disharmony' affecting the individuals who come to see them. They try to work out whether the individual has a blocked, deficient or disturbed 'energy' (ch'i). Once they discover how the individual's 'energy' is blocked, the Chinese herbalist will prescribe a range of herbal medicines and give advice on how they can restore their normal energy balance.

If you visited a Chinese herbalist they would ask you what kind of 'complaint' you are suffering from. You would need to tell them where it is located, whether it comes and goes, how intense it is,

Health ideas from the past

- Ancient Egyptians used a sand-paste to clean their teeth.
- Aboriginal peoples used a casing of mud and clay to set broken limbs, and cleared their camps of human waste and debris to stop their enemies stealing their spirits
- Aztec Indians used human hair to stitch (suture) body wounds.

Over to you!

Are you superstitious about anything? Think about your superstitions and how they affect the ways that you act or behave. Are any of your superstitious beliefs linked to ideas about health or ill-health?

Over to you!

The six people described opposite have different lifestyles, attitudes, values and needs. In some ways they may be 'healthy', in other ways they may not be. Read through each case study and answer the questions at the end.

Lois, age 30, has a job as a stockbroker. She buys and sells shares and must reach certain targets each week. She works out in the company gym each morning and then works very hard from 7.30 a.m. to 7.30 p.m. five days a week. She admits to feeling stressed most of the time. Before going home, she usually goes for a few drinks with her colleagues to wind down. She has made a lot of money but says that she has little time for other things.

Richie is a 27-year-old packer in a factory. He says his job is very boring. His life really revolves around sport and fitness training. He goes to a gym five nights a week to do weight training. Before work each day, he jogs or swims. He cycles everywhere he goes. Richie is very concerned about his diet and his physical appearance. He thinks about exercise even when he isn't doing it. He always wants to do more to improve his body. He has recently started taking anabolic steroids to help him build up his physique.

Amira describes herself as 'just a housewife'. She is 23 and has two children under five. She lives on income support, but occasionally gets help from her mother who lives a few miles away. She says that the children take up most of her time so she doesn't go out very often. Her favourite pastime is television. After the children are in bed she likes to watch soap operas and quiz shows. She always has a box of chocolates, some crisps and a few cans of lemonade while she watches TV.

Linda is a 19-year-old student of geology. In her first year at university, she joined a rock climbing group and went on most of their climbing trips. She recently went on a trip to Snowdonia. This time, she says, she 'just lost her nerve'. She got stuck on a cliff face and had to be taken off by rescue helicopter. She's been feeling 'on edge' ever since and has fallen behind in her studies this term.

Alex, age 47, gave up his job as a business studies lecturer two years ago to live in France and write books. He used to spend a great deal of time out of doors, cycling around the countryside. Last year he damaged his ankle in a fall and can no longer ride very far. Although he's made a few friends, he rarely has enough money to go out. Last winter he felt lonely. He caught pneumonia because he couldn't afford to heat his house. He's now working as a tourist guide to make money until he gets a book published.

Gary is a 55-year-old nurse working on a hospital medical ward. He works seven days a week, sometimes doing two seven-hour shifts (one in the morning the other in the afternoon) and finishing at 9.30 p.m. He's very concerned about hygiene and always uses disposable gloves at work. Gary washes his hands several times during the day. He carries an extra suit of clothing to change into between shifts. He's worried he might contract a serious disease and insists that his house is cleaned every day, with a fresh set of bed linen put on every other day. His spare time is spent sleeping.

- In what way is each person healthy or unhealthy? Make notes of your ideas. You might want to give each person a score (10 = extremely healthy, 1 = extremely unhealthy) for physical, emotional, social and intellectual health.

- Compare and discuss your ideas and scores with other people in the class.

- What sort of approach to health are you using in making your decision about each person? (Hint: is your approach to health positive, negative, holistic or based on another type of definition?)

what makes it better or worse (e.g. food, activity, time of day) and what you have done about it. This information tells the herbalist about your 'patterns of dysfunction'. The herbalist would also feel your pulse and look closely at your tongue for signs of 'imbalance'. According to the Chinese system, healthy people need to achieve a mind-spirit balance, an energy balance, a blood balance and a body fluids balance. The herbal medicines that are often prescribed are said to strengthen the individual's organs or to 'clear' from their body the unhealthy factors that are preventing balance and blocking energy flows.

Investigate ...

Produce a range of questions that explore ideas about health and wellbeing. Use your questions to carry out a survey of friends, relatives or school colleagues to find out how they think about health and wellbeing. Summarise your results by comparing what different people say about the various approaches to 'health' we have looked at.

Knowledge Check

1 Name three ways of defining 'health'.

2 How would a care practitioner using a negative definition go about assessing an individual's health?

3 Which approach to health and wellbeing focuses on the 'whole person'?

4 What does the term 'wellbeing' mean?

5 Explain why a person who is physically fit and the correct weight for their height might not be healthy.

6 When is a person 'healthy'? Write an answer to this in your own words.

7 Explain why most people living in modern Western societies no longer believe that health and illness result from the action of 'evil spirits'.

8 Name two physical features that a Chinese medical herbalist would look at closely when assessing a person's health problems.

9 What, according to Chinese herbal medicine, happens to cause a person to be unwell?

10 Describe the purpose of the herbal medicines that are prescribed by Chinese herbal practitioners.

11 Explain, using examples, how ideas about 'health' can vary over time and between different cultures.

Chapter checklist

The box below provides a summary of the areas covered in chapter 10. Tick the areas that you feel you understand and would be confident about when writing your assignment. If there are any areas that you don't understand or are not confident about, you will need to return to them before you begin planning or writing your assignment.

Definitions of health and wellbeing
- Disease and illness ☐
- Positive definitions ☐
- Negative definitions ☐
- Holistic definitions ☐

The social construction of health and wellbeing
- Changing definitions over time ☐
- Cultural differences in definitions ☐
- Life stage differences ☐

Assessment Guide

Your learning in this unit will be assessed through a controlled assignment task. This will be set by the OCR awarding body and marked by your tutor.

The assignment will require you to produce a health improvement plan for an individual. You can develop a plan based on improving your own health and wellbeing or find a volunteer who is willing to be the focus of your project.

Your final plan will need to:

- Define health and wellbeing.

- Identify the health and wellbeing needs of the person whom your health improvement plan is based on.

Chapter 10 provides full coverage of different ways of defining health and wellbeing. Studying and referring back to chapter 10 should provide you with the background information needed to complete this part of the controlled assessment task.

Chapter 11

Interpreting physical measures of health

Key issue: How can an individual's physical health be measured?

The previous topic outlined a variety of factors that can affect a person's health and wellbeing. These include factors that promote good health, such as exercise and a balanced diet, and cigarette smoking which is harmful to health. But how can we know whether a person is healthy or not? One way is to measure specific aspects (indicators) of their physical health. This topic will focus on what these indicators are, how they can be measured and how the results of health assessments can be used to develop realistic health improvement plans.

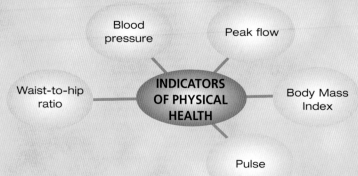

Figure 3.2 Indicators of physial health.

Chapter 11 will help you to understand how and why physical health is measured. It won't teach you how to make these measures yourself but will help you to understand how they are used by health care practitioners to develop realistic health improvement plans for service users.

Ways of measuring physical health

You've probably had aspects of your physical health measured many times. This will have happened when you visited your GP (family doctor) or if you've ever been to hospital for assessment or treatment. You've probably also watched television programmes set in hospitals where people seem to spend a lot of time checking the state of their patients' health.

So, how can health care practitioners tell if a person is physically healthy or not? There are, in fact, many different ways of measuring physical health. They are all based on the same basic idea – the health care practitioner measures and records something and then compares the individual's 'score' against a standard scale. In order to interpret the results of any physical measurement procedure, a health care practitioner has to take into account the individual's age, sex and lifestyle. This is important because a pulse rate of 100 beats per minute would be fast for an adult but normal for a baby, for example. You are probably familiar with the way that blood pressure and pulse are measured. However, there are a range of other techniques that provide useful information about physical health too.

Blood pressure

Health care professionals routinely measure their patient's blood pressure as well as their pulse rate. Blood pressure measurement is a direct way of checking heart functioning, and indirectly physical fitness.

When a person's blood pressure is checked, two measurements are taken. The force, or pressure, which the blood puts on the walls of the artery when the heart beats is one of these measurements. This is known as the **systolic blood pressure**. The continuous pressure that the person's blood puts on the arteries between heart beats is the second measurement of blood pressure. This is known as the **diastolic blood pressure**. A person's blood pressure reading is recorded and written as two numbers. The systolic measure comes first, followed by the diastolic measure. On average, a healthy young adult will have a blood pressure reading of 120/80 mm Hg (millimetres of mercury).

Blood pressure is measured with an instrument called a sphygmomanometer or 'sphyg' for short. Some health care professionals use electronic sphygs which measure automatically and display the results on a screen. The other way of measuring blood pressure is to use a manual sphyg.

A person's blood pressure fluctuates throughout the day and night. It increases when the person is active and decreases when they are inactive, resting or sleeping. A person's blood pressure will usually be taken when they are resting. A younger adult should have lower blood pressure than an older adult. If a person's blood pressure is higher or lower than average for their age, it will need to be checked on several more occasions to establish whether this is caused by a health problem. Consistently high blood pressure (hypertension) is linked to a higher risk of heart attacks and strokes. Low blood pressure (hypotension) may be an indicator of heart failure, dehydration or other underlying health problems.

Peak flow

A person's respiratory health (breathing) can be assessed by recording simple physical measurements. One way of doing this is to use a peak flow meter. You may have seen or used a peak flow meter, especially if you have asthma or have had other respiratory health checks. A person is asked to take a deep breath and then breathe out as hard as they can into the peak flow meter.

A peak flow meter measures the maximum rate at which air is expelled (pushed out) from the lungs when a person breathes out as hard as they can. This is an example of a pulmonary function test. A healthy adult should record a peak flow result of 400–600 litres of air per minute. Peak flow tests are used to monitor several aspects of respiratory function. For example, the

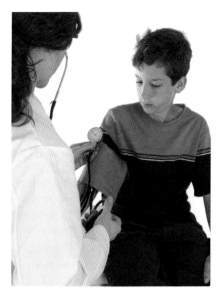

Blood pressure monitoring.

 Over to you!

Find out what effect each of the following can have on a person's blood pressure:

- a diet high in fat and salt
- regular exercise
- stress
- cigarette smoking.

peak flow meter can be used to diagnose whether a person has a problem with the use of their lungs, because there is a standard scale of expected scores against which the results can be compared. People with chronic (long-term) asthma usually record a measurement that is lower than 350 on the peak flow scale when they breathe out as hard as they can.

Body Mass Index

The relationship between height and weight can be an indicator of good or ill-health in adults. Health professionals recommend that a person's weight should be in proportion to their height. A person is considered obese when their weight is more than 20 per cent above the average weight for people of the same height. People who are obese or whose weight is much greater than recommended run the risk of developing a range of health problems.

Health professionals use the Body Mass Index (BMI) to assess whether a person is overweight. Unlike blood pressure measurement, you don't need to undertake any training to measure a person's BMI. Body Mass Index is calculated by dividing a person's weight in kilograms by their height in metres squared. This produces a number which is then checked against the categories in the table below.

Using a peak flow meter.

Figure 3.3 BMI table.

Female BMI	Indicates	Male BMI	Indicates
Under 18	Underweight	Under 18	Underweight
18–20	Lean	18–20	Lean
21–22	Normal	21–23	Normal
23–28	Overweight	24–32	Overweight
29–36	Obese	32–40	Obese

In most cases a person's BMI result will provide some useful information about their physical health. Being over or underweight can have significant negative effects on physical health, for example. However, one of the limitations of BMI scores is that they don't take a person's body shape and composition into account. A very fit and muscular person, such as a rugby player or weightlifter, may have a lot of heavy muscle and little fat. Their BMI score may still suggest they are overweight or even obese when this isn't the case.

Waist-to-hip ratio

Measurement of a person's hip/waist ratio provides a way of assessing the proportion of body fat that is stored around their waist and hips. People tend to store fat either around their middle (giving them an apple shape) or around their hips (giving them a pear shape). People who carry extra fat around their waist have an increased risk of developing health problems compared to people who carry extra weight around their hips or thighs.

The hip/waist ratio is calculated by measuring the circumference of the waist (located just above the hip bone) and dividing it by

Health problems associated with obesity

- arthritis
- high blood pressure
- increased risk of stroke
- diabetes
- gallstones
- heart disease.

the circumference of the hips at their widest point. A hip/waist ratio of about 0.7 for women and 0.9 for men is associated with good general health and fertility. Research has shown that women within the 0.7 range are also less likely to develop diabetes, cardiovascular disorders or ovarian cancers. Men within the 0.9 range are also healthier, more fertile and less likely to develop prostate or testicular cancers.

Resting pulse and recovery pulse after exercise

The pulse rate, both before and after exercise, is often used to determine a person's general health or physical fitness. The pulse rate indicates how fast the heart is beating. For adults, the average (or normal) resting rate is usually between 70 and 80 beats per minute. Babies and young children normally have a faster pulse rate than adults.

The pulse can be felt at any artery. In conscious people, it is usual to use the **radial artery**, which can be felt at the wrist. In unconscious people, the **carotid artery**, which can be felt at the neck, may be used (Most conscious people would find it uncomfortable if you pressed on their carotid artery!). A person's pulse rate increases when they exercise, when they are emotionally upset, or if they develop a form of heart or respiratory disease. Unfit people, smokers and overweight people have a faster resting pulse rate than normal.

Knowledge Check

1 Identify five different indicators of physical health that health care practitioners can measure and monitor.

2 Identify and describe two methods of measuring a person's cardiac (heart) health.

3 Using your own words, explain what the systolic and diastolic numbers in a blood pressure reading are measuring.

4 Explain what a high diastolic measurement would tell you about a person's blood pressure.

5 Explain the purpose and use of a peak flow meter.

6 Identify the two measures needed to calculate a person's Body Mass Index (BMI).

7 What effects can obesity have on an individual's health and wellbeing?

8 What can an individual's waist-to-hip ratio reveal about their health?

9 Describe how a person's pulse can be taken.

10 Why is it important to take account of a person's age, sex and lifestyle when interpreting health measurements?

Investigate ...

Measure your own, or another person's, pulse rate (using the radial pulse!) for one minute. Compare the resting pulse rate with the pulse rate taken after some brief exercise.

Over to you!

1 Is your BMI measure within or outside of the normal range? If outside, how can you adjust your health-related behaviour to bring it within the normal, healthy range?

2 You can find more information on weight, BMI and weight measurement on several websites. Try those listed below or carry out a search of your own:

- www.teenagehealthfreak.com
- www.surgerydoor.co.uk
- www.weightlossresources.co.uk

Some websites will calculate your BMI for you if you know your height and weight figures.

Over to you!

How might each of the following factors have an impact on an individual's pulse rate?

- Stress
- Blood loss
- Drugs
- Strenuous exercise
- Age
- Infection
- Sleep.

Chapter checklist

The box below provides a summary of the areas covered in chapter 11. Tick the areas that you feel you understand and would be confident about when writing your assignment. If there are any areas that you don't understand or are not confident about, you will need to return to them before you begin planning or writing your assignment.

Health assessment measures
- Blood pressure ❑
- Peak flow ❑
- Body Mass Index ❑
- Hip/waist ratio ❑
- Resting and recovery pulse rates ❑

Factors affecting interpretation of health assessment measures ❑

Assessment Guide

Your learning in this unit will be assessed through a controlled assessment task. This will be set by the OCR awarding body and marked by your tutor.

The assignment will require you to produce a health improvement plan for an individual. You can develop a plan based on improving your own health and wellbeing or find a volunteer who is willing to be the focus of your project.

Your final plan will need to:

- Provide information about the state of the individual's physical health and their intellectual, emotional and social wellbeing.

- Provide evidence that you can calculate two physical measures of the individual's health (Pulse, peak flow, blood pressure. BMI or waist-to-hip ratio, for example).

- Present an analysis of your findings , identifying two physical needs that the plan is going to focus on.

Chapter 11 provides full coverage of a range of ways of measuring physical health and interpreting findings. Studying and referring back to chapter 11 should provide you with the background information needed to complete this part of the controlled assessment task.

Chapter 12

Factors positively affecting health and wellbeing

Key issue: What factors contribute positively to health and wellbeing throughout a person's life?

Would you like to be healthy? Most people would answer 'yes' to this question. Research has shown that people say being healthy is just as likely to make them feel happy as winning lots of money. Winning lots of money relies on luck. However, being healthy is a bit easier to achieve if you understand how different factors affect health and wellbeing. These include:

- *Physical factors* such as a balanced diet, regular exercise, sufficient sleep and personal hygiene.
- *Social factors* such as supportive relationships, stimulating work, education, leisure activity, work-life balance.
- *Economic factors* such as adequate financial resources.
- Use of health monitoring and illness prevention services (such as **screening** and **vaccination**).
- Use of **risk management** to protect health and promote personal safety.

Chapter 12 will help you to gain an understanding of how each of these factors can affect health and wellbeing in a positive way.

Physical factors

A person who has a balanced diet, exercises regularly, has sufficient sleep (rest) and who maintains good standards of personal hygiene has a relatively healthy lifestyle.

A balanced diet

Food plays a very important role in health. The food we eat should be nutritious if it is going to be beneficial to our physical health. This means it should contain a variety of **nutrients**. Nutrients are naturally-occurring chemical substances found in the food we eat. The five basic nutrients help the body in different ways:

- Carbohydrates and fats provide the body with energy
- Proteins provide the chemical substances needed to build and repair body cells and tissues
- Vitamins help to regulate the chemical reactions that continuously take place in our bodies

- Minerals are needed for control of body function and to build and repair certain tissues.

As well as eating food that contains a balance of these five nutrients, we also need to consume fibre and water. Although these are not counted as nutrients they are vital for physical health.

The components of a balanced diet.

A healthy intake of food, also known as a **balanced diet**, contains suitable amounts of each of the five basic nutrients. The amount and types of foods that are healthy for a person to eat, varies for each individual. The following factors will affect how much and what types of food we need to consume:

- age
- gender
- body size
- height
- weight
- the environment (for example, whether you live in a cold or a warm country)
- the amount of physical activity you do in your daily life.

Nutrition is very important in the early years of life. Babies and infants need the right types of food to help them grow and develop normally, and to prevent them from developing certain illnesses. Children and adolescents also need the right types of food to promote their physical growth and to provide 'fuel' or energy for their high level of physical activity.

People who have special diets, for example vegetarians and vegans, leave out or include specific food groups to meet their personal values or special physical needs. Vegetarians don't eat meat or fish but they can still get all the nutrients they need. They can get proteins from cereals, beans, eggs and cheese. Vegans, who eat no animal products at all, can still get all their essential nutrients provided their food intake is varied. For example, they can get protein from nuts and pulses.

Over to you!

Family member	Day	Breakfast	Lunch	Snacks	Dinner
Tom age 40	Saturday	Boiled egg, toast, coffee	Ham roll, crisps,	Doughnut, coffee	Pizza, salad, baked beans, baked potatoes, beer, chocolate cake
	Sunday	Fried egg, bacon, toast, coffee	Roast chicken, roast potatoes, peas, carrots, tinned fruit, ice cream, white wine	Chocolate bar, coffee	Cheese and pickle sandwich, fruit cake, tea
Laura age 30	Saturday	Boiled egg, toast, tea	Crispbread, cottage cheese, herb tea,	Apple, diet coke	Pizza, salad, diet coke, orange, coffee
	Sunday	Toast, marmalade, orange juice, tea	Roast chicken, peas, carrots, ice cream, wine, coffee	Banana, diet coke	Fruit cake, tea
Rachel age 8	Saturday	Cornflakes, orange juice	Ham roll, crisps, blackcurrant squash	Chocolate bar, cola drink	Pizza, salad, baked potato, blackcurrant squash, chocolate cake
	Sunday	Fried egg, toast, orange juice	Roast chicken, roast potatoes, carrots, ice cream, wafers, grape juice	Cheese sandwich,	Chocolate milkshake; sponge cake
Danny age 3	Saturday	Ready breakfast cereal, milk	Tuna sandwich, apple, orange juice	Chocolate bar, milk	Pizza, salad, blackcurrant squash, chocolate cake
	Sunday	Toast, savoury spread, milk	Roast chicken, roast potato, peas, ice cream, wafers, grape juice	Chocolate milkshake	Fruit yoghurt, sponge cake, blackcurrant squash
Audrey age 73	Saturday	Grapefruit, crispbread, marmalade, tea	Roll, cottage cheese, tomato, herb tea	Apple	Pizza, salad, chocolate cake, tea
	Sunday	Boiled egg, toast, tea	Roast chicken, roast potato, peas, carrots, tinned fruit, ice cream, wine, coffee	Nothing	Tuna sandwich, fruit cake, tea

This is a diet record sheet showing the weekend food consumption for members of the James family. Use the diet sheet to answer these questions.

1   Which nutrients can be found in the foods eaten by the family?

2   What effect does each nutrient have on the body?

3   How nutritional is this family's diet?

4   Do you think that individual family members are getting a balanced diet?

5   Are there any deficiencies or excesses in their nutritional intakes?

Using examples from the record sheet, write a paragraph explaining your views on the last three questions. What advice would you give to the parents of Danny and Rachel about the type of diet needed to promote healthy growth and development in children?

Investigate ...

Monitor your diet over a 3-day period by keeping a food diary. List all of the food you eat (including meals and snacks). Identify the range of nutrients that you consume in each meal or snack. Does your diet over the three days suggest that you are or are not eating a balanced diet?

Regular exercise

Do you like doing exercise? Some people really enjoy playing sports, going to the gym or taking exercise classes. You might be one of them. Or you might be one of the large number of people who don't do enough exercise. Unfortunately exercise isn't as popular as eating food and is one of the things in lists of top health tips that many people struggle with. But it's still important, and is very good for your physical health.

Regular exercise has a positive effect on both physical and mental health. But it's important not to do too much exercise. People are advised to find a balance between physical activity and rest in order to maintain good physical health and a sense of wellbeing. Too much exercise can lead to excessive weight loss and may result in physical damage or chronic injuries, to joints or ligaments for example.

So, what kinds of exercise should you do? The type and level of exercise that an individual can do safely will depend on their age, gender and health status. For example, moderate exercise can be safely undertaken by older and less physically mobile people, including women in the later stages of pregnancy and people with physical disabilities. Younger people who are physically fit can safely undertake more vigorous exercise.

Benefits of exercise

Exercise…

…keeps the heart healthy

…improves circulation

…helps muscles, joints and bones to remain strong

…improves stamina

…reduces blood pressure

…increases self-esteem and self-confidence

…helps to control and maintain weight

…makes you feel more energetic

…is a good way of socialising

…helps the body to stay supple and mobile.

Sufficient sleep

Do you get enough rest and sleep? How much sleep do you need to be healthy? If you want to be healthy you've got to take rest and sleep seriously. Not everyone does. Some people work too much and spend their life feeling tired. This isn't healthy.

People should rest every day to maintain their health and wellbeing. The amount of sleep a person needs varies according to their age. Babies, young children, older people and pregnant women tend to need a period of rest (lack of exertion) during the day.

Most healthy adults and older children need to rest only at the end of their active day. Even so, people need varying amounts of sleep depending on their life stage and physical needs. For example, a four-year-old child sleeps an average of ten to fourteen hours a day whilst a ten-year-old needs about nine to twelve hours. Most adults sleep from seven to eight and a half hours every night. Others require as few as four or five hours or as many as ten hours each night. Most people find that they need slightly less sleep as they grow older. A person who slept eight hours a night when they were thirty years old may need only six or seven hours when they are sixty years old.

Personal hygiene

Good personal hygiene, including washing your skin and hair regularly, keeping your nails clean and brushing your teeth, contributes to the maintenance of physical health and wellbeing as well as to social and emotional wellbeing. Being clean helps to keep the human body in good condition because it prevents the growth of bacteria, viruses and fungi that will live on and feed off unclean skin. Regular washing and dental care also ensure that you smell fresh and clean. This is important in modern society as people expect others to maintain good standards of hygiene and make judgements about us based on our physical appearance and standards of hygiene and dress.

Knowledge Check

1 Identify four different physical factors that affect health and wellbeing.

2 Name the five basic nutrients that are part of a balanced diet.

3 Identify at least two sources of each nutrient in the food you eat regularly.

4 Describe the factors that affect how much food a person should eat.

5 Explain why a varied and balanced diet is especially important for babies and children.

6 What are the health benefits of taking regular exercise?

7 Why is it important for people of all ages to have sufficient sleep?

8 Describe how good personal hygiene contributes to an individual's health and wellbeing.

Social factors

Social factors refer to relationships with others and the activities that people take part in as a member of wider society. Social factors that can affect health and wellbeing include, for example, supportive relationships, stimulating work, education, leisure activity and achieving an appropriate work-life balance. In particular, there are strong links between social factors and our mental health and social wellbeing.

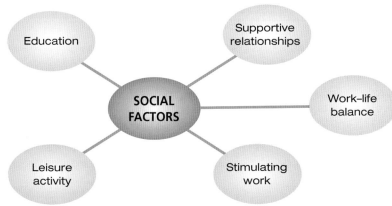

◄ Figure 3.4 Social factors affecting health and wellbeing.

Supportive relationships

Do you have good friends and relatives who you care about? Hopefully you will be able to think of a variety of people to whom you are emotionally close. These people are good for your health and wellbeing. You may have disagreements and fall out with family members and close friends from time to time, but you shouldn't underestimate the important effect they have on your emotional wellbeing and mental health.

Relationships with family members and friends are supportive, and have a positive effect on mental health when the people involved feel emotionally close, cared for and able to trust each other. We need supportive relationships in each life stage to

Case study

Robbie is one year old. Monica, his mum, is 22 years old and a lone parent. She has recently found out that she has to go into hospital for an eye operation. Monica is upset and feels frightened about how this might turn out. Her worst fear is that something might go wrong and she won't be able to care for Robbie afterwards. She is also upset about the prospect of being separated from Robbie for a week whiles she is in hospital.

- How might Robbie react if he feels insecure and unsupported when Monica is in hospital?
- Who would you seek support from if you were in Monica's situation?
- What kinds of support do you think Monica needs at the moment?
- What do you think other members of Monica's family could do to be supportive whilst she is in hospital?

experience wellbeing, and to support our social and emotional development. Babies need to form a close attachment to an adult carer (usually a parent) so that they can experience an emotionally secure relationship. Children also need supportive relationships with their parents (or carers) and with friends to develop their self-concept and self-esteem. Not having friends can lead to a child feeling 'left out' and having low self-esteem. During adolescence close, supportive relationships with friends and parents provide people with a 'safe place' when they feel stress and pressure. These supportive relationships help to boost self-esteem, a sense of belonging and of feeling valued by others. People who experience supportive relationships with family members and friends are more likely to experience a positive sense of social and emotional wellbeing and better mental health than people who lack support and are more socially isolated. Researchers have shown that people who lack close, supportive relationships are much more likely to experience depression.

Stimulating work

For many people, work has a positive effect on their health and wellbeing. Work is good for mental health and social wellbeing when it provides an individual with:

- a sense of purpose and identity ('what do you do?')
- self-reliance
- self-esteem and a sense of self-worth
- social relationships.

Employment obviously provides the income people need for their financial wellbeing but it also provides people with social contacts and support and a sense of achievement. Work can make a positive contribution to a person's physical health as well as their intellectual, emotional and social wellbeing if it involves safe, stimulating and satisfying work.

Education

A person's educational achievements affect their outlook on life, their sense of emotional wellbeing and their self-esteem. People feel proud of passing exams and gaining qualifications, and upset about failing them. Personal, social and health education programmes are now also a part of every school's curriculum.

 ## Over to you!

What types of jobs do you think would be mentally demanding and good for your sense of wellbeing? List five jobs that would stimulate you intellectually and be emotionally satisfying.

Children and young people now learn about physical, mental, emotional and sexual health as well as how the use of alcohol, tobacco and illegal drugs can affect their health and wellbeing. Increasingly schools and colleges are also focusing on healthy eating and educating pupils and students about the need to consume a balanced diet. These kinds of educational experiences often shape the attitudes of children and young people and help to make them more informed and more able to make healthy lifestyle choices. More informal educational approaches are also used to target adults and older people with forms of health education - through leaflets, booklets, articles and programmes in the media, for example – in order to provide information and shape attitudes towards living a healthier lifestyle.

Leisure activity

Leisure time, including having hobbies, enjoying a social life and simply relaxing, is part of a healthy life. The leisure activities that people take part in during their non-work time contribute to health and wellbeing because they:

- help people to form social relationships with each other
- provide opportunities to communicate with and feel valued by others
- enable people to develop social skills
- provide opportunities to develop and use physical and intellectual abilities and skills, depending on the leisure activity
- provide people with an important sense of belonging to a group or team.

Work-life balance

If you want to live a healthy life, it is important to have a balance between work and non-work activity. Some people live for their work and can't think of a better way to spend their time than by having a busy work life. For many people, work is an important source of self-esteem and status. Work provides a feeling of being successful, of having a purpose and of being useful. However, even though work can be good for health and wellbeing, too much of it and a lack of rest, recreation and social activity can lead to people feeling stressed , being too tired and feeling unsupported and socially isolated.

Having a poor work-life balance is an increasing problem in present day society where jobs can be very demanding and people's work hours can be very long. If you want to live a healthy life, it's important to have a balance in your life between work and non-work time.

Education promotes wellbeing.

 Over to you!

What kind of leisure activities do you regularly take part in? What impact does your choice of leisure activity have on your health and wellbeing?

Poor work–life balance leads to stress.

 Over to you!

What kind of work-life balance do you have? How do you ensure that there is more to your life than school or college work? Are there any changes you could make to improve your work-life balance?

Economic factors

Money is an economic factor linked to health and wellbeing because it affects an individual's quality of life, their lifestyle choices and the opportunities open to them. A person's health and wellbeing won't be good simply because they have a lot or even sufficient money to live on. The economic links between money and health are indirect – it is what money can buy and how people use their money that is important.

Adequate financial resources

People need enough money (adequate finance) to afford the basic necessities of life, such as food, housing and clothing, which directly affect physical health. People with more money generally have better housing and may eat better quality food. In this way money does affect basic physical health.

People who have a good income are also less likely to worry about being able to cope with everyday life. They don't experience the same stresses as people who are worried about paying their rent or feeding their children, for example. Having a good income allows people to buy luxuries such as holidays, cars, electrical goods and other desirable things. It also has a positive effect on self-esteem as money is highly valued in Western societies. People with lots of money are often seen in a positive way. Being rich and successful is seen as desirable.

Knowledge Check

1 Identify four different social factors that can affect an individual's health and wellbeing.

2 How can relationships with family and friends contributes to health and wellbeing?

3 Describe how educational experiences can affect an individual's health behaviour and lifestyle.

4 Name one positive effect that work can have on a person's health or wellbeing.

5 Which aspects of health and wellbeing are most likely to be affected by having stimulating work?

6 Describe ways in which taking part in leisure activities promotes health and wellbeing.

7 What does a good work-life balance involve?

8 Identify an economic factor that can affect health and wellbeing.

9 Describe two ways in which income can have a positive effect on a person's physical health and wellbeing.

Health monitoring and illness prevention

Health care practitioners provide a range of services that are designed to prevent people from becoming ill and to promote a healthy lifestyle. Services are usually provided for particular client groups, or to deal with particular health problems. For example, illness prevention services include:

- **Vaccinations** against infectious diseases such as polio, diphtheria and measles; against viruses, such as influenza (flu), that affect many older people; and against tropical diseases, such as malaria, that can affect overseas travellers visiting areas where the virus is prevalent.

- Advice and information services to help people change their unhealthy behaviour and live healthier lives. GPs, for example, provide advice about stopping smoking and ways of losing weight.

- Classes where health workers teach people ways of improving their health. For example, relaxation, pilates and yoga for people who are stressed, or opportunities for people to meet and talk about their problems.

The general health of the UK population is much better now than it was at the beginning of the twentieth century. The evidence for this can be seen in the much higher proportion of children who survive early childhood and the fact that both men and women can now expect to live much longer lives. The widespread use of screening and vaccination has been important in this.

Screening

Screening is a health monitoring strategy. It is used to detect disease in individuals who have no obvious signs or symptoms of that disease. The aim of screening is to identify disease early enough to treat people and hopefully prevent them becoming more unwell. Common screening tests for adults include blood pressure measurement, blood cholesterol tests, cervical smears and mammograms for breast cancer. Screening tests can help with early diagnosis of health problems and plays a key part in enabling early treatment. However, screening tests can also lead to misdiagnosis and give some people who were thought to be clear of a particular disease a false sense of security if symptoms do occur at a later stage.

Vaccination

Vaccination is an illness prevention strategy. It involves giving an individual a vaccine (usually but not always by injection) that produces immunity to a disease. Vaccinations are the most clinically effective and cost-effective way of preventing infectious diseases. Babies and young children are given a number of vaccines as part of an immunisation programme (see figure 3.6) to protect them from infectious diseases. Older people (65+ years) and those with chronic heart and respiratory diseases are also encouraged to have an influenza ('flu) vaccination each year.

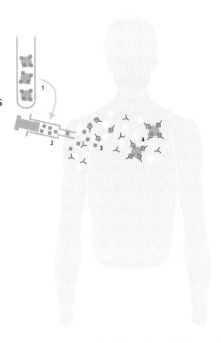

Screening is a preventative health strategy.

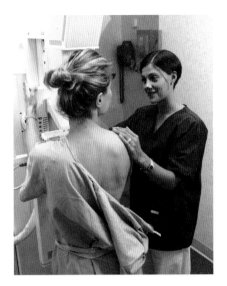

Figure 3.5 How a vaccine works. ▶

A vaccine is made from the disease-causing organism (1).
It is injected into the bloodstream (2) so that the body produces antibodies that neutralise it (3). The body then remains ready to produce an immune response against future infections by the organism (4).

Vaccine	When given
Diptheria Tetanus Pertussis (whooping cough) Polio Hib (*Haemophilus Influenzae*) Pneumococcal infection	2 months
Diptheria Tetanus Pertussis (whooping cough) Polio Hib (*Haemophilus Influenzae*) Meningitis	3 months
Diptheria Tetanus Pertussis (whooping cough) Polio Hib (*Haemophilus Influenzae*) Meningitis Pneumococcal infection	4 months
Meningitis C and Hib	Around 12 months
MMR (Measles, mumps, rubella) Pneumococcal infection	Around 13 months
Diptheria Tetanus Pertussis (whooping cough) Polio MMR	3 years
Human papillomavirus (cause of cervical cancer)	Girls 12–13 years
Diptheria Tetanus Polio	13–18 years

Figure 3.6 Typical immunisation programme

 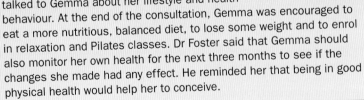

Case study

Gemma is 30 years old. She has been trying to get pregnant since marrying Phil 2 years ago. When she made an appointment with her GP, Gemma was hoping that there might be a quick and simple solution to the problem. Dr Foster, her GP, said he would need to take a range of health measures and carry out some checks to assess her current state of physical health. He also talked to Gemma about her lifestyle and health behaviour. At the end of the consultation, Gemma was encouraged to eat a more nutritious, balanced diet, to lose some weight and to enrol in relaxation and Pilates classes. Dr Foster said that Gemma should also monitor her own health for the next three months to see if the changes she made had any effect. He reminded her that being in good physical health would help her to conceive.

- What aspects of Gemma's physical health would you expect Dr Foster to check?
- How could Gemma monitor her own health over the next three months?
- What kind of health monitoring and screening services are available to young women like Gemma in your local area?

Health monitoring can also be carried out using simple self-monitoring techniques that can be learnt, such as breast or testicle self-examination. Checking your weight, looking after your skin and hair and having regular dental check ups and eye tests are also ways of monitoring personal health. Using health monitoring and illness prevention services, and assessing your own health regularly, are important to achieve and maintain good physical health and wellbeing.

Investigate ...

Look at the immunisation programme in figure 3.6. Research three of the diseases that are listed. Use the information to make a leaflet or poster that informs parents about the dangers of these diseases.

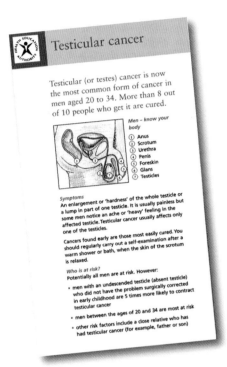

Testicular cancer

Testicular (or testes) cancer is now the most common form of cancer in men aged 20 to 34. More than 8 out of 10 people who get it are cured.

Men – know your body
1. Anus
2. Scrotum
3. Urethra
4. Penis
5. Foreskin
6. Glans
7. Testicles

Symptoms
An enlargement or 'hardness' of the whole testicle or a lump in part of one testicle. It is usually painless but some men notice an ache or 'heavy' feeling in the affected testicle. Testicular cancer usually affects only one of the testicles.

Cancers found early are those most easily cured. You should regularly carry out a self-examination after a warm shower or bath, when the skin of the scrotum is relaxed.

Who is at risk?
Potentially all men are at risk. However:
- men with an undescended testicle (absent testicle) who did not have the problem surgically corrected in early childhood are 5 times more likely to contract testicular cancer
- men between the ages of 20 and 34 are most at risk
- other risk factors include a close relative who has had testicular cancer (for example, father or son)

Risk management and personal safety

The final advice for achieving health and wellbeing is to stay safe. Accidents are responsible for around 10,000 deaths each year in the UK. Most people who die as the result of an accident are under the age of 35. Accidents are the most common cause of death in people under the age of 30, and also result in a large amount of serious injury and disability. If you want to be healthy, accidents are best avoided.

Statistics also show that young people are more likely to experience violent crime or attack than other sections of the population. But, how do you avoid being the victim of an accident or a potential attacker? Life isn't completely risk free but there are plenty of ways of reducing the risks and avoiding the hazards that are part of modern life.

If you want to stay safe and healthy, assessment of your own and other people's health and safety should be a part of your everyday life. This doesn't mean you should hibernate and try to live a risk-free life, but that you should be alert to potential hazards and dangers in everyday situations. **Risk assessment** is the procedure you go through when you question whether what

Over to you!

What do you think are the potential hazards in your everyday environment? Think about your journey to school, the environment where you spend your social time and your home environment. Are there any situations, or places, you avoid because you think the risk of an accident or attack is too high? Make a list of the main hazards to your health and safety and identify what you can do to stay safe and reduce the risk of accidents or personal injury.

you're about to do will be safe. For example, is it a good idea to accept a lift in a car if the driver has been drinking in the pub with you all night? What might the dangers be? Should you fill your room with candles and burn them for the nice smell because it helps you get to sleep? What might the dangers be? Shouldn't you make sure that somebody walks home with you or picks you up if you're out late at night? You probably know by now what the risks and dangers are of not taking these personal safety precautions. Avoiding accidents and staying safe is achieved through everyday risk assessment, by adjusting your behaviour or ensuring that other people behave safely whether at home, at work or when you're out enjoying yourself.

The Living Room

Knowledge Check

1 Name two methods used by health care practitioners to prevent ill-health.

2 Describe one way in which a person can monitor their own physical health.

3 Name three health problems or diseases that people can be screened for.

4 Explain what screening involves.

5 Identify four infectious diseases which children under the age of 1 are vaccinated against.

6 Explain what vaccination involves and how a vaccine works.

7 Approximately how many people die each year in the UK as a result of accidents?

8 Explain what the term risk assessment means and how this can contribute to an individual's health and wellbeing.

Chapter checklist

The box below provides a summary of the areas covered in chapter 12. Tick the areas that you feel you understand and would be confident about when writing your assignment. If there are any areas that you don't understand or are not confident about, you will need to return to them before you begin planning or writing your assignment.

Physical factors
- Balanced diet ❏
- Regular exercise ❏
- Sufficient sleep ❏
- Personal hygiene ❏

Social factors
- Supportive relationships ❏
- Stimulating work ❏
- Education ❏
- Leisure activity ❏
- Work-life balance ❏

Economic factors
- Adequate financial resources ❏

Health monitoring and illness prevention
- Screening ❏
- Vaccination ❏

Risk management and personal safety ❏

Assessment Guide

Your learning in this unit will be assessed through a controlled assessment task. This will be set by the OCR awarding body and marked by your tutor.

The assignment will require you to produce a health improvement plan for an individual. You can develop a plan based on improving your own health and wellbeing or find a volunteer who is willing to be the focus of your project.

Your final plan will need to:

- Identify factors that have a positive impact on the individuals health and wellbeing.

- Explain how the individual's lifestyle affects their physical health.

Chapter 12 provides full coverage of a range of factors that can have a negative effect on physical health and wellbeing. Studying and referring back to chapter 12 should provide you with the background information needed to complete this part of the controlled assessment task.

Chapter 13

Risks to health and wellbeing

Key issue: What factors are risks to health and wellbeing and how do they have a damaging effect?

A range of factors can put an individual's health and wellbeing at risk. Chapter 13 explains how a person's physical and mental health as well as their social wellbeing can be harmed by different physical, lifestyle, social, economic and environmental factors. These include:

- *Physical factors* such as genetically inherited diseases and conditions and lack of sleep.
- *Lifestyle factors* such as substance misuse, poor diet, lack of regular physical exercise, unprotected sex and lack of personal hygiene.
- *Social factors* such social isolation, too much stress and poor work-life balance.
- *Economic factors* such as unemployment and poverty.
- *Environmental factors* such as inadequate housing and pollution.

Physical factors

The physical factors that affect health and wellbeing are those things that have a direct influence on a person's physical health experience. They include:

- genetically inherited diseases and conditions
- lack of sleep.

Genetically inherited diseases and conditions

Each human body cell contains two sets of 23 chromosomes – one set from each parent. The genes we inherit from our parents are the biological 'instructions' or codes that tell our body's cells how to grow. Some people inherit one or more genes that are defective or faulty. These faulty genes can, but won't always, result in a person experiencing a disease or condition that has a negative effect on their health and wellbeing.

Dominant gene defects

We inherit one set of genes from each of our biological parents. Some of these genes are identical, whilst others differ. For example, we may inherit a blue eye colour gene from one parent and a brown-eye-colour gene from the other. Where this happens, one gene will be dominant over the other. In this case, the brown eye colour gene wins! However, if the dominant gene is also a faulty or defective gene, the child will inherit the disease or condition for which it provides instruction. For example, people who inherit the defective gene leading to Huntington's disease have a fifty per cent chance of developing the disorder. Huntington's disease is a slowly progressing, fatal brain disorder which develops in middle age and results in dementia and uncontrollable movements. There is now a diagnostic test for people with a family history of Huntington's disease to assess the risk of them passing the defective gene to their offspring.

Recessive gene defects

A gene that isn't dominant is known as a recessive gene. Normally the genetic information in the recessive gene will be overruled by that in the dominant gene. This happens in the case of eye colour: the blue eye-colour gene is recessive. However, if a person inherits two faulty or defective copies of a recessive gene this will have an effect on their health and wellbeing. A person who inherits just one copy will not have the disease or condition but will be a 'carrier' and may pass it on to their children. Cystic fibrosis is a disease inherited as a result of recessive gene defects. Even though about one in every 25 people is a carrier of the faulty recessive gene, only one in every 2,000 children is born with cystic fibrosis.

Chromosomal defects

Some inherited conditions result from a person being born with the wrong number of chromosomes. These include Down's syndrome, Klinefelter's syndrome and Turner's syndrome. All these conditions affect the growth and development of the people who inherit them.

The conditions and disorders that result from dominant and recessive gene defects and chromosomal defects are relatively rare. Other more commonly experienced health problems that also have a significant genetic component to them include:

- eye disorders, such as glaucoma
- high blood pressure
- heart conditions
- high cholesterol
- haemophilia.

Investigate ...

Tuberous sclerosis, achondroplasia (dwarfism), Marfan's syndrome and neurofibromatosis are all conditions that can be inherited as a result of dominant gene defects. Use medical dictionaries, encyclopedias and the Internet to investigate one or more of these conditions. Identify the possible effects that each condition may have on a person's health and wellbeing.

Investigate ...

Cystic Fibrosis, Friedrich's ataxia and sickle cell anemia are all conditions that can be inherited as a result of recessive gene defects. Use medical dictionaries, encyclopedias and the Internet to investigate these conditions. Identify the possible effects that each can have on a person's health and wellbeing.

Case study

Ajay Khan is 20 years of age. He is an active, sporty person who tries to keep his weight within acceptable limits and who manages his diet carefully. Ajay avoids eating fatty food wherever he can, has never smoked and doesn't drink. Ajay is very health-conscious because he is aware of his family history of high blood pressure and heart disease. Ajay's father and grandfather both had high blood pressure and both died of heart conditions in their mid-fifties. Ajay's GP has told him he needs to be aware that there is a genetic component to these health problems and that he may be susceptible to them unless he manages his lifestyle carefully.

- What does Ajay's GP mean when he says that there is a 'genetic component' to high blood pressure and heart disease?

- Identify two lifestyle factors that can contribute to heart disease.

- What is Ajay doing that might help to reduce his genetic risk of heart disease and high blood pressure?

Even though a person may be genetically vulnerable to a particular disorder, lifestyle and other biological factors can limit or even prevent some genetically inherited conditions from occurring.

Lack of sleep

What happens if you don't get enough rest and sleep? People who are deprived of sleep lose energy and become irritable. After two days without sleep, concentration becomes difficult. Other negative, and potentially dangerous, effects of sleep loss include:

- mistakes in routine tasks
- slips of attention
- dozing off for periods of a few seconds or more
- falling asleep completely
- difficulty seeing and hearing clearly
- confusion.

Lack of sleep can be very dangerous. For example, many car accidents are caused by people falling asleep while driving and losing control of their vehicle.

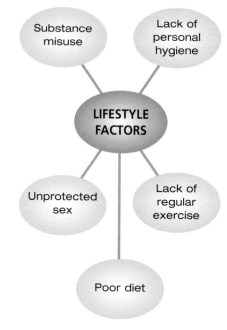

Knowledge Check

1 What are genes?

2 Explain how a person's genes can have a negative effect on their physical health and development.

3 Name one inherited disorder that results from a recessive gene defect.

4 Explain how a person inherits a disorder as a result of recessive gene defects of their parents.

5 Describe the effects that Huntington's disease can have on a person's health, wellbeing or development.

6 How might insufficient sleep lead to health and wellbeing problems?

Lifestyle factors

An individual's health, wellbeing, growth and development are partly influenced by the way in which they choose to live their life. The choices a person makes about drugs, alcohol and smoking, their diet, exercise and whether they have unprotected sex, for example, have definite consequences for their health and wellbeing.

Substance misuse

Substance misuse is widespread in many countries, including the United Kingdom. The substances that people are most likely to misuse and which have significant consequences for health and wellbeing are:

- legal and illegal drugs
- solvents
- tobacco
- alcohol.

Misuse of any of these substances can have a range of adverse effects on am individual's physical and mental health and may even prove fatal.

Misuse of drugs and solvents

Drug misuse is very high up the list of ways to harm your health. Damage to health from drug misuse can be sudden and catastrophic (people die) or it can occur over a longer period of time. Either way, drug misuse is something to avoid if you wish to live a long and healthy life.

Drugs are chemical substances that affect the body's chemistry and functioning. Drugs are widely used, and also widely misused, in the United Kingdom. They can be obtained through:

Figure 3.7 Lifestyle factors affecting health.

- a doctor's prescription if they are for medical treatment
- over the counter, by purchasing them in a chemist, supermarket or other shop (these drugs include medicines and legal substances such as alcohol and tobacco)
- buying 'street' and medicinal drugs illegally.

Over to you!

What does figure 3.8 reveal about the differences in drug-taking between males and females? Approximately, what percentage of men in England and Wales used cannabis in 2004/5?

Percentages

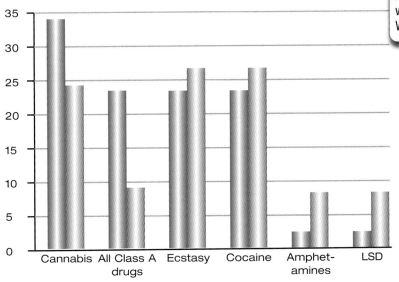

Males

Females

Figure 3.8 Prevalence of drug misuse by 16 to 24 years olds in the previous year, 2004/5, England and Wales.

For many years, newspapers and television have featured stories and programmes about drug misuse. Drug misuse is now a major cause of health problems and premature death in the United Kingdom. All sections of the population are affected by it, but young people are the most likely to risk their health through drug misuse. There are many complex reasons for this.

Any drug, whether it is legal or illegal, can cause harm if it is misused. For example, whilst medicines are used to treat disease and illness, they can also have physical and psychological side-

Over to you!

Why do you think some people take illegal drugs? Make a list of possible reasons. Why do other people avoid using them? Make another list of possible reasons.

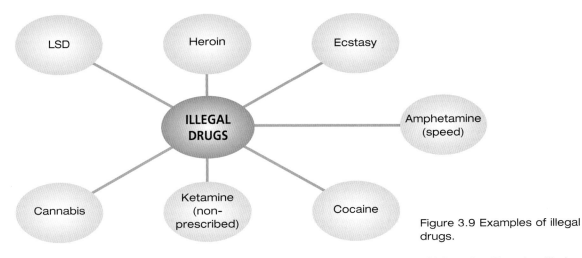

Figure 3.9 Examples of illegal drugs.

effects. The doctor who prescribes them will know about these possible effects and will take care to monitor the patient. To limit side effects, the doctor will prescribe only the dose required. People may misuse prescription drugs by taking more than their doctor prescribes, or they may take medicine not prescribed for them. They then run the risk of experiencing harmful and even fatal side-effects.

If taken over long periods, some drugs cause people to become psychologically dependent on them. This applies to medicinal drugs as well as to illegal 'street' drugs. Long-term users often suffer very unpleasant side-effects and withdrawal symptoms when they try to stop taking these drugs.

Non-prescription drugs are usually illegal. Alcohol, cigarettes and medicines bought from chemists or supermarkets are the exceptions. People who use 'street' drugs such as heroin, cocaine, marijuana and ecstasy are usually trying to get the short-term feelings of mental pleasure, stimulation and physical energy that the drugs often give. However, in the longer-term all 'street' drugs present major risks to the user's health. They usually have damaging effects on physical health, as well as on social, psychological and financial wellbeing.

Solvents are chemical substances made for industrial and scientific use. They are used in the production of cleaning fluids, ink, glue, aerosols and cigarette lighter fuel. People who misuse them are typically teenagers or young adults. After alcohol and tobacco, solvents are the main drugs that young people are most likely to experiment with. Solvent misuse has a number of bad effects on, and dangers to, health:

- cigarette lighter fuel (butane gas) that is sprayed in the mouth cools the throat tissues causing swelling, and sometimes suffocation

- some solvents contain poisonous substances such as lead

- solvent misuse causes people to feel reckless, making users less able to deal with danger

- solvents are flammable. There is an increased fire risk if the user is smoking

- solvents cause people to hallucinate

- long-term misuse may cause damage to liver, kidneys, lungs, bone marrow and the nervous system.

Tobacco smoking

Do you smoke cigarettes? If not, you probably know people who do. Smoking cigarettes is a prominent part of some people's social life. However, despite it being legal for people age 18 or over to buy and smoke tobacco, cigarettes have got a very bad reputation with health professionals.

Cigarettes, and tobacco smoking of any kind, have no health benefits at all. Instead, smoking cigarettes directly damages your physical health. This is one of the most important pieces of information that health professionals regularly give out to people. Their advice is always to stop smoking. You should be told this if you smoke cigarettes. People who fail to take note of this warning run a considerable risk of causing themselves long-

Investigate …

How much do you know about the effects and health risks of 'street' drugs? Improve your knowledge and understanding by finding out about them on these websites:

www.talktofrank.com

www.teenagehealthfreak.com

Print off, or make notes about, the possible health effects of the main 'street' drugs that you investigate.

Over to you!

You can improve your knowledge and understanding of solvent abuse by looking at the www.re-solv.org website.

term health damage and dying, as a direct result of their smoking habit. The health problems associated with smoking tobacco include:

- coronary heart disease
- stroke
- high blood pressure
- bronchitis
- lung cancer
- other cancers, such as cancer of the larynx, kidney and bladder.

Smoking cigarettes is harmful to health because the smoke inhaled and substances circulated deep into the body are harmful. These substances include nicotine, carbon monoxide and tar.

Nicotine is a powerful, fast-acting and addictive drug. Smokers absorb it into their bloodstream and feel an effect in their brains seven to eight minutes later. Some smokers say this is 'calming'. However, the physical effects of smoking also include an increase in heart rate and blood pressure and changes in appetite. Cigarette smoke contains a high concentration of carbon monoxide, a poisonous gas. Because carbon monoxide combines more easily with haemoglobin (the substance in blood that carries oxygen), the amount of oxygen carried to a smoker's lungs and tissues is reduced. This reduction in oxygen supply to the body then affects the growth and repair of tissues, and the exchange of essential nutrients.

The carbon monoxide inhaled by a smoker can also affect their heart. The changes in the blood associated with smoking can cause fat deposits to form on the walls of the arteries. This leads to hardening of the arteries and to circulatory problems, causing smokers to develop **coronary heart disease**.

Cigarette tar contains many substances known to cause cancer. It damages the cilia, small hairs lining the lungs that help to protect them from dirt and infection. Because these lung protectors get damaged, smokers are more likely than non-

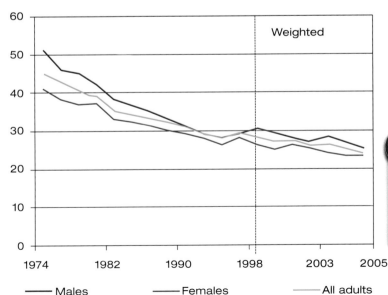

— Males   — Females   — All adults

Figure 3.10 Percentage of adults who smoke cigarettes by sex. Great Britain 1974–2005

Over to you!

What does the graph reveal about trends in cigarette smoking? Approximately, how many females smoked cigarettes in 2003?

UNIT 3

Smoking during pregnancy

When women smoke during pregnancy, the ability of the blood to carry oxygen to all parts of the body is reduced. This affects the flow of blood to the **placenta**, which feeds the foetus. Mothers who smoke during pregnancy have a greater risk of suffering a miscarriage. Women who smoke tend to give birth to premature or underweight babies who are more prone to upper respiratory tract infections and breathing problems. The risk of cot death among these babies is also increased.

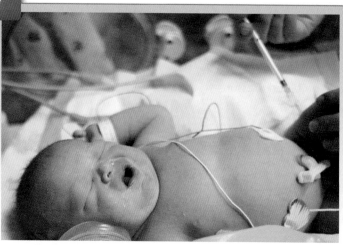

smokers to get throat and chest infections. About 70 per cent of the tar in a cigarette is deposited in the lungs when cigarette smoke is inhaled.

The use of tobacco is now less widespread and less socially acceptable than it was twenty years ago. However, in 2005, 24 per cent of adults were still smokers and there were approximately 106,000 smoking-related deaths. Teenage girls are one of the few social groups who are now more likely to smoke than in the past. Tobacco use is therefore still a major cause of preventable disease and early death in the UK.

Excessive alcohol intake

Alcohol is a very popular, widely available and accepted part of social life in the United Kingdom. Many people enjoy a drink and there is usually nothing wrong with that. In small, controlled quantities alcoholic drinks can be part of a pleasurable social occasion. In fact, some types of alcoholic drink, such as red wine, have been shown to be good for health.

When consumed, alcohol is rapidly absorbed into the bloodstream. The amount of alcohol concentrated in the body at any one time depends on how much a person drinks, whether the stomach is empty or full and the height, weight, age and sex of the drinker. Nearly all the alcohol a person drinks has to be burnt up by the liver. The rest is disposed of either in sweat or urine. The human body can get rid of one unit of alcohol in one hour. Smaller than average people, younger or older people and people who are not used to drinking are more easily affected by alcohol and take longer to get it out of their bodies.

The health risks associated with alcohol result from consuming it in large quantities, either regularly or in binges. People who frequently drink excess amounts of alcohol have an increased risk of:

- high blood pressure
- coronary heart disease
- liver damage and cirrhosis of the liver
- cancer of the mouth and throat

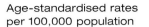

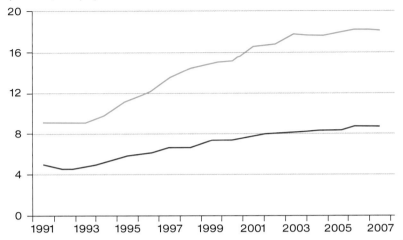

Age-standardised rates
per 100,000 population

Figure 3.11 Alcohol-related
deaths by year, 1991–2007

— Male

— Female

- psychological and emotional problems, including depression
- obesity.

Alcohol is a depressant. This means that it reduces certain brain functions and affects judgement, self-control and coordination. This is why alcohol causes fights, domestic violence and accident-related injuries. There were 8724 alcohol-related deaths in 2007. The number of alcohol-related deaths for both men and women has increased significantly since the start of the 1990s (see figure 3.11).

Health professionals recommend safe limits of alcohol consumption. The recommended limits for women are two to three units a day, or less. It is recommended that men limit their consumption to between three and four units a day or less. One unit of alcohol is the same as one small glass of wine, half a pint of ordinary strength lager, beer or cider, or a 25ml pub measure of spirits. If men and women follow this guide there should be no significant risks to their health from alcohol. However, if women regularly drink three or more units and men drink four or more units a day, the risk to health is increased.

You should be aware that these recommended limits are based on 'pub measures'. People who drink at home, or buy alcohol from an off-licence or supermarket to consume elsewhere, usually pour themselves larger measures of wines and spirits or consume stronger beer than that sold in licensed premises.

 Over to you!

In general, has the trend in alcohol related deaths gone up or down since 1991? Approximately, how many females per 100,000 population died as a result of alcohol-related causes in 2003?

 Over to you!

Using the Internet, investigate the health impact of drinking excessive amounts of alcohol. Produce a poster designed to inform 14–16 year old adolescents about the links between alcohol consumption and health problems.

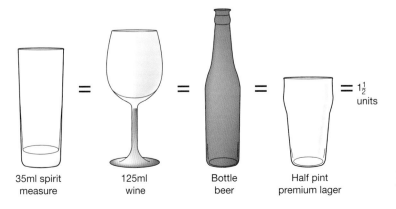

35ml spirit measure = 125ml wine = Bottle beer = Half pint premium lager = $1\frac{1}{2}$ units

Figure 3.12 Each of these contains 1.5 units of alcohol.

Case study

Jodie started drinking when she was 14 years of age. She used to drink in her local park with some older teenagers and a couple of her friends. At weekends Jodie drank a couple of bottles of cider and any vodka that was available. Jodie thought that drinking was fun and that it made her happy. She realised when she was 19 years of age that the opposite was true. Jodie found herself thinking about alcohol during work and would go to the pub for a few drinks at lunchtime. Jodie was eventually sacked from her job as a trainee hairdresser for coming to work smelling of alcohol. After making a promise to her mum and dad Jodie hasn't drunk any alcohol for three months. They told her about the physical effects that binge drinking and long-term alcohol abuse could have on her health.

- Suggest some reasons why young teenagers like Jodie start drinking alcohol.
- Identify four effects of binge drinking or long-term alcohol abuse on physical health.
- What are the recommended limits (in units) for alcohol consumption that Jodie should stick to if she does start drinking alcohol again?

Unbalanced, poor quality or inadequate diet

A number of key points have been made about the positive impact of a balanced diet on health and development. An unbalanced diet, however, can have negative effects on an individual's physical health and development and on social and emotional wellbeing:

- Over-eating can lead to weight gain and **obesity**. This occurs where a person eats a diet containing more energy than they are able to use up in their daily activity. Obesity is linked with a range of health problems, including coronary heart disease and type II diabetes.

- An inadequate diet is one that is insufficient to meet an individual's energy needs (too little food) or one that is lacking in nutrients (lack of nutritious food). Nutritional deficiencies such as **kwashiorkor** and **marasmus** are rare in the UK but can occur where children do not receive a sufficient, balanced diet.

- Diets that are high in sugar or fat or which lack certain food groups, such as vitamins and minerals from vegetables, are not nutritious and can be harmful to a person's physical health, growth and development. Anaemia (iron deficiency), rickets (calcium and vitamin D deficiency) and scurvy (vitamin C deficiency) can result from poor diets.

- Being significantly over- or under-weight can lead to physical and mental health problems and problems with emotional wellbeing as both adults and children get teased and feel devalued in comparison to people of normal weight.

Lack of regular physical exercise

Lack of regular physical exercise can lead to ill-health and disease. For example, lack of exercise is linked to an increased risk of diseases such as coronary heart disease, stroke, obesity (being excessively overweight or very fat) and osteoporosis (brittle bones). Obesity is now a major health problem in the UK and is closely linked to people over-eating and not exercising. There are many reasons why people don't take more exercise. These include not having enough time, not liking sport and being frightened of injuries.

Case study

Jack is 14 years old. He lives on a small estate on the edge of town with his parents. Jack plays a lot of computer games on his console. He's also a keen keyboard player, practising for a couple of hours each day. Jack is popular at school, partly because he is very funny. He uses his humour to defend himself when people laugh at his size. Jack is about 3 stone overweight. His parents are concerned about this although his mum insists he does not overeat. She believes that lack of exercise has led to his weight problem.

- What factors might be contributing to Jack being overweight?
- Why is Jack's weight likely to lead to health problems if he doesn't do something about it?
- Suggest three ways Jack could increase the amount of exercise he takes each day.

Unprotected sex

The main health risk of unprotected sexual activity is from **sexually transmitted diseases**. There are at least thirty different types of sexually transmitted disease. Each year they affect about one million men and women in the United Kingdom. Sexually transmitted diseases are caught by having unprotected sex with an infected person. A person can become infected with a sexually transmitted disease after a single act of unprotected sex with another infected person. Young sexually active people are most at risk of catching a sexually transmitted disease. The most common sexually transmitted disease is **chlamydia**. It can cause serious problems such as pelvic inflammatory disease (PID) and inflammation of the fallopian tubes (oviducts) if it is not treated. However, it isn't fatal. People recover after treatment.

Over to you!

Use medical reference books or a website such as www.teenagehealthfreak.com or www.avert.org to find out more about the causes, symptoms and consequences of the sexually transmitted diseases referred to above.

Figure 3.13 – Examples of sexually transmitted diseases

Girls	Boys
• A vaginal discharge that is thick or smelly, has a different colour, is more copious than usual or causes itching may indicate you have thrush or trichomoniasis. • If it hurts when you pass urine (water), you may have cystitis (inflammation of the bladder) or thrush. • If your vagina itches or gets sore, you may have thrush. • If you develop warty lumps around your vagina or anus (back passage), you may have genital warts.	• If blood or a discharge comes out of your penis, or passing urine (water) is painful, it may mean you have gonorrhoea, non-specific urethritis or chlamydia. • If you get warty lumps on or near your penis or anus (back passage), you may have genital warts. • If you get painful sores or blisters on or near your penis or anus (back passage), you may have herpes. • If the tip of your penis or area around your anus (back passage) is red and itchy, you may have thrush. • If you have an itchy scrotum and pubic hair, you may have crabs (pubic lice – small wingless insects that live in pubic hair and feed on blood).

UNIT 3

HIV and AIDS

The human immunodeficiency virus (HIV) that causes acquired immune deficiency syndrome (AIDS) is a sexually transmitted disease which attacks and destroys the body's natural defence mechanisms. HIV can be transmitted through three different routes:

- sexual intercourse (anal or vaginal)
- contaminated blood transfusion
- drug abusers sharing non-sterile needles.

People who do not use condoms and spermicides during sex run a higher risk of catching sexually transmitted diseases and of suffering the various health consequences. Unprotected sex, involving anal or vaginal penetration, allows the release of infected semen or the transfer of vaginal secretions into the body.

By the end of 2007, there had been 18,324 AIDS-related deaths in the United Kingdom and, in total, nearly 577,400 people were reported to have been infected by the HIV virus (www.avert.org/uksummary.htm).

Lack of personal hygiene

Personal hygiene and body odour (smell) are very sensitive topics for most people. It is not good to have a reputation for body odour (BO) and bad breath! On the other hand, being clean and smelling pleasant are good for your reputation, social life and self-esteem. In fact, good personal hygiene is an important way of maintaining good health.

A person who fails to maintain good personal hygiene can experience a range of health and social problems. Health problems, such as skin conditions (sores, rashes), result from poor personal hygiene when the bacteria and fungi which naturally grow on, and in, the body are not removed. The body conditions that help bacteria and fungi to grow are:

- moisture from sweat
- warmth from body heat
- food from the dead cells and waste products in sweat.

The areas of the body that need most cleaning are those where sweat is excreted – for example, under the arms, the groin area, the feet, the scalp and hair. Failing to take a daily bath or shower or to wash the skin and clean your teeth, result in a build up of bacteria, dirt and odour. You should note that acne (spots, zits, pimples) is something that happens to most teenagers and some adults and is not caused by poor personal hygiene. Cleaning the skin thoroughly and keeping skin pores clear helps to reduce, but cannot prevent, acne. It is caused by hormone imbalances.

Health problems can also result from poor dental hygiene. Brushing the teeth properly and using dental floss keeps the teeth clean and helps to prevent decay, gum disease and bad breath. Factors contributing to bad breath include:

- gum infections
- eating strongly flavoured food like garlic
- rotting teeth

Over to you!

Why do you think that younger people, especially teenagers, take risks with sex? Discuss this in a small group and then compare your ideas with those of other groups in the class. Make a list of the most common reasons discussed in the various groups.

Good oral hygiene is important for health.

Case study

Sandra Davis is a single mother of three children. She has just got a job and needs to arrange childcare to cover the time that she'll be at work. You're one of three people who have answered her advert for a childminder for Dion, aged three, Sonia, aged six, and Jay, aged nine. In the interview, Sandra explains the arrangements. The children will arrive at your house at about 8.30 a.m. Sandra will pick them up again after work at 4 p.m. Sandra's next questions is: 'What will you do to ensure that each of my children maintains good personal hygiene throughout the day?'

- Write an answer explaining what you think the priorities are and indicate what you would do to set and maintain standards of good hygiene practice for each child.

- decaying food stuck between the teeth
- throat infections
- smoking
- not drinking enough water.

Not looking after your personal hygiene can lead to health problems, such as skin infections. However, the social problems that result from being smelly and unclean are just as great. Personal hygiene problems will have a negative effect on a person's relationships and social life. This is likely to lead to the person feeling rejected, isolated and having low self-esteem.

Knowledge Check

1 Identify three different forms of substance misuse that are a risk to health.

2 Explain why solvent misuse is a risk to health and wellbeing.

3 Name three diseases associated with cigarette smoking.

4 Describe the physical effects on the body of inhaling cigarette smoke.

5 Explain what statistics on smoking reveal about the trends of cigarette smoking in the UK.

6 Name three long-term effects that drinking too much alcohol can have on a person's health and wellbeing

7 What factors should a person take into account when assessing how much it is safe for them to drink?

8 Describe how diet is linked to ill-health.

9 Identify two health problems that can result from not taking enough regular exercise.

10 Explain why unprotected sex is a high risk activity that can lead to health problems.

11 Name three sexually transmitted diseases that can be transmitted through unprotected sex.

12 Describe two ways in which a person can minimise the risk of catching a sexually transmitted disease.

13 How can a lack of personal hygiene have a negative effect on an individual's health and wellbeing?

14 Describe how a lack of personal hygiene can lead to health and wellbeing problems.

UNIT 3

Social factors

Social factors are those things that influence our relationships with, attachments to and feelings about ourselves and other people in our life.

Social isolation

Human beings need each other – we are social animals. Spending time and mixing with others has a positive effect on an individual's social and emotional wellbeing. Social relationships with friends and family provide:

- opportunities to develop close relationships and express a range of positive and negative feelings in a safe, supported way
- opportunities to give and receive emotional support and feel valued by others
- an important boost to self-esteem and contribute to our sense of personal identity
- protection against feeling isolated, lonely and depressed.

People who become socially isolated lack the support and companionship that friends, family members and work colleagues offer. As a result their emotional wellbeing and mental health will tend to suffer. People who experience social isolation tend to have higher rates of depression and anxiety and may use alcohol, drugs or self-harm as a way of coping with or drawing attention to their situation.

Stress

People often talk about 'feeling stressed' and stress has a bad reputation with health professionals. So, what is it? Stress is a response to the demands made on a person. Where the demands outweigh a person's ability to cope or adapt, they feel under pressure, threatened, tense or strained. This is 'stress'. It has both psychological and physical symptoms.

Extreme stress, either sudden or more long-term, produces uncomfortable symptoms and can lead to health problems. Stress becomes harmful when it is continuous, disrupts everyday life and relationships and becomes too difficult to cope with. Some people experience temporary health problems from which they recover when they manage to reduce their stress levels. For other people, stress has long-term health effects on both their physical and mental health. Stress can trigger mental health problems such as depression and anxiety-based illnesses.

Over to you!

What impact might not having friends or being excluded from a friendship group have on an adolescent's personal development?

Short term symptoms of stress

- muscle pain
- headaches
- feeling sick
- trembling
- sweating
- dry throat
- disturbed sleep
- changes in appetite
- stomach upset
- fast pulse rate
- feeling faint or dizzy
- irritability
- poor concentration
- feeling panicky.

Health problems associated with stress

- anxiety and depression
- eczema
- asthma
- migraine
- angina (pain around the heart muscle)
- high blood pressure
- heart attack
- stomach ulcers
- accidents.

Case study

Neville is a 37-year-old plumber. He wants to retire as a rich, happy man when he is 50. Neville runs his own plumbing company, working between 60 and 80 hours every week. He is feeling under a lot of pressure at the moment. Neville has complained to his wife that he has had a headache for a week, feels faint at times and is having trouble sleeping. Neville will not go and see his GP as he says he is too busy. His wife is trying to persuade him to take a holiday but he is reluctant to do so because of the amount of work he has to do.

- What symptoms of stress does Neville have?
- What might be causing Neville's current stress problems?
- Explain what might happen to Neville's health and wellbeing if he continues to experience high stress levels.
- Suggest some changes that Neville could make to his lifestyle to reduce his high stress levels.

Many different factors can cause 'stress'. Exams, assignments or being asked questions in class might do it for you. Other common causes of stress in people's lives include relationship problems, money worries, poor living or work conditions, having too much work to do and general lack of satisfaction in life.

What can people do to reduce or minimize stress? Exercise, recreation and leisure activity are particularly important for reducing stress levels. Having supportive relationships and satisfying work also helps. Increasingly, people use sports activities to help them to relax and de-stress. Massage, talking to others about problems and feelings, thinking positively and being assertive (saying 'no' to extra work!) are all good ways of reducing stress levels.

Poor work-life balance

People who work excessively long hours, perhaps combining employment and studying, doing more than one job or by pouring all their time into their work, tend to have a poor work-life balance. This means that work dominates their life to the extent that they have little time or energy for personal and family relationships, leisure activities and other non-work interests. People who have a poor work-life balance have an increased risk of experiencing high stress levels, physical and mental fatigue, low emotional wellbeing and relationship breakdown. The high stress levels that result from a poor work-life balance can lead to a range of physical health problems from cardiovascular disease to alcohol misuse.

Over to you!

Identify three occasions when you've felt very stressed. What were your symptoms? What caused your stress? Make a note of these points or discuss them with a colleague in your class.

Knowledge Check

1 Describe how an individual's health and wellbeing may suffer if they become socially isolated.

2 Briefly, explain what 'stress' is.

3 Identify five physical symptoms of stress

4 Describe how stress can have a negative effect on an individual's physical health.

5 Using examples, describe the reasons why teenagers sometimes experience levels of stress that can harm their health or wellbeing.

6 Explain why having a poor work-life balance is a risk to an individual's health and wellbeing.

Economic factors

An individual's health and wellbeing can be affected by a number of money-related or economic factors. Economic factors have a strong influence on the kinds of opportunities that a person is able to enjoy in each life stage. A lack of work and poverty are associated with a range of health and social problems.

Unemployment

A person is unemployed when they don't have work. Unemployment is something that people of working age worry about and hope they can avoid. Losing a job or not being able to obtain work has a variety of effects on people:

- being unemployed can reduce self-esteem if an individual feels rejection or devalued by the loss of their job
- unemployed people complain that they feel they don't 'fit in', and can become socially isolated if they are unable to participate in the normal activities and lifestyle of others in their community
- financial problems occur very quickly when people have no income. For some people this leads to poor diet, lack of heating and loss of good housing
- people who experience long-term unemployment can feel hopeless, lose motivation and self-confidence and turn to harmful substances such as tobacco or alcohol to cope with the negative feelings they experience
- unemployment can lead to emotional strain, anxiety and depression that damages an individual's relationships and their long-term mental health
- long-term unemployed people are more likely to suffer from respiratory problems, alcohol related disease, arthritis and mental illness.

Poverty

People who live in absolute poverty have insufficient income to meet their basic needs. People who live in relative poverty have

Over to you!

Unemployment usually means a person has a lower income than if they were in work. Explain how this direct effect of unemployment might have an indirect or knock-on effect on an individual's health and wellbeing. Think about the things that people need money for and what might have to be sacrificed if income is reduced.

Case study

Desmond is 35 and has been unemployed for the last six months. He currently lives on his own in a council-owned maisonette. He finds the days very long, boring and stressful. When he does get an interview for a job, he says that he finds the situation very difficult. In particular, he has a lack of self-confidence when talking about his skills and personal qualities. Desmond has had a variety of different jobs in both the building and catering industries in recent years. Currently all the jobs that he sees seem to require computer skills and experience. Desmond doesn't have access to the Internet at home and is cautious about using computers. He says that he feels that he's been 'left behind' and thinks he might be unemployable now. Desmond has no real plans for the future at the moment. He says that he's getting depressed and becoming demotivated in his search for work.

- How is unemployment affecting Desmond's emotional health and wellbeing?
- How might long-term unemployment affect Desmond's physical health?
- What advice or information would you give to Desmond to help him to improve his health and wellbeing?

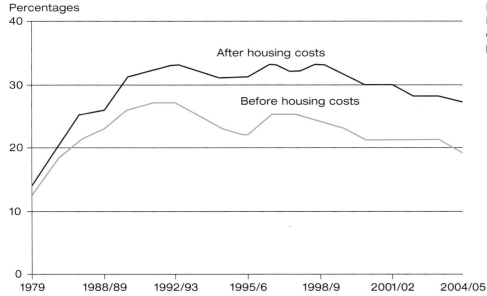

Figure 3.14
Proportion of
children living in
poverty

enough money for their basic needs but relatively little money compared to other people. People living in relative poverty can afford the essentials but are unable to enjoy other activities and material possessions that others in their community take for granted. A person is defined as living in poverty in the UK if their income is less than 60% of the average household income.

There are very strong connections between poverty and ill-health. The reasons for this are not completely clear-cut. It is possible that people who experience ill-health are unable to work as effectively or as frequently as people who are in good health and so earn less money. However, poverty and low income can also be a cause of ill-health. Poverty affects an individual's ability to afford a good diet, comfortable housing conditions, stress-relieving holidays and leisure activities, for example. Statistics show that people living in poverty are more likely to experience:

- high infant mortality rates
- greater risk of low birth weight
- higher rates of mental health problems
- higher rates of long-term illnesses.

A person facing financial difficulties may not be able to afford the basic necessities of life (food, shelter, clothing) and may have to make difficult decisions about how to spend the little money they do have. This might lead to them eating a poor diet, living in poor housing conditions and experiencing high stress levels. As a result a person facing financial difficulties is likely to experience a decline in their physical health, emotional and psychological problems, or low self-esteem. A person's financial difficulties may be short-term and might be resolved when they do find work or are able to change their living circumstances. In these situations, people often learn things about themselves and how they should live their life that are helpful to them. However, where a person is unable to change their circumstances, the financial difficulties that they face may result in them making fundamental decisions – about moving house, relocating to another area or changing career – that have a lasting impact on their personal development.

Over to you!

What proportion of children were living in poverty (before and after housing costs) in 2001/02?

Promoting Health and Wellbeing

Over to you!

When we say that people need 'enough money', what do we mean? 'Enough' for what? For the basic necessities of life usually.

- Identify what you think are the basic necessities of life by completing this checklist.
- How much money would a person need (each week, month or year) to afford your list of basic necessities?

heating ❏	toys for children ❏
an indoor toilet ❏	a warm waterproof coat ❏
satellite TV ❏	a refrigerator ❏
a damp-free home ❏	access to a personal computer ❏
a washing machine ❏	carpets ❏
a bath or shower ❏	three meals a day ❏
a foreign holiday ❏	a bedroom for each child ❏
beds for everyone ❏	two pairs of all-weather shoes ❏
a mobile 'phone ❏	party celebrations ❏
money for public transport ❏	a roast dinner once a week ❏

Knowledge Check

1 Identify two economic factors that have an impact on health and wellbeing

2 Describe the ways unemployment can have an impact on a person's health and wellbeing.

3 When is a person living in 'poverty'?

4 According to government statistics, what proportion of children were living in poverty in 2004/05?

5 Describe ways in which poverty can have an impact on an individual's physical health and wellbeing.

Environmental factors

The physical environment in which a person lives can have a direct effect on their health and wellbeing. If the quality of the physical environment is poor because of air and noise pollution or poor housing or the type of area in which the person lives limits their opportunities or causes them to feel stressed, their health and wellbeing may suffer.

Inadequate housing

A person's housing provides them with physical shelter and protection. This is important for physical health. However, the place where you live and spend most of your time is more than just somewhere to stay and keep warm and dry. 'Home' also provides people with a sense of emotional wellbeing and psychological security.

Poor housing can have a direct effect on a person's physical health. For example, lack of adequate heating, dampness and overcrowding can lead to respiratory disorders, stress and mental health problems. Lack of basic amenities (a shower or bath, for example), sharing facilities between too many people (kitchen or bathroom, for example) and cold, damp or unsafe buildings make some homes unfit to live in. Poor conditions like these can

lead to health problems. Lack of security, too much noise and lack of privacy can also lead to high stress levels and loss of wellbeing.

Cold and damp housing aggravates many medical conditions, including asthma, bronchitis and other respiratory diseases, and rheumatism and arthritis. These conditions affect people of all ages, but are particularly serious for babies, infants and older people. Older people with low incomes sometimes have to choose between buying food and heating their homes. The consequence of not having enough heating can be hypothermia – a fall in body temperature to below 35°C (normal body temperature is 37°C).

Overcrowding encourages the spread of infection and infectious diseases such as tuberculosis and dysentery. Children who live in overcrowded homes are more likely to be victims of accidents. Sleeplessness and stress are also associated with overcrowding.

People living in high-rise tower blocks or bedsits may suffer from poor emotional wellbeing because of social isolation. This in turn can lead to depression and low self-esteem. Many high-rise blocks of flats were built in the UK during the 1950s and 60s (in the post-war years) when there was an acute housing need. The government's long-term plan is now to phase these buildings out and gradually replace them with more appealing housing that is suitable for the wider community. Most housing blocks built in the last few years do not extend beyond four floors.

Over to you!

What is healthy housing? Identify the features you feel are important in making a person's housing 'healthy'. Alternatively, identify the negative features that you would look out for if you were house or flat-hunting. Explain, in terms of their effect on health and wellbeing, why you would try to avoid housing that had these negative features.

Case study

Courtney is three years old. She lives with her mum in a bedsit flat on the edge of a large city. Courtney's mum is very caring and spends all of her time looking after her daughter. The flat where they live is cold and damp. A lot of traffic passes directly in front of the flat and there are few places where Courtney can play outside in the local area. As a result, Courtney doesn't go out very often. She also gets colds and chest infections quite often and is underweight for her age. Courtney's mum has very little money to spend on food, heating or clothes as she is unemployed and claiming benefits. She has recently applied to the council for a change of flat as she believes that her current housing conditions are harming Courtney's health and development.

- Identify two features of the bedsit flat in the case study that may have a negative effect on health

- Describe two modifications to the bedsit flat that would be beneficial for Courtney's health.

Environmental pollution

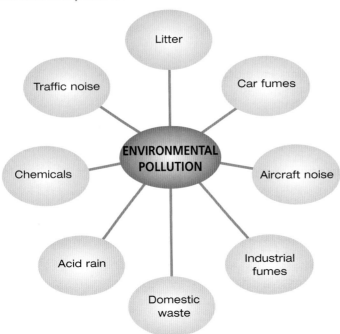

Figure 3.15 Forms of environmental pollution.

Pollution happens when our natural surroundings (including the air, water and landscape) are contaminated with poisonous or harmful substances. Usually, though not always, this involves the release of high concentrations of a substance, such as human sewage or chemicals. Environmental pollution can remain in the environment for a long time, causing health problems for whole populations for many years.

Pollutants can affect the air, sea, waterways and land. Factories and cars that produce carbon-based fumes are common sources of air pollution. Often we only think about the smoke and fumes that we can see in the environment. However, other air pollutants are less visible. For example, 'acid rain' is ordinary rainwater that has become acidic because it picks up residues of sulphur and nitrogen oxides that are produced by cars, power stations and other factories, often long distances away from where the rain falls. Acid rain is thought to make respiratory problems, such as asthma, worse because it irritates surface membranes in the lungs.

You may also have heard about 'greenhouse gases' and the 'ozone layer'. Greenhouse gases are chemicals which, when released into the atmosphere, reduce the ozone layer high above the Earth. The ozone is a layer of oxygen high in the atmosphere that acts as a sunscreen. Holes in the ozone layer, caused by the emission of greenhouse gases, result in harmful ultraviolet light beaming down from the sun. This type of pollution increases the risk of skin cancers.

Noise pollution

Noise pollution occurs when human or machine-made sound disrupts the activity or balance of a person's everyday life. Transport systems, particularly cars, airplanes and trains, are the main source of noise pollution. People who live in densely populated residential areas may also experience noise pollution, especially if they live near to industrial buildings.

 Over to you!

Can you think of sources of environmental pollution that effect your everyday surroundings? Identify as many as possible. Think about pollution of the air, water and general environment.

 Over to you!

Sources of noise pollution
- Car engines and alarms
- Airplanes
- Trains
- Audio entertainment systems
- Power tools and construction work
- Office machinery
- Factory machinery
- Domestic appliances
- Lighting hum
- Barking dogs
- Noisy people.

Noise pollution can lower the quality of life of those people who are exposed to it. Chronic exposure to excessive noise is linked to tinnitus, increased stress levels, disturbed sleep patterns and hearing loss. The World Health Organisation (WHO, 2008) has also produced research linking noise pollution to premature death from heart disease that is triggered by exposure to excessive levels of noise. It estimated that 3,030 of the 101,000 deaths from coronary heart disease in the UK in 2006 were caused by chronic noise exposure. The WHO guidelines on noise pollution say that chronic exposure to noise of 50 decibels or more – light traffic noise – may lead to cardiovascular problems. People who are exposed to 42 decibels or more are likely to experience sleep disturbance.

Chapter checklist

The box below provides a summary of the areas covered in chapter 13. Tick the areas that you feel you understand and would be confident about when writing your assignment. If there are any areas that you don't understand or are not confident about, you will need to return to them before you begin planning or writing your assignment.

Physical factors
- Genetically inherited diseases ☐
- Lack of sleep ☐

Lifestyle factors
- Substance misuse ☐
- Poor diet ☐
- Lack of regular exercise ☐
- Unprotected sex ☐
- Lack of personal hygiene ☐ ☐

Social factors
- Social isolation ☐
- Too much stress ☐
- Poor work-life balance ☐

Economic factors
- Unemployment ☐
- Poverty ☐

Environmental factors
- Inadequate housing ☐
- Pollution ☐

Knowledge Check

1 Describe how inadequate housing can lead to ill-health.
2 Identify three physical health problems associated with inadequate housing.
3 Explain how a person's housing conditions can affect their emotional wellbeing.
4 Identify five different sources of pollution that can be harmful to health.
5 Using examples, explain what air pollution is and describe how it can affect health and wellbeing.
6 Identify five examples of noise pollution.
7 Describe the links between noise pollution and health problems.

Assessment Guide

Your learning in this unit will be assessed through a controlled assessment task. This will be set by the OCR awarding body and marked by your tutor.

The assignment will require you to produce a health improvement plan for an individual. You can develop a plan based on improving your own health and wellbeing or find a volunteer who is willing to be the focus of your project.

Your final plan will need to:

● Identify features of the individual's lifestyle that have affected their physical health.

Chapter 13 provides full coverage of a range of factors that can have a negative effect on physical health and wellbeing. Studying and referring back to chapter 13 should provide you with the background information needed to complete this part of the controlled assessment task.

Promoting Health and Wellbeing

Chapter 14

Health promotion and improvement methods

Key issue: How can individuals be motivated and supported to improve their health?

Have you ever set yourself a goal of 'being healthier' or 'getting fit'? A common time to do this is just after Christmas, when people often feel they've had too much to eat or drink, or a few months before going on holiday. We've probably all wanted to improve our health and wellbeing at one time or another. However, health improvement needs to be based on more than good intentions. Chapter 14 will help you to apply the knowledge and understanding you have about factors that affect health and wellbeing and about measures of health to health improvement situations. It will show you how to design a health and wellbeing improvement plan for an individual or group of individuals. Your plan will need to include:

- An assessment of the present health status of the individual or group.

- Appropriate health promotion materials to motivate and support the person or people involved.

- A clear health and wellbeing improvement plan that includes both short- and long-term targets.

- An assessment of the difficulties the person may experience in implementing the health and wellbeing improvement plan.

- An outline of support needed to implement the plan.

Designing a health improvement plan

You may have been on a diet in order to lose weight, tried to give up smoking, joined a gym or taken up a sport to 'get fit'. All these things are examples of health improvement activities. Some people feel very guilty about being 'unhealthy' and despite trying various ways of improving their health, feel as though they never quite succeed. This is particularly the case with regular dieters. Despite this, the good news is that it is possible to improve your health and wellbeing. The solution is to choose an effective way of doing so rather than to follow the latest diet or fitness fads.

Figure 3.16 A HIP process.

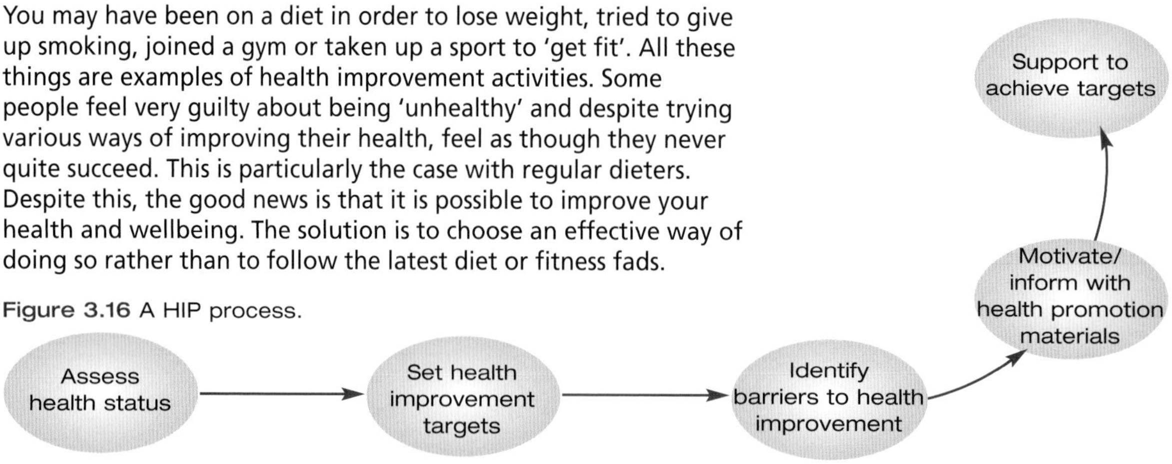

Assess health status → Set health improvement targets → Identify barriers to health improvement → Motivate/ inform with health promotion materials → Support to achieve targets

Assessing health status

Health improvement planning should begin with thorough and honest health assessment. This involves collecting basic health-related information and also measuring physical health indicators. Figure 3.17 identifies the lifestyle issues that a health care professional might ask about and the range of physical measures they may take as part of an individual's health assessment.

Figure 3.17 Health assessment information.

Lifestyle information	Physical measures
Dietary intake Amount of sleep Units of alcohol consumed Exercise pattern Use of cigarettes or drugs	Height Weight Pulse (before and after exercise) Blood pressure Cholesterol levels Blood glucose levels Body Mass Index (BMI) Hip/waist ratio

The information that the health practitioner collects is used to provide a baseline, or starting point, from which to work. The service user who is motivated to improve their health may be asked to complete a questionnaire or might be interviewed about their health and wellbeing by the health care practitioner to obtain this information. In some cases service users are asked to keep a health and lifestyle diary for a couple of weeks. The aim is to record what they eat and drink, their sleep and exercise pattern, and their cigarette and alcohol consumption, for example. The health diary, combined with physical measures, enables the practitioner to identify some of the factors (such as lack of exercise, poor diet) that may be contributing to a health problem (such as obesity). It also provides a basis on which to set realistic improvement targets.

Before any health improvement targets are identified, it is important to compare the service user's physical health measures to those recommended or expected for someone of their age and physical characteristics. This allows the care practitioner to identify whether, and if so how far, any of the person's physical health indicators (blood pressure, for example) are outside the expected range and a cause for concern. The health care practitioner will then know which areas they need to concentrate on to improve the service user's physical health and wellbeing.

 Investigate ...

Talk to somebody who helps others to 'get fit' – such as a PE teacher, a personal fitness trainer or an aerobics instructor. Find out how they assess fitness, how they set targets and what methods they use to motivate people to improve their fitness.

Case study

Philip (17), Lara (19), Erica (44) and Pauline (62) all work in a nursing home for older people. They have recently volunteered to take part in a health improvement programme being run by the local primary care trust. Each member of the group has agreed to have their physical health measured and to provide some basic lifestyle information. This will help the primary care staff to assess their current state of health and develop a health improvement plan for each individual. The health measurements that have been recorded are provided below.

Measure	Philip	Lara	Erica	Pauline
Height	6′1″	5′8″	5′4″	5′2″
Weight	13.5 stone	7 stone	14 stone	8.5 stone
Resting pulse	80 per minute	65 per minute	125 per minute	87 per minute
Blood pressure	120/80	90/65	200/135	135/85
Cigarettes per week	None	Smokes 10 cigarettes a day	Smokes 10 cigarettes a day	None
Units of alcohol per week	Drinks beer. 6 units per week	Drinks vodka. 30 units per week	Drinks lager. 40 units per week	Drinks wine. 10 units per week
Hours of exercise	Football 3 hours. Gym 3 hours	Gym 7 hours	None	Yoga. 2 hours. Walking 2 hours
Diet	Eats a regular balanced diet	Eats snacks and salads. Avoids fatty food	Eats a lot of burgers, chips and kebabs	Eats a regular balanced diet

- Who do you think is the most healthy and least healthy person out of the four people in this group? Give clear reasons for your choices.

- Describe the ways in which the remaining two members of the group appear to be healthy or unhealthy.

- Identify three lifestyle factors that should be taken into account when interpreting the various health measurements.

Setting health improvement targets

The next stage is to set targets for improvement. Health care practitioners must ensure that the health improvement targets they set for service users are safe, realistic and achievable. For example, it is important not to plan for unrealistically rapid weight loss that can only be achieved through 'crash dieting' or exercise binges. People regain weight lost in this way very quickly and can damage their physical health in the process. Instead, there should be a clear, logical plan for setting particular health improvement targets that can be achieved in a reasonable timescale. Many health care practitioners set short, medium and long-term targets, and build in regular reviews, so that service users can see their progress and address any difficulties they are having in reaching the targets.

The methods that are used to work towards, and achieve, health improvement targets should be safe and, ideally, should fit in with the service user's current lifestyle. For example, improving

Case study

Chris Henry was very fit during his early twenties. He remembers going to the gym a couple of times a week, playing football at weekends and even ran thirteen miles in a half-marathon when he was 30 years old. Chris is now 45 years of age. He's become overweight and unfit during the last ten years. He says this has happened because he stopped taking part in sport and increased his drinking and smoking. Chris is now very keen to improve his health generally and his physical fitness in particular. He realises that he'll never be as fit as he was in his twenties but thinks that losing two stone in weight and improving his stamina will benefit his health.

- Identify the baseline measures that should be taken before Chris begins his health improvement plan.

- Suggest three health targets that could be a part of Chris's health improvement plan.

- What types of exercise would you recommend for Chris as a way of reducing his weight and improving his stamina?

- Apart from increasing the amount of exercise he does, how else could Chris change his lifestyle to reach his health improvement goals?

physical fitness can be achieved in many different ways. Walking more, cycling to school or work or going to an exercise class once a week are all relatively straightforward and won't disrupt a person's lifestyle too much. Running a marathon or swimming the English Channel may enable the person to achieve the same weight loss or fitness targets but probably aren't realistic or safe methods of doing so! An individual is not likely to achieve or benefit from such ambitious targets.

It is important to view health improvement as a gradual process that needs to be worked at. Sudden changes in weight, fitness or behaviour are unlikely to be maintained. If you need to develop a health improvement plan for another person, remember to take their age and physical characteristics into account when conducting the health assessment. You will also need to ensure that the person agrees with the health improvement targets and is personally motivated to achieve them. If not, they'll never reach them.

Using health promotion materials

There are a range of different types of health promotion material available on a wide variety of health-related subjects. Health care practitioners use health promotion materials to raise awareness of health issues, to motivate people to change their health behaviours and to support people who set themselves health improvement targets. The particular type of health promotion material that a health care practitioner chooses will generally be selected because of its particular advantages and because it is appropriate in the circumstances. Figure 3.18 identifies a number of different types of health promotion material and outlines some of their strengths and limitations.

Over to you!

Develop a simple but realistic plan for improving your personal health and wellbeing.

- Collect information about the health-related aspects of your lifestyle and record as many of your basic physical indicators of health as you can. You may want to produce a diary for the first part of this task and get some help in doing the second part.

- Compare your personal results to those recommended for someone of your age and physical characteristics.

- Identify those aspects of your health you need to improve and set yourself a couple of short, medium and long-term targets.

- Identify ways of working towards and reaching your targets.

Investigate ...

Visit places in your local area where you would expect to find health promotion information. These might include your GP surgery, local library, a sports centre or a youth club. Identify examples of health promotion material on display. Write a brief report describing the information that was available, explaining who it was aimed at and what the health messages were. You could also say whether you think the material and the way it was presented was effective and what other information could be displayed or provided to promote health improvement.

Figure 3.18 Strengths and limitations of health promotion materials

Health promotion material	Strengths	Limitations
Leaflets	<ul><li>Can be read in own time</li><li>Easy and cheap to make</li><li>Can summarise a lot of information</li></ul>	<ul><li>Information can be too general</li><li>Requires good reading skills</li><li>Easy to ignore or lose</li></ul>
Videos	<ul><li>Can show real-life situations</li><li>Easy to use and engage with</li><li>Can be seen by a lot of people</li></ul>	<ul><li>Requires specialist equipment</li><li>Can become outdated quickly</li><li>Viewers may not think about what they watch</li></ul>
Posters	<ul><li>Easy way to raise awareness of a topic or issue</li><li>Can give basic information to a lot of people</li><li>Easy and cheap to produce</li></ul>	<ul><li>Can deteriorate quickly</li><li>People learn to ignore them/don't read</li></ul>
Websites	<ul><li>Can provide a lot of information to a lot of people</li><li>Can be easily updated</li><li>Can be viewed/used in own time</li><li>Can be eye-catching and interactive</li></ul>	<ul><li>Requires computer and internet access</li><li>Not suitable for all age groups</li><li>Need to know website exists and be able to find it on Internet</li></ul>

Identifying barriers to health improvement

A number of factors are likely to influence the effectiveness and ultimately the success of a health improvement plan. These are summarised in the table below:

Figure 3.19 Factors affecting health improvement plans

Factor	Positive effect	Negative effect
Motivation	The person has enough willpower and the desire to succeed	The person lacks commitment and loses heart easily
Involvement	The person identifies their own targets	The person doesn't understand or agree with the targets
Values	The person sees health and fitness as important	The person doesn't see the need to change their health behaviour
Stress levels	The person is not too stressed by work and personal life	The person is already very stressed and can't cope with more changes
Peer and social pressure	The person responds positively to encouragement of others to change health behaviour	The person feels embarrassed by or rejects encouragement of others to change health behaviour
Self-concept	The person is able to adjust their self-concept to see themselves as fit and 'healthy'	The person is reluctant to change self-concept or doesn't accept they can be fit and 'healthy'.

Case study

Men don't often talk to each other about their personal health and wellbeing. They are also less likely than women to visit their GP if they do have health concerns. This means that some men don't get the appropriate treatment for health problems that could be prevented or cured. Avoiding contact with health care services and being unaware of disease symptoms may result in some men developing serious health conditions, such as testicular or prostate cancers, that become untreatable.

● Suggest some aims for a health promotion campaign targeted at men.

● What methods could be used to promote both health awareness and a preventive approach to health with men as the target group? Explain why you would use these methods.

● What barriers would your health promotion campaign have to overcome before it made a difference to men's health?

Over to you!

Teenagers are very sensitive to being 'told what to do' even if this is intended as health promotion advice. Imagine that you are a health promotion officer. You've been asked to:

● Identify three key health topics affecting teenagers.

● Suggest a health message for each topic about which teenagers ought to be aware.

● Propose a way of getting each health message across to the teenage target group.

Think about this health promotion challenge and write down your suggestions.

Implementing a health improvement plan

An individual who has begun their health improvement plan and is working to achieve their targets is likely to need help and support to keep going and reach their goals. Health care practitioners use a range of strategies to support the implementation of health improvement plans that they develop with service users. These include:

● using diaries and record-keeping forms to help the person monitor their own progress and their feelings about the plan or the targets they have to achieve

Case study

Elsie Stevens is a 60-year-old woman. Since recently retiring from her job as a secretary, Elsie has decided that she needs to get fit to make the most of her retirement. Elsie currently does no exercise at all. She is two stone overweight. In her youth, Elsie was a keen swimmer and also enjoyed walking.

● Suggest three types of exercise Elsie could take as a way of reducing her weight and getting fitter. Explain how these particular choices would benefit Elsie and also fit into her lifestyle.

● Plan a three-month exercise/activity programme for Elsie based on the range of opportunities and facilities available in your local area. Set out your programme in a table format.

- encouraging people to attend support groups, or contribute to online forums with other individuals who are also seeking to improve their health. Some health care practitioners help service users to establish supportive 'buddy relationships' with others in a similar position so that they can talk to and support each other

- using substitutes, such as nicotine patches, or recommending lower fat or lower calorie alternatives to foods that a person has difficulty giving up

- reward systems, such as scoring or grading improvements, identifying a slimmer of the week or month, for example, or encouraging the person to treat themselves as a personal reward for making progress towards their targets

- review meetings that acknowledge difficulties and give positive feedback to the person for their efforts and the progress they have made. Review meetings also allow the health care practitioner and the service user to adjust targets if they reach them early or if they appear to be unrealistic.

Knowledge Check

1 Identify three factors that must be assessed before a health improvement plan can be written.

2 Describe how health behaviour and lifestyle can be assessed as part of a health improvement programme.

3 Explain why individual health assessment and target setting are essential before an effective health improvement plan can be constructed.

4 Explain why it might be damaging to an individual's health to set unrealistic health improvement targets.

5 Identify a range of factors that are likely to affect the success of a health improvement plan.

6 Describe four different forms of health promotion material that can be used to deliver health improvement messages to the general population.

7 How can an individual be motivated and supported to improve their health?

Chapter checklist

The box below provides a summary of the areas covered in chapter 14. Tick the areas that you feel you understand and would be confident about when writing your assignment. If there are any areas that you don't understand or are not confident about, you will need to return to them before you begin planning or writing your assignment.

Health improvement planning

Assessment of health status ❏

Identifying health improvement targets ❏

Designing health improvement plan ❏

Using health promotion materials ❏

Assessment of barriers to health Improvement ❏

Ways of supporting health improvement efforts ❏

Assessment Guide

Your learning in this unit will be assessed through a controlled assessment task. This will be set by the OCR awarding body and marked by your tutor.

The assignment will require you to produce a health improvement plan for an individual. You can develop a plan based on improving your own health and wellbeing or find a volunteer who is willing to be the focus of your project.

Your final plan will need to:

● Identify health improvement targets for your chosen individual.

● Explain how the targets address the individual's needs.

● Describe the possible impact on their health should the individual meet these targets.

● Analyse and explain the possible risks to health of the targets.

● Explain the support that might be required for the individual to achieve the goals set for them.

Chapter 14 provides full coverage of health improvement planning. Studying and referring back to chapter 14 should provide you with the background information needed to complete this part of the controlled assessment task.

Safeguarding and Protecting Individuals

Introduction

The focus of this unit is on safeguarding and protecting individuals. You will learn about:

- Safeguarding individuals and the consequences of a lack of safeguarding.

- How the spread of infection can be prevented in order to protect care service users.

- Basic first aid procedures for injuries and health emergencies that could occur in care settings.

- How to recognise potential risks to safety and how to reduce risks to safety in care settings.

The key to considering safeguarding and protection issues is to think about 'who is at risk' and 'why are people ill-treated'. People who neglect and abuse others can be professional care workers, informal carers, parents, visitors or organisations. Those who do ill-treat people are often called 'perpetrators' of abuse. By the end of this unit you should understand why some groups and individual's require safeguarding and protecting from perpetrators of abuse, the kinds of risks that they face and how primary and secondary care workers can reduce risks and protect service users in care settings.

Chapter 15

Safeguarding individuals

> ### Key issue: Who requires safeguarding and the consequences of a lack of safeguarding

To get started on this unit you need to understand a basic point about many care service users. This is that people in care settings are often vulnerable. In particular, service users may have to rely on others because they are ill or because they have emotional or developmental problems. Some care service users are also vulnerable due to their age (young or old) or because they have physical, sensory or learning disabilities and special care needs. Part of the care workers role is to offer protection to vulnerable service users and to ensure that each individual's best interests are safeguarded.

Chapter 15 will develop your knowledge and understanding of:

- a range of groups who are vulnerable
- the reasons why vulnerable people may need to have their interests protected by care practitioners
- the possible effects of ill-treatment
- the laws and guidance on safeguarding that have been developed to protect vulnerable groups.

Vulnerable groups

Health and safety, infection control, first aid and security provision are all important issues in any care setting. This is because care service users tend to be more vulnerable to harm, exploitation and abuse when they are unwell. A number of different groups of care service users are often seen as being vulnerable to hazards or exploitation and in need of protection and safeguarding (see figure 4.1).

Children are vulnerable and in need of safeguarding by responsible adults (parents and teachers, for example) because they depend on others to meet their basic physical, emotional, safety and security needs. Children are likely to be vulnerable and in need of safeguarding if they are:

- left to look after themselves without adult protection

Figure 4.1 Examples of vulnerable groups.

- People who reside in care settings
- Children
- People with mental illness
- VULNERABLE GROUPS
- Children in care
- People with learning difficulties
- People with disabilities
- Older people

Case study

Beverley, aged 15, suffered neglect and abuse at the hands of her mother and step-father for six years before the local authority and police became aware of the situation. From the age of nine when her mother remarried, Beverley was forbidden to play with her two half-brothers. She was also locked in her room at night, given too little to eat and made to do all the household chores for her family. Beverley was deliberately excluded from family life by her parents. They made her use an outside toilet, stopped her having any books in her room and starved her of love and affection, even though she could see her siblings being hugged and cuddled. Because she was shabbily dressed, underweight and often unkempt Beverley was bullied at school. Beverley was frightened of her mother who didn't want to be near her, shouted at and hit her and always made her stay at home on family days out. Beverley eventually told a teacher at school what her life was like at home. A doctor who examined her said that she was underweight, had eyesight and teeth problems and had suffered emotional abuse and neglect. Beverley and her half-brothers were removed from the family home by social workers. Her parents admitted charges of cruelty and neglect and were given community sentences.

- Identify reasons why an adolescent like Beverley is vulnerable to neglect and abuse.
- In what ways was Beverley subjected to ill-treatment?
- How did care practitioners intervene to safeguard Beverley's interests and wellbeing?

- verbally abused by being regularly shouted at
- exposed to violent scenes at home
- neglected by parents who put their own needs before those of their children
- emotionally ill-treated by being deprived of love or physical contact
- bullied at school or by neighbours or family.

Several inquiries into residential child care services in the United Kingdom over the last thirty years have highlighted that *children in care* often have additional safeguarding and protection needs. Some forms of institutional care have in the past allowed unscrupulous members of staff to exploit and abuse the children they were supposed to be caring for. Accounts of being emotionally ill-treated by being deprived of love or physical

Investigate ...

Using the Internet and other sources, find out about the case of Victoria Climbie, an 8-year-old girl who was abused and killed by people who were supposed to be caring for her. Make brief notes about what happened to Victoria and try to identify why she was vulnerable and who should have provided her with protection.

Case study

The Waterhouse Report, published in 2000, investigated and described a large number of allegations about the abuse of children in care homes in North Wales between 1974 and the late 1980s. The report describes sexual abuse of boys by care staff and paedophiles from outside of the care system. The inquiry also heard a range of allegations about the physical and emotional abuse that ranged from hitting and throttling to the bullying and belittling of children. Punishments used by staff included forcing children to scrub floors with toothbrushes and making them carry out garden tasks using cutlery. The Waterhouse Report said that the quality of care, and standard of education, in all the homes it investigated were below acceptable levels.

- Identify the types of abuse and ill-treatment that children experienced in care homes in North Wales between 1974 and the late 1980s.
- Who were the main perpetrators of the abuse that these children suffered?
- Why are children in care particularly vulnerable and in need of safeguarding and protection?

Case study

Charlotte Cohen is 80 years of age. She has lived in a residential home for the last 5 years. Charlotte's room is on the second floor of the home. Over the last 6 months Charlotte has become more confused and has started to wander around the home, once going out and walking in the main road until a passer-by stopped her and brought her back. The staff now describe Charlotte as 'a bit of a handful' and have complained to the care home manager that they need an additional member of staff on duty to look after her. Whilst they are waiting for the manager to agree to increase the number of staff on duty, the care workers at Charlotte's home have taken to keeping her in her room for most of the day. They do this by wedging the door open and then place a small table across the opening to stop Charlotte from getting out. Charlotte complains loudly about this every morning, tries to remove the table but eventually gives up and sits in a chair staring at the doorway. The staff have told her daughter who is very upset about this and has demanded that it be stopped that they 'don't have the time' to stay with Charlotte all day and that 'it's for health and safety reasons – at least we know where she is'.

- Do you think that the care workers at Charlotte's residential home are guilty of abuse?
- What factors have led to this situation occurring?
- What effects do you think this treatment is likely to have on Charlotte?

contact, being physically abused (for example by being slapped or hit) and being sexually abused have led to many changes in the way that care is provided for looked after children. People working in residential services for children are now subject to extensive Criminal Records Bureau (CRB) checks, are managed more closely and generally do their best to support and protect the children they work with.

People who reside in care settings can become very dependent on care workers and may lose their independent living skills. This is particularly the case where a care setting has a 'routine' that limits or even removes the everyday choices that residents have about issues such as when and what to eat, when to get up or go to bed and what to do with their time. As a result some people who reside in care settings can lose the ability to make personal decisions, may become too compliant and can find it hard to say no to people they see as being in positions of 'authority'. In residential settings where staff are poorly trained, stressed, overworked and poorly managed standards of care can deteriorate and residents can be vulnerable to:

- unacceptable practices such as verbal abuse (shouting and swearing),
- humiliating, rough and harassing treatment
- forcible isolation where they are denied access to the outside world or to a particular service or facility.

People with disabilities may be vulnerable to exploitation or ill-treatment because of their physical or sensory (hearing, visual or speech) impairments. Problems with mobility, communication or just seeing and hearing other people can restrict an individual's ability to meet their own needs and manage their personal safety and security if another unscrupulous person decides to exploit or take advantage of this.

People with mental illness suffer a range of distressing, sometimes frightening and often disabling symptoms that can

Investigate ...

Use the Internet and other sources of information such as your school, college or local library to find out about the causes and effects of mental illness that make people vulnerable. The Mental Health Foundation, MIND and Young Minds all have websites that provide a good range of useful information on this issue.

Case study

Edward Jones is 26 years of age. He lives alone in a first floor flat near to the city centre. Edward moved to this flat a year ago after being discharged from a local mental health unit. Edward's mental health is much better than it used to be. He spent 3 years in hospital after having a breakdown. This was triggered by a series of events that included the death of his girlfriend in a car accident, being made redundant and then being attacked and badly beaten by a gang of teenagers whilst walking home late at night. Edward has worked hard to recover from these traumatic events. He still sees a community mental health nurse every fortnight and takes medication to help him cope with anxiety and depression. Edward has recently revealed to his nurse that a group of children and his next door neighbour have been harassing him, shouting obscenities through his letter box, calling him 'nutter' and spitting at him when they see him. Edward is worried that this will make him ill again but he doesn't know how to stop it happening.

- What kinds of abuse and ill-treatment is Edward experiencing?
- Why do you think people are behaving like they are towards Edward?
- What impact might the behaviour of local children and Edward's neighbour have on his health and wellbeing?

preoccupy them and limit their ability to use their judgement effectively. If an individual is taking medication, this might make them feel sleepy or slow their thinking down. Similarly if they have a very low mood or experience 'voices' or other disturbing symptoms, they may be too preoccupied to meet their basic needs or to be aware of potential threats or hazards to their personal safety.

People with learning difficulties have a restricted ability to learn and a limited level of intelligence. As a result, individuals in this group may not be able to identify potential threats to their personal safety or wellbeing and may find it difficult to know whether other people have their best interests at heart. People

Case study

A review of care at Orchard Hill hospital and some community homes in Surrey for people with learning difficulties was carried out in 2006. This happened in response to a number of serious incidents, including allegations of physical and sexual abuse. A member of staff was jailed for six years in 2006 after pleading guilty to sexual activity with a woman resident. The review concluded that "outmoded, institutionalised care" at the hospital and in the community homes had led to the neglect of people with learning disabilities. It said that "impoverished and completely unsatisfactory" living conditions, poor staff training and failures in management were partly responsible for the unacceptable standards of care. Examples of poor care included people being wrapped in blue tissue paper at mealtimes and being fed too quickly to enable them to enjoy the food. The review said the needs of individuals had been sacrificed in favour of the needs of the institution.

The residents with learning disabilities who lived at Orchard Hill were not supported to become independent, but instead were "institutionalised".

- What kinds of abuse or ill-treatment were experienced by the residents of the Surrey hospital and community homes described above?
- What factors may have led to the situation described occurring?
- What does the term 'institutionalised care' mean and why is this type of care more likely to lead to the abuse and ill-treatment of vulnerable service users?

with learning difficulties who use care services rely on care workers to treat them as valued people and to respect their rights and interests. They will often be very trusting and will not expect a care worker to do anything that might harm them. However, in some situations unscrupulous care workers have used the power and influence they have over individuals with learning difficulties to abuse and exploit them.

Older people, particularly those who become physically and mentally frail, perhaps as a result of confusion and memory loss or other age-related conditions, are vulnerable to exploitation by unscrupulous people who seek to take advantage of them. Older people living alone are particularly vulnerable if they become isolated and lack the support of family, friends or neighbours. The UK Study of Abuse and Neglect of Older People carried out in 2007 found that:

- men aged 85 and older are more likely to have experienced financial abuse than men in the younger age groups

- older people living alone, receiving services, in bad health and older people who are divorced, separated or lonely have an increased risk of financial abuse and exploitation

- a quarter of perpetrators live in the older person's home

- about 30% of financial abuse is committed by domiciliary care workers.

Financial abuse of elderly people

Say the word "abuse" and most people automatically think sexual or physical. But, for older people living in their own homes, financial abuse has been revealed as the second most prevalent form of abuse, behind neglect.

According to the recent government-funded report on abuse and neglect of older people in the UK, financial abuse affects 7 in 1,000 older people and includes theft of money, possessions or property, fraud, embezzlement and extortion.

The report reveals that family members are the most common perpetrators, something that comes as no surprise to Gary FitzGerald, chief executive of Action on Elder Abuse. An analysis of more than 400 calls about financial abuse to the organisation's helpline in 2006 revealed that £2.1m was reported as stolen, defrauded or coerced from elderly victims and nearly a quarter of callers claimed their houses had been sold or taken without their consent. Most victims were women older than 81, and most perpetrators were their sons and daughters aged between 41 and 60.   (**Source** – www.communitycare.co.uk)

1 Which two forms of abuse are older people living at home most at risk of experiencing?

2 Who is most likely to financially abuse older people?

3 What effect might this kind of abuse have on an older person who experienced it?

It should be clear from the case studies and the explanations provided that some groups of vulnerable people are at risk of abuse, neglect and ill-treatment unless they receive appropriate protection and safeguarding. Abuse and neglect are most commonly perpetrated by parents on children, by one partner on another and by carers on vulnerable people who are unwell, frail or who have developmental problems. The different forms of abuse that members of vulnerable groups experience include:

- physical abuse
- sexual abuse
- emotional and psychological abuse
- financial exploitation
- neglect.

As you will have realised from reading the case studies and studying the previous section, abuse and neglect can occur for a variety of reasons.

Reasons for abuse and ill-treatment

The perpetrator, or person who carries out abuse, neglect or ill-treatment, is ultimately responsible for their actions and generally won't be allowed by their employers, the Police or the courts to make excuses for harming a vulnerable relative or service user. However, there are a number of reasons why an abuse situation may have developed (see figure 4.2).

It is helpful for care workers to be aware of factors that contribute to the ill-treatment of vulnerable people. This enables them to alert their colleagues, managers and employers to circumstances, care practices or the behaviour of some individuals that could lead to the abuse, neglect or exploitation of service users. For example, when care workers are poorly trained, are unsupervised or lack support, managers should be alerted because this can lead to neglect and abuse of service users. Similarly, where a care worker is working on their own with service users, or if there are an inadequate number of staff or informal carers to look after people who use services, standards of care practice can fall to unacceptable levels. In these

Over to you!

Think about somebody you know (of any age) who you think of as 'vulnerable'. Does the person belong to any of the groups listed above? In what way(s) is this person 'vulnerable? Make a list of the factors that you think make them particularly vulnerable to abuse, exploitation, neglect or some other form of harm.

Over to you!

Look back at the case studies in the earlier part of this chapter. Why do you think that the perpetrators in each case of ill-treatment behaved in the way that they did? Jot down some ideas about the range of possible reasons for abuse and ill-treatment.

Figure 4.2 Reasons for abuse and ill-treatment.

circumstances it is often complaints from service users or their relatives that brings abuse and neglect to light. Ensuring that all the practice standards of care workers are monitored, that regular training and updating is provided and that care workers have enough support to provide good quality care are ways of reducing the risk of abuse and neglect.

The effects of a lack of safeguarding

Care practitioners are expected, and required by their employers and professional bodies, to keep themselves and service users safe and secure. Where this does not happen, service users can be affected in a variety of different ways. These include:

Physical effects

- A person who is being physically abused may suffer injuries as a result of being hit, slapped or treated roughly.

- Depending on the severity of what has happened, the abused person could be left with long-term physical damage or a disability.

- The effects of a lack of safeguarding can cause a person to turn their anger against themselves through self-harming behaviour or may lead them to use alcohol and drugs as a way of coping with the distressing feelings they are left with.

- Extreme or prolonged physical abuse can result in a person experiencing injuries that ultimately result in their death.

Emotional and psychological effects

- A vulnerable person who experiences abuse is likely to have low self-esteem, lack confidence in themselves and find it difficult to trust other people.

- People who have experienced emotional abuse and neglect often find it difficult to form relationships of their own and may have difficulty expressing their feelings towards a partner and their children due to a lack of previous, positive role models.

- Abuse can lead individuals to develop negative self-concepts in which they see themselves as less valuable and not worthy of other people's attention.

Effects on behaviour

- An individual who is or has been abused may become more aggressive towards others as a way of protecting themselves and also as a way of expressing their anger and upset about what has happened to them.

- People who have been physically and emotionally abused can become fearful, withdrawn and may be reluctant to make relationships or have close contact with others in order to avoid being hurt again.

- The behaviour of children and young people who suffer abuse or neglect often deteriorates and they are more likely to underachieve at school, drink alcohol and take drugs as ways of coping with their distress.

- Children and young people who have been sexually abused may express inappropriate sexual behaviour at a young age and may find it difficult to form close relationships with others.

Case study

Damien's parents had a very strict approach to discipline. All three of their boys were hit with a cane if they misbehaved. Damien's parents felt it was 'fair' to ask each boy directly about any misbehaviour they were accused of. They believed that this gave the boys a chance to explain and to apologise before they received their punishment. Damien's father carried out the canings when he arrived home from work. Damien's two older brothers often blamed him when their mother accused them of taking food, breaking toys or messing up the house. Damien learnt that protesting his innocence only led to harsher punishment.

As he grew up Damien grew used to being hit and thought it was normal to be shouted at and treated in an emotionally cold way by your parents. Damien has also suffered from recurring episodes of depression since he was a teenager. These often revolve around the idea that he is a bad person. Damien has been happily married for five years and now has very little contact with his family. Damien's wife would like them to have children but he doesn't believe he would make a good father and tries to avoid discussing the issue with her.

- What kinds of ill-treatment did Damien experience when he was growing up?

- Which aspects of Damien's development and wellbeing seem to have been affected by his ill-treatment?

- What kind of long-term impact has Damien's experience of ill-treatment had on him?

Knowledge Check

1 Identify five different groups of care service users who are vulnerable to abuse and neglect.

2 Identify five different types of abuse or ill-treatment that vulnerable people may experience.

3 What does the term 'perpetrator' mean?

4 Describe two situations in which a child may be vulnerable and in need of safeguarding.

5 Explain why children in care are a vulnerable group who require safeguarding and protection.

6 Give two examples of the ways in which people residing in care settings are vulnerable to ill-treatment.

7 Identify three different types of disability that may make individuals who experience them more vulnerable to abuse or ill-treatment.

8 What is financial abuse and who are the main perpetrators of it when if affects older people?

9 Identify five different factors that are thought to increase the risk of vulnerable people experiencing abuse or ill-treatment in care settings.

Legal protection for vulnerable people

A number of different laws have been passed to protect and safeguard the interests of vulnerable children and adults. Health, social care and early years practitioners should be aware of these laws and should know how they apply to the work they do with service users (see figure 4.3 for example).

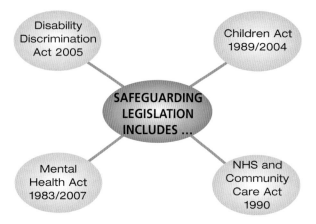

Figure 4.3 Examples of safeguarding legislation.

The Children Act 2004

This piece of legislation updated the Children Act 1989 following an inquiry into the death of Victoria Climbie in 2000. The Children Act 1989 established that care workers should see the needs of the child as **paramount** (most important) when making any decisions that affect a child's welfare. Under the 1989 Act local authorities were required to provide services that met the needs of children identified as being 'at risk'. The goal of the Children Act 2004 is to improve the lives of all children who receive informal or professional care. It covers all services that children might use, such as schools, day care and children's homes as well as health care services. The Children Act 2004 now requires care services to work collaboratively so that they form a protective team around the child.

The Children Act 2004 resulted from a report called *Every Child Matters* that led to significant change in the way services for children and young people are provided in the UK. You will probably recall that the aims of the *Every Child Matters* programme (www.everychildmatters.gov.uk) are that all children should:

- be healthy
- stay safe
- enjoy and achieve
- make a positive contribution
- achieve economic wellbeing.

The ongoing *Every Child Matters* programme of children's service development ensures that safeguarding remains the key priority for everyone who is part of the children's workforce. People who work with children, young people and vulnerable adults now have to have their background checked by the Criminal Records Bureau (CRB) to ensure they are a suitable person to be working with vulnerable people. In 2009, a Vetting and Barring Scheme that is administered by the Independent Safeguarding Authority and the Criminal Records Bureau will require all adults who work with children to register with them. Equivalent agencies called Disclosure Scotland and Access Northern Ireland operate in other parts of the UK.

Mental Health Act 2007

This legislation updated the Mental Health Act 1983, which was the main piece of law affecting the treatment of adults experiencing serious mental disorders in England and Wales. The Mental Health Act 2007 seeks to safeguard the interests of adults who are vulnerable because of their mental health problems by ensuring that they can be monitored in the community by care practitioners and admitted to hospital if they don't comply with treatment. The Mental Health Act 1983 and 2007 also protect the rights of mental health service users in a number of ways. Both Acts give individuals the right to appeal against their detention in hospital and gives them some rights to refuse treatment. The new 2007 Act now gives individuals detained in hospital the right to refuse certain treatments, such as electroconvulsive therapy, and ensures that a person can only be detained in hospital if appropriate treatment is available for them.

Disability Discrimination Act 2005

This Act safeguards the rights of disabled people by making 'less favourable treatment' of disabled people in employment, the provision of goods and services, education and transport unlawful. The aim of the Act is to ensure that disabled people receive equal opportunities and that employers, traders, transport and education providers make 'reasonable adjustments' to their premises and services to allow access.

NHS and Community Care Act 1990

The NHS and Community Care Act (1990) introduced community care for adults with social care and support needs. Under the Act all local authorities are required to assess the social care and support needs of adults who have a physical disability, disabling illness, terminal illness, sensory impairment, learning disability or mental health problem. The local authority must then purchase care services to meet the individual's needs. The Act safeguards the interests of vulnerable adults by ensuring that they are appropriately catered for in the community.

 Investigate ...

Use the Equality and Human Rights Commission website (www.equalityhumanrights.com) to find out about the rights of disabled people and those with mental health problems.

 Case study

Simon Evans is 37 years of age. He has received assistance and treatment from health and social care workers for mental health problems since the age of 19 when he had his first admission to hospital. Simon usually takes medication to help him to cope with the distressing 'voices' and ideas that he experiences when he is unwell. When he takes his medication, Simon is generally well and is able to work as a Library Assistant at a local college. However, Simon sometimes stops taking his medication when he feels well. This can lead him to relapse as his symptoms return quite quickly.

- Identify one piece of legislation that could be used to protect Simon when he becomes unwell.

- Why might Simon be vulnerable when he becomes unwell?

- What legal responsibilities do Simon's local authority have with regard to providing him with appropriate support services?

Knowledge Check

1 Identify three different laws that are designed to protect vulnerable people.

2 Describe the aims of the *Every Child Matters* programme.

3 What is a CRB check and why do care workers have to have them done?

4 Explain how the Disability Discrimination Act 2005 protects disabled people.

5 How does the NHS and Community Care Act 1990 protect adults with social care and support needs?

Chapter checklist

The box below provides a summary of the areas covered in chapter 15. Tick the areas that you feel you understand and would be confident answering exam questions about. If there are any areas that you don't understand or are not confident about, you will need to return to them before you begin your exam revision.

Vulnerable groups ☐

Reasons for abuse and ill-treatment ☐

Effects of a lack of safeguarding ☐

Legislation to protect vulnerable people
Children Act 2004 ☐
Mental Health Act 2007 ☐
Disability Discrimination Act 2005 ☐
NHS and Community Care Act 1990 ☐

Assessment Guide

Your learning in this unit will be assessed through a one hour written examination taken online.

The examination will consist of a series of short and longer answer questions covering all aspects of this unit. You will need to show that you understand:

● Which groups are vulnerable to ill-treatment.

● How and why ill-treatment occurs.

● The effects of a lack of safeguarding of vulnerable people.

● The legislation that is designed to protect vulnerable people from ill-treatment.

Chapter 15 provides full coverage of all of the topics you may be asked about in the examination.

Chapter 16

Infection control

Key issue: Preventing the spread of infection

Preventing infection is one way of protecting people who use services; it is important for care settings to follow basic measures that will help to reduce the risk of the spread of infection in care settings. In chapter 16 you will learn about:

- Types of infection that are a risk to health
- Basic procedures that prevent the spread of infection
- Practical procedures and medical treatments that can prevent the spread of infection
- The importance of good food hygiene practices in care settings
- Legislation that promotes good infection control practice.

Everyone working in care settings should be aware of the importance of infection control and the need to follow basic infection control procedures. Service users are vulnerable to infection because of their poor physical health and can suffer serious complications or additional health problems if they contract an infection.

Basic infection control procedures

Infection control and high standards of hygiene are important health and safety issues in all care settings. Care practitioners working in hospitals or other residential care settings should see infection control as a high priority area because of the increasing problems and potentially fatal consequences of infections for vulnerable care service users. Many of the bacteria and viruses that cause infections are present in everyday life. However, hospitals and residential care settings are also places where new and more unusual infections may also be present and can be contracted. People who are physically frail or who are suffering from significant health problems tend to be more vulnerable and susceptible to common infections.

Care workers should be aware of, and follow, basic infection control procedures to minimise the risks of infection. These include:

- personal hygiene issues relating to dress, hair care, footwear and oral hygiene
- the use of personal protective clothing such as aprons, gloves and masks

Effective cleaning is central to infection control.

- the importance of following standard health, safety and hygiene precautions in the workplace
- correct hand-washing procedures.

Figure 4.4 Methods and modes of infection.

Method of transmission	Mode (How it is spread)	Example
Airborne	Droplet	Coughing; sneezing
Instilled	Liquid	Splashes to eye
Ingested	Contaminated food/water	Eating raw or undercooked meat, eggs, unprocessed cheeses
Insects	Injected	Mosquito or flea bites
Direct contact	Touching; absorption	Not covering open wounds; incorrect disposal of waste products
Indirect contact	Animals	Worms
Infestation	Fomites	Scabies in bed linen

Personal hygiene

Personal hygiene standards and hygiene practices in the care workplace are sensitive and important issues for care workers. Nobody wants to have their personal hygiene standards questioned by colleagues or service users. However, everybody working in care is expected to have clean and tidy hair, nails, skin and work clothing. Care workers should:

- wash regularly to ensure their skin is clean and free of odours
- keep cuts covered with plasters or clean dressings
- keep their nails clean and short
- use tissues or handkerchiefs when coughing or sneezing
- wear clothes that are clean and tidy
- have clean teeth
- wash their hands after using the toilet, handling food or touching clients when providing care.

In many health and early years settings in particular, care work involves being physically close to, and often touching, service users. The risk of infection being spread between people (cross-infection) and of food contamination increases where care workers don't maintain good standards of personal hygiene. These care workers are likely to produce, carry and pass on more disease-carrying bacteria, viruses and fungi than workers who do have good personal hygiene standards.

 Investigate ...

Use the Internet and library sources to find out about the causes and effects of:

- Ringworm
- Scabies
- Impetigo
- Halitosis
- Athletes foot
- Body odour.

Produce a table summarizing the causes and effects of each of these problems and also suggest how they can be prevented or dealt with through personal hygiene routines.

Case study

Methicillin-Resistant *Staphylococcus Aureus* (MRSA) is an infection that has become a serious problem in care settings, both nationally and globally. The overuse of antibiotics is one of the main reasons for this bacteria's resistance to some antibiotics. However, low standards of hygiene and poor use of infection control techniques in care settings have also played a significant part in the spread of MRSA.

Ineffective hand washing by health-care workers before and after dealing with MRSA-positive individuals is the main cause of MRSA infection in care settings. However, if basic good hygiene precautions are followed, MRSA-positive individuals are not a risk to others. Studies show that hand decontamination with alcohol disinfectant is effective in combating MRSA, especially when combined with good hand hygiene practice.

- Identify the main reason for the development of MRSA.

- What factors have played a significant part in the spread of MRSA?

- What basic infection control techniques are effective in combating the MRSA virus?

Personal protective equipment

Care practitioners who provide forms of personal care for service users, such as washing, toileting and wound care, should have access to personal protective equipment (PPE) and should always use the correct equipment for the task they are performing. Items of PPE that are commonly available in care settings include disposable gloves, masks and aprons. Care practitioners should always use PPE when changing dressings, performing **aseptic techniques** and when disposing of bodily products such as blood, faeces, urine and vomit.

Hand-washing procedures

The risks of infection and **cross infection** are greatly reduced by good hand hygiene. In fact, this is the single most important infection control measure. Care practitioners who have direct physical contact with service users should wash their hands thoroughly with a decontamination agent and dry them before and after working with each individual. Research carried out by the National Patient Safety Agency shows that infection rates are reduced by between 10 and 50 per cent when healthcare workers clean their hands regularly. Many care organisations advise care practitioners not to use a service user's own soap or towel when cleaning their hands to minimise cross-infection risks.

Over to you!

How frequently do you wash your hands each day? Make a note of the occasions when you have washed your hands today. Do you always wash your hands after using the toilet or before and after touching food?

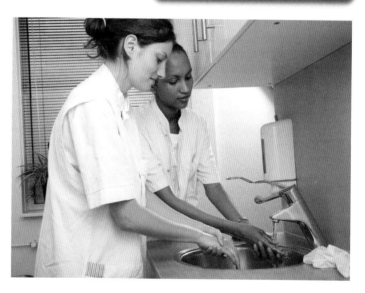

Hand-washing is a high priority in care settings.

Environmental hygiene

The environment in which care is provided, including equipment, furniture and fixtures and fittings in bedrooms, living areas and bathrooms, should be kept clean and maintained to a high standard. It is important that care workers understand the different ways of cleaning and sterilising an environment (see figure 4.5.).

Figure 4.5 Ways of cleaning a care environment.

General cleaning (dusting, vacuuming)

Disinfecting floors, surfaces, equipment

CLEANING METHODS INCLUDE ...

Removal of waste and rubbish

Sterilisation of equipment

General cleaning, disinfecting and sterilising

Cleaning, disinfection and sterilisation are all procedures that are used to decontaminate equipment, clothing or buildings. Decontamination reduces the risk of cross infection and is important in the overall control of hospital acquired infections such as MRSA (see above).

Cleaning is the process of removing contaminants such as dust, soil, micro-organisms and organic matter (e.g. blood, vomit) from equipment, clothing or buildings. Domestic staff and specially trained cleaners are generally responsible for cleaning the floors, surfaces and fixtures and fittings in a care setting. Every care setting should have an ongoing cleaning plan that ensures dust, everyday dirt and any spillages or waste products are removed quickly to minimise the risk of infections developing and spreading. Care practitioners should always report lack of cleanliness and should always ensure that they leave bathrooms, kitchens and treatment areas clean and tidy.

Disinfection is used to reduce the number of micro-organisms that are present in a care setting. Disinfection won't kill or remove all of the micro-organisms present in a care setting but will reduce their number and ensure they are not harmful to health if carried out on a regular basis. Domestic and cleaning staff generally have the task of disinfecting equipment and areas of the care environment that may harbour infectious organisms. Care workers should also disinfect equipment such as commodes and non-disposable bedpans by cleaning them thoroughly with detergent and hot water after use.

Case study

Gemma is a nursery nurse, working at the Cheeky Monkey day nursery for children under 5 years of age. She is currently working with the youngest children who are between 1 and 3 years of age. Riley, aged 2, was sick shortly after eating his fruit and biscuit snack this morning. He vomited into a box of toys as well as onto the nursery floor. Gemma phoned Riley's mum to come and collect him after she had cleaned him up and changed his clothes. She wiped the sick off the floor with some paper towels but has forgotten about the box of toys.

- What should Gemma do to decontaminate the areas where Riley was sick?

- What might happen if Gemma does not decontaminate the floor and the box of toys properly?

- How could Gemma protect herself from cross-infection whilst dealing with this situation?

Sterilisation destroys all microbes but can only be carried out using specialist equipment. Surgical instruments, needles, urinary and other **catheters** have to be sterilised to ensure they are completely free from any infection because they are inserted into the body. **Autoclaving** is the commonest method of sterilising equipment in health care settings. An autoclave machine is often found in hospital settings where **invasive** medical procedures are carried out. Equipment is placed inside it and subjected to pressurized steam in order to sterilise it.

Dealing with spillages

Spillages of liquids or body products in care settings should always be treated as health and safety hazards. Wet and slippery floors cause many accidents in care settings. As a result, care organisations usually have a set of policies and procedures for dealing with different types of spillage. The actual procedure that is used for any particular spillage is likely to depend on the substance involved and the level of risk associated with it. In some care settings cleaners and porters are responsible for dealing with spillages because they have received special training to do so. Hygiene standards and infection control procedures can break down and cause health and safety problems where there is confusion, disagreement about or delay in cleaning up. Blood and body-fluid spillages should be cleaned immediately, for example, to prevent accidents and infection occurring.

Disposal of hazardous waste

Various kinds of clinical, food and everyday waste are produced in care settings. Each of these types of waste present an infection hazard unless it is correctly dealt with. Care organisations have

Figure 4.6 Methods of waste disposal.

Type of waste	Method of disposal
Soiled linen	Soiled sheets, towels and clothing should be kept separately from other used linen and clothing. In hospitals and care homes, they are often put in a red bag to show they are soiled. Soiled linen should be washed separately from other linen and should be dealt with as soon as possible.
Non-soiled linen	Non-soiled linen should be placed in an ordinary laundry bag using the individual's preferred method in the home care setting.
'Sharps'	'Sharps' such as used needles, cannulas and blades should be disposed of in a yellow sharps bin. This must be sealed before incineration.
Body products	These include body fluids such as blood, urine and sputum as well as other waste products such as vomit and faeces. Spillages should be cleared up and flushed down a sluice, toilet or sink. The spillage area should be cleaned and disinfected.
Clinical waste	This includes dressings, bandages and swabs, for example. In residential care settings it should be disposed of in a marked clinical waste bin containing a yellow clinical waste bag.
Household waste	This should normally be disposed of as domestic rubbish in black bags or using the waste disposal system provided by your local authority.
Left-over food	Food that is directly left over from individuals' meals should be disposed of in a kitchen bin immediately after the meal is finished. Staff employed to work in the food preparation and serving areas should normally receive food hygiene training which covers ways of dealing with food waste.

Case study

Rishna Khan is halfway through a nurse training placement on a children's ward. She did her first ever night shift last week. Rishna was working with two qualified nurses and two experienced health care assistants. Whilst Janine, her qualified supervisor, was on her break Rishna realised that Toby, a 6 year old boy with a broken leg, had been incontinent of faeces and needed cleaning and changing. Rishna panicked because she had never dealt with this situation before. Instead of changing Toby, she hid in the toilet for a few minutes until one of the health care assistants noticed that Toby was sobbing. Whilst her colleague cleaned and dressed Toby, Rishna offered to take the soiled linen and night clothes away.

- Identify reasons why Rishna should have got some help for Toby from one of her colleagues straight away.

- Describe the potential hazards that need to be dealt with in order to provide care for Toby.

- How could Rishna maximise health and safety and minimise the risk of infection in the way that she deals with Toby's soiled sheets and night clothes?

detailed policies and procedures on safe waste disposal. Waste disposal policies give details of the procedures that care workers are expected to follow when faced with different kinds of waste. Often this includes the colour coding of waste disposal bags (see figure 4.6). Care practitioners should always wear protective gloves when handling waste, such as used needles, dirty linen or bedpans, that carry an infection risk. Dirty or soiled clothing and bed linen should always be bagged and machine-washed in accordance with an organisation's hazardous waste policy and procedures.

One of the basic principles of safe waste disposal is that care workers should limit how much they move the waste that they are disposing. For example, it is better to bring the correct waste disposal bag to a person's bedside or to the treatment area rather than to take clinical waste through the care setting whilst looking for a suitable bag to put it in. This reduces the risk of cross infection occurring in different areas of the care setting.

Disposal of medication

Medicines that are no longer required by a service user should be safely disposed of. Failure to dispose of unwanted medication can lead to confusion and mistakes being made by service users, their relatives and care practitioners. Some medications may be toxic or may be dangerous if consumed by physically healthy adults or children. However, disposal of medicines should be carried out carefully in order to prevent others coming to harm and to protect the environment. For example, unused medication should not be thrown in the rubbish bin, flushed down the toilet or poured down the sink. All of these methods of disposal lead to the medication polluting the environment. Unused medication should, where possible, be returned to a GP or to a hospital or community pharmacy for safe disposal.

Vaccination and immunisation

As we have seen in chapter 12, vaccination is an illness prevention strategy. When a vaccine is introduced into a person's body, usually by injection, it stimulates the body to produce antibodies that can neutralise or destroy a disease-carrying organism. Vaccinations are the most clinically effective and cost-effective way of preventing infectious diseases. Babies and young children are given a number of vaccines as part of an immunisation programme to protect them from infectious diseases. Care workers are also encouraged, and are sometimes required by the employers, to have a range of vaccinations – or boosters - to protect them against infectious diseases such as Hepatitis C, polio, tuberculosis, rubella and tetanus.

Reporting infection control problems

Care practitioners are expected to report diseases, illnesses and conditions which occur in care settings that are infectious or which present a significant risk to health, safety or hygiene. The Reporting of Injuries, Diseases and Dangerous Occurrences Regulations (RIDDOR) 1995 identify a range of situations that must, by law, be recorded and reported to the **Health and Safety Executive**. These include:

- death in the workplace
- injuries that lead to 3 or more days off sick
- a range of infectious diseases and illnesses including malaria, tetanus, typhoid, typhus, measles and salmonella.

Environmental problems such as overflowing drains, the presence of hazardous chemicals (including cleaning substances) and gases must also be recorded and reported on. The Control of Substances Hazardous to Health (COSHH) Regulations say that a COSHH file containing a list of all the hazardous substances and their location should be available in every care setting. The COSHH file should also provide safety details about the risks and effects of each hazardous substance as well as information on how to deal with them in an emergency.

Vaccination protects against infection.

 Investigate ...

Use the Health Protection Agency website (www.hpa.org.uk) to find out about healthcare associated infections. Make some notes about the symptoms of the Norovirus and the ways it can be contracted.

 Knowledge Check

1 Identify three different methods of transmitting infectious diseases.

2 Explain why infection control is a high priority issue in care settings.

3 Why is it important for care workers to wash their hands after going to the toilet?

4 What does the term cross-infection mean?

5 Describe three examples of personal protective equipment that can be used to minimise the risk of cross-infection.

6 Describe what MRSA is and explain how care practitioners can minimise the risk of becoming infected or cross-infecting others with it.

7 Identify three methods of decontamination that help to control infectious organisms.

8 Describe a safe method of disposing of soiled linen in a hospital setting.

9 Identify examples of diseases, illnesses and conditions that have to be reported under the RIDDOR 2002 regulations.

Safeguarding and Protecting Individuals

Food safety and hygiene

Care workers may from time to time be asked to prepare a snack for a service user or a visitor to the care setting. As a result, they must understand and must follow good food hygiene practices in order to prevent food poisoning from occurring. Good food hygiene results from people taking care to ensure that food is stored, handled and cooked in ways and under conditions that prevent contamination. The health of vulnerable service users, their visitors and care workers themselves may be at risk from food poisoning and severe cases can even be fatal where people are already very sick or frail.

Good standards of food hygiene are essential in care settings.

Understanding food hygiene

Care workers should be aware that the three main elements of good food hygiene are hygiene control, temperature control and pest control.

Hygiene control

Hygiene control involves following food preparation, handling and storage practices that prevent food becoming contaminated by bacteria. The main sources of food contamination are:

- food-to-food contamination, such as bacteria being transferred from raw to cooked meat
- equipment to food contamination, such as bacteria growing on and being transferred from unclean surfaces, unclean utensils or unclean cloths
- food-handler-to-food contamination, such as using unclean hands or fingers to taste food or poor personal hygiene
- contamination by pests, pets or microbes when food is left to stand at room temperature.

Care workers should understand that the risk of food contamination is reduced by:

- washing hands thoroughly with soap and water before handling food
- hand washing after using the toilet, touching service users, coughing or sneezing or handling any kind of food or other waste

 Case study

Tyrone Ward admits people over the age of 65. The people who are admitted to the ward are often confused and are sometimes also physically frail or have long-term physical health problems. Mike Andrews, the ward manager, has just received phone calls from three different members of staff. The three staff members have all reported in sick for a third day, saying that they have the symptoms of food poisoning. One of the staff members believes that she became sick after eating an egg sandwich from the ward's dinner trolley earlier in the week. Mike Andrews is now worried that some of the patients may also have eaten some of these eggs sandwiches.

- Why might this episode of staff sickness turn out to be a health and safety issue?
- Who else may be at risk if the cause of the staff member's sickness is a food hygiene problem?
- Is Mike required to report this situation?

- wearing protective clothing, particularly an apron when preparing or serving food
- keeping nails short and hair clean and tied back
- covering all cuts or wounds with a waterproof dressing
- covering and storing raw and cooked foods (especially meat) in different fridges or in different areas if there is only one fridge available. Raw food should always be kept in a lower part of the fridge if kept with cooked food
- using separate chopping boards for raw and cooked meat and for non-meat foodstuffs
- checking packaging to ensure that food products are only used and consumed within their 'use by' dates. This is particularly important for meat and dairy products.

Figure 4.7 Sources of food poisoning.

Source	Symptoms
Salmonella A bacterium found in faeces of infected people and in poultry, eggs, meat and water	• Abdominal pain, watery and bloody diarrhoea • Headaches • Nausea and vomiting
Campylobacter This is a bacterium usually found in undercooked meat (esp poultry), unpasteurised milk and untreated water	• Severe diarrhoea and abdominal pain • Blood in faeces
Bacillus cereus This is the bacterium found in rice dishes and sometimes in pasta, meat and vegetable dishes, dairy products, soups and sauces	• Diarrhoea and abdominal pain • Nausea and vomiting
Clostridium perfringens This is the bacterium that occurs naturally in the intestines of people and animals	• Diarrhoea and abdominal pain
Escherichia coli (E Coli) E coli is a bacterium that occurs naturally in the intestines of people and animals. Most types of E coli don't cause illness – some release toxins that contaminate food and water	• Stomach cramps and diarrhoea • Vomiting • Blood in faeces
Staphylococcus aureus This is a bacterium that is found in the nose and throat. It can produce toxins that contaminate food	• Diarrhoea and abdominal pain • Severe vomiting

 Case study

Erica Jordan is 18 years of age. She has just got a summer job working in the catering department of her local hospital. Erica's job is to plate up the food that patients order so that it can be put into heated trolleys and delivered to them on the wards. Erica is looking forward to getting paid for the work but isn't really taking the job seriously. In the first couple of days her supervisor told her off for not wearing a hat and gloves when working and for not washing her hands after handling raw meat. Today one of Erica's colleagues saw her using the same spoon to serve rice, then lamb curry and then sponge pudding. Erica put the serving spoon in her mouth between serving each dish.

- Identify two symptoms of food poisoning that can result from poor food hygiene practices.
- How might Erica's behaviour lead to food contamination?
- What should Erica do differently to minimise the risk of food contamination occurring?

Case study

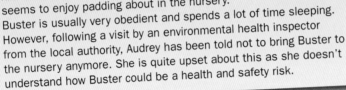

Audrey has been a volunteer nursery assistant at the Elim Pre-School group for two years. She works at the nursery every Tuesday and brings Buster her labrador dog with her. The children like Buster a lot and spend time patting and stroking him. Buster is very placid, used to children and seems to enjoy padding about in the nursery. Buster is usually very obedient and spends a lot of time sleeping. However, following a visit by an environmental health inspector from the local authority, Audrey has been told not to bring Buster to the nursery anymore. She is quite upset about this as she doesn't understand how Buster could be a health and safety risk.

- Identify reasons why Buster is a health and safety risk at the nursery.
- Explain how Buster's presence might lead to food hygiene problems at the nursery.
- Suggest how health and safety risks can be minimised to allow children to touch and play with pets.

Temperature control

The bacteria that cause food poisoning need food, warmth, moisture and time to grow. Maintaining correct food temperature is therefore an effective way of preventing food poisoning bacteria from growing. Bacteria do not grow below 5 degrees Celsius or above 63 degrees Celsius. Bacteria can grow and thrive in the danger zone between these points. As a result, basic temperature control rules are:

- keep hot food hot
- keep cold food cold
- keep prepared food out of the temperature danger zone.

Pest control

If food is badly stored or food preparation areas become infested with pests such as rats, mice or cockroaches, the risk of contamination and food poisoning rises considerably. Pests eat and spoil food and transfer bacteria to food. They should be kept away from food through safe storage and regular cleaning of food preparation areas. Unsafe and careless disposal of food waste attracts pests and creates additional infection risks.

Legislation and infection control

A number of different laws have been passed to try and promote good infection control. Some of these laws, such as the Health and Safety at Work Act 1974 place general duties and responsibilities on employers and employees that should result in the provision of safe and clean food preparation environments and good standards of food hygiene practice. The Reporting of Injuries, Diseases and Dangerous Occurrences Regulations (RIDDOR) 1995 is also designed to have a broad impact on the care workplace but covers infection control issues through the reporting of infectious illnesses and diseases. Laws that are specifically designed to promote food safety include:

- **The Food Safety Act 1990**
  This states that people working with food must practice good food hygiene in the workplace. Food provided for service

Investigate ...

The Food Standards Agency provides comprehensive and up to date information and advice on food hygiene through their eat well website (www.eatwell.gov.uk). You can find out about ways of preventing food poisoning by reading the Germ Watch section of the site.

users and visitors must be safely stored and prepared and must not be 'injurious to health'. Local authority environmental health officers enforce this law.

- **The Food Safety (General Food Hygiene) Regulations 1995**
This refers to the need to identify possible risks surrounding food hygiene and to put controls in place to ensure any risk is reduced. These regulations also specify how premises that provide food should be equipped and organised.

Chapter checklist

The box below provides a summary of the areas covered in chapter 16. Tick the areas that you feel you understand and would be confident answering exam questions about. If there are any areas that you don't understand or are not confident about, you will need to return to them before you begin your exam revision.

Basic infection control procedures
- Personal hygiene ☐
- Personal protective equipment ☐
- Hand-washing procedures ☐

Environmental hygiene
- Cleaning, disinfecting and sterilising ☐
- Dealing with spillages ☐
- Disposal of hazardous waste ☐
- Disposal of medication ☐

Vaccination and immunisation ☐

Reporting infection control problems ☐

Food safety and hygiene
- Hygiene control ☐
- Food poisoning ☐
- Temperature control ☐
- Pest control ☐

Legislation and infection control
- Health and Safety at Work Act 1974 ☐
- RIDDOR 1995 ☐
- The Food Safety Act 1990 ☐
- The Food Safety (General Food Hygiene) Regulations 1995 ☐

Knowledge Check

1. Why should care workers have an understanding of food hygiene principles?
2. Describe three methods of food contamination.
3. Explain how care workers who prepare food can reduce the risk of food contamination.
4. Describe the sources and symptoms of two forms of food poisoning.
5. What are the temperature control rules that care workers should be aware of?
6. Why is pest control vital in food preparation and serving areas of a care setting?

Assessment Guide

Your learning in this unit will be assessed through a one hour written examination taken online

The examination will consist of a series of short and longer answer questions covering all aspects of this unit. You will need to show that you understand:

- Basic infection control procedures.
- How infection can be minimised and dealt with in care settings through environmental hygiene methods.
- The role of vaccination and immunisation in reducing infection.
- The reporting of infectious diseases and conditions that occur in care settings.
- The principles of food safety and hygiene.
- Legislation affecting food hygiene and safety.

Chapter 16 provides full coverage of all of the topics you may be asked about in the examination.

Safeguarding and Protecting Individuals

Chapter 17

First aid practice

Key issue: How to use first aid to deal with minor injuries

Chapter 17 focuses on first aid. You need to know about basic first aid practices and the procedures first aiders use to respond to injuries and health emergencies that can occur in care settings. These will include:

● The principles of first aid
● The responsibilities of the first aider
● Casualty management and how to prioritise needs
● Information that should be given when calling the emergency services.

Chapter 17 looks at a number of situations that are classed as health emergencies. Studying them should help you to understand why immediate first aid is required in each situation. However, this does not mean that you would have the practical skills to provide first aid in any of these situations. If you wish to become a first aider, you will need to complete a practical first aid course in which you learn and demonstrate your ability to perform a range of practical skills under the supervision of a qualified first aid instructor.

The principles of first aid

First aid is urgent treatment given to an individual who has suffered a sudden injury or ill-health. There are a range of reasons why a service user, a visitor or a care practitioner may require first aid in a care setting. An individual may develop unexpected health problems or may become the victim of an accident, for example. The aims of first aid are to:

● preserve a casualty's life
● prevent further harm occurring to the casualty
● promote or support the process of recovery.

Situations in which first aid is required are best dealt with by people who have received appropriate training and who have up-to-date first aid skills. Ideally there should be a trained first aider on duty in every care setting. However, there are situations where there is no trained first aider on hand. In these situations it is helpful to be aware of the

basic response procedure that first aiders apply. This is summarised as the five-step 'DR ABC' procedure, that is:

- **D**anger – firstly, assess the situation, checking for any signs of continuing danger to yourself or the casualty and then call for help. If the situation is safe enough the next step is to check the casualty's response.

- **R**esponse – make contact with the casualty by gently shaking or touching them whilst speaking loudly to establish whether they are conscious. If the person does not respond, check their ABC immediately.

- **A**irway – check that there is no obstruction in the mouth or throat blocking the person's airway. The airway can become obstructed by the tongue or another object or food that hasn't been swallowed properly. If the airway is not cleared the person would be unable to breathe and would die.

- **B**reathing – check that the person is breathing freely. This is done by looking for chest movements, listening for breathing sounds and feeling for air by putting your cheek close to the casualty's mouth. If the casualty is breathing, putting them in the recovery position (see page 232) should keep their airway clear.

- **C**irculation – check that the person has a pulse. If the casualty has stopped breathing, they probably won't have a pulse. Where there is no sign of breathing or pulse, the first aider needs to perform a combination of chest compressions and rescue breaths. Breathing oxygen into the casualty's airway and then compressing the chest to pump it around the person's body can sometimes keep the person alive until the emergency services arrive.

Over to you!

Make a list of ten different first aid situations. Have you ever experienced any of these situations or helped out when a person required first aid? Make a note of the kinds of skills and personal qualities that you think a first aider needs to deal with accidents and unexpected health problems.

Over to you!

Why do you think it is vital to assess any accident situation for danger before trying to help the casualty? When might it be too dangerous or risky to intervene?

Figure 4.8 – 5 step DR ABC procedure.

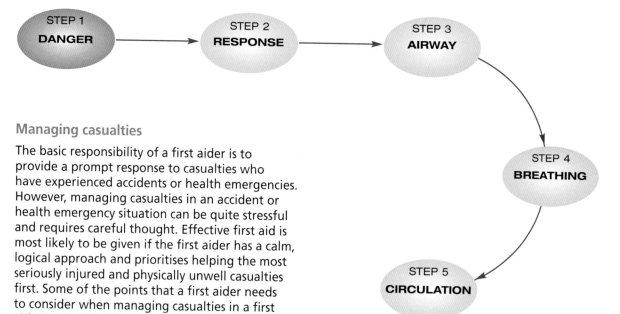

Managing casualties

The basic responsibility of a first aider is to provide a prompt response to casualties who have experienced accidents or health emergencies. However, managing casualties in an accident or health emergency situation can be quite stressful and requires careful thought. Effective first aid is most likely to be given if the first aider has a calm, logical approach and prioritises helping the most seriously injured and physically unwell casualties first. Some of the points that a first aider needs to consider when managing casualties in a first aid situation include:

- Initial observation of the casualties is the point at which the first aider should establish some priorities.

- If an accident or health emergency involves more than one casualty, first aiders are taught to respond to any unconscious casualties first.

- Checking any unconscious casualty's airway, breathing and circulation (ABC) is the first aider's main priority as the person will die if any of these vital body functions are absent.

- Conscious casualties who are unable to walk or move themselves are usually the next priority.

- A conscious casualty may be suffering from serious fractures, head injuries or have bleeding wounds that need immediate attention.

- A first aider should not move or lift an immobile casualty unless the person is in danger of experiencing further harm – such as being run over if they have collapsed into the road. Moving a person who is conscious but immobile can be dangerous if the person has unseen spinal injuries, fractures or open wounds.

- Where a casualty is bleeding, the first aider should do all they can to minimise the risk of cross-infection between themselves and the casualty. Where possible direct contact with open wounds and the casualty's blood should be avoided by using gloves if they are available in a first aid box and by covering cuts and wounds with appropriate dressings and bandages.

- If a casualty has some injuries or is confused or shaken by the accident but doesn't require immediate first aid it is the first aider's responsibility to arrange for them to be taken to hospital for further examination and possible treatment.

- A first aider should always remain with the casualty until help arrives. This ensures the safety of the casualty, provides reassurance and comfort especially if the person is shocked or in pain and allows the first aider to monitor the individual's condition in case this deteriorates.

Every first aider has a responsibility to act safely and within their skill level so that the casualty doesn't experience further harm or injury as a result of their intervention. Following the 'DR ABC' procedure (see above), assessing whether there are ongoing risks

Case study

Sian, aged 17, is standing by the side of the school playing fields with a couple of friends watching the Year 11 rugby team playing against another local school. Sian winces every time the players crash into each other when they make tackles. The game looks very aggressive and dangerous to Sian and her friends. Just as they agree that playing rugby must hurt, two players from the opposing team collide as they run for the ball. There is a loud crack as they bang heads and then fall down. One of the boys has blood running down his face and is groaning as he lies on the floor. The other boy is silent and completely still. The referee hasn't noticed what has happened and the game is continuing further up the field. Sian is trying to remember her recent lesson about first aid and the emergency response procedure.

- What should Sian do now?

- Which casualty should Sian go to first (explain why)?

- How could Sian check that the unconscious player is breathing?

to the casualty's health or safety and getting help from the emergency services are the kinds of immediate actions that help to preserve life, prevent further harm and promote recovery. If the person who responds first to an accident or health emergency isn't a trained first aider it is still possible for them to be helpful in an assisting role or by getting help for the casualty from designated first aiders or emergency services.

Calling emergency services

First aid situations are extremely varied. Some situations, such as when an individual falls and grazes or cuts their skin, are relatively minor. A competent first aider should be able to deal with minor injuries like these without calling for help. However, in other life threatening situations, such as when a person collapses into unconsciousness, the emergency services should be called as soon as possible. In care settings all care workers should know who to call for help and how to contact emergency services. In most instances the names and telephone numbers of designated first aiders are provided on posters or notice boards that are displayed prominently in public areas of the care setting. If a situation is serious, the care worker should either phone, or instruct somebody else to phone, 999 for an ambulance. The emergency operator who answers will ask the caller to give them the following kinds of information:

- which services they require (police, ambulance and/or fire service)
- their name and the number of the phone they are calling from
- the location of the accident or incident
- the number of casualties involved
- what has happened (including signs, symptoms and state of casualties)
- whether the casualty is conscious or not.

It is important for the caller to listen carefully to the emergency operator, to provide the information they ask for and to remain as calm as possible, even though this may be difficult in the circumstances.

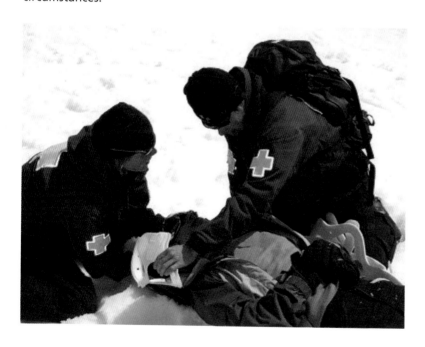

Case study

Daniel, aged 19, is walking home along Long Lane, a country road, late at night. He left a party about an hour ago because he wasn't feeling very well. As he rounds a bend about a mile away from his house, Daniel sees a small car that has gone off the road and which is now upside down in a ditch. The accident has happened about three hundred metres from Southdown Farm. There seem to be two people in the car, both are groaning but are unable to get out. Daniel can smell petrol but there is no fire.

- What should Daniel do now?
- What information should Daniel be able to give to the emergency operator?
- What are the risks to Daniel's health and safety in this situation and how can he reduce these risks?

Knowledge Check

1 List the three main aims of first aid.

2 Briefly explain, using the five-step DR ABC approach what a first aider should do when they arrive at the scene of an accident.

3 Why is it vital to check the airway of an unconscious casualty as quickly as possible?

4 Explain why moving an unconscious casualty might be a dangerous thing to do.

5 How can a first aider minimise the risk of cross-infection when they are dealing with a casualty who is bleeding?

6 List the kinds of information that an emergency call handler (999 operator) is likely to ask a caller for.

Investigate ...

Find out about work roles in the emergency services – such as paramedics, emergency services call handler and emergency medical practitioner – and watch the video called 'ramp' about a skateboarding accident at the Step into the NHS website (www.stepintothenhs.nhs.uk).

Common first aid situations

We have already covered the basic response procedure that first aiders use when dealing with accidents or health emergencies. Ensuring safety, obtaining help and assessing and supporting casualties immediately are all important parts of the first aider's role in any emergency situation. However, there are also times when a first aider is required to carry out first aid interventions to help a casualty who has suffered injuries or whose life may be in danger. The following explanations aim to make you more aware of what a first aider is likely to do in different types of emergency situations. You should not attempt to carry out any of the procedures described until you have completed a recognised first-aid course with a fully qualified first aid assessor. It is important that you accept the limitations of your own ability in this area and do not try to act beyond your level of competence in treating other people's injuries.

Once you have studied and understood the section that follows, you should be able to recognise the key signs of a number of common health emergencies and know how to carry out procedures for dealing with them. These health emergencies are:

- burns and scalds

Over to you!

What might be the consequences if an untrained and inexperienced person tries to perform first aid in an accident or emergency situation?

- wounds and bleeding
- fractures relating to limbs and body
- loss of consciousness
- breathing difficulties caused by conditions such as asthma and anaphylactic shock.

Burns and scalds

A burn happens when a person experiences tissue damage due to dry heat. A scald also results in tissue damage but the cause is wet heat, such as very hot water or chemicals. Burns and scalds damage the blood vessels that lie below the skin as well as the skin itself. When this occurs, a colourless fluid contained in the blood called plasma leaks out. A large burn or scald can result in significant blood and plasma loss and will cause the person to go into shock.

Older and very young people have very sensitive skin that is particularly susceptible to burns and scalds. Hot baths and showers, kettle steam, hot drinks and sitting too close to a heat source can cause accidental burns to the skin of the infants and older people. The signs and symptoms of burns depend on their severity:

- First-degree burns to the top layer of skin produce a patch of redness, swelling and pain.
- Second-degree burns damage the layers of skin beneath the surface and produce blisters, pain and redness.
- Third-degree burns are the most damaging kind as they damage the different layers of skin and the tissue underneath. The area affected can look waxy white, leathery brown or charred.

The aims of first aid treatment for burns and scalds are to prevent shock, avoid infection and relieve pain. Immediate first aid for burns and scalds involves:

- Cooling the affected area with water for at least 10 minutes and for 20 minutes if the burn is a chemical burn. This helps to reduce the pain and stops plasma loss by closing damaged blood vessels.
- If the burn or scald is severe (second or third-degree), dial 999 for an ambulance as soon as possible.
- Making the casualty as comfortable as you can, encouraging them to lie down if possible. Monitor the person for signs of shock (see below).
- Wearing disposable, protective gloves remove any jewellery, watch or clothing in the burn area, unless the person's skin is already sticking to it.
- Removing clothing that has been burnt onto the skin as this is sterile and will protect against infection.
- If the burnt or scalded area of skin is exposed, cover it gently with a clean, non-fluffy material – such as a lint free dressing, cloth, plastic bag or kitchen film as this will help to protect it against infection.

When treating burns and scalds it is important not to apply any lotions, ointments or creams to the skin. First aiders also know that they shouldn't use adhesive dressings or break any blisters that develop. Running water is the only cleaning and cooling solution that should be used. Any burn that is larger than a postage stamp or deeper than a ten pence piece must be seen and treated by an expert burns practitioner.

Wounds and bleeding

A wound is a break in the surface of the skin. Cuts, grazes, puncture wounds and lacerations to the body, or the opening of surgical wounds, can result in anything from a trickle of blood to more significant and dangerous bleeding where blood is flowing or spurting out. Fast flowing or spurting bleeding occurs because the blood is being lost from an artery and is being pumped by the heart at high pressure. This kind of blood loss must be stopped very quickly. Cuts or wounds that result in bleeding from veins and tissues can still be alarming and should also be dealt with quickly but are not as dangerous.

External wounds and bleeding are usually quite obvious, though a person's clothes can sometimes hide their injuries. In addition to the signs of blood, an individual who is bleeding may also:

Basic wound care.

- feel faint and dizzy
- look pale in the face and around the lips
- develop cold, clammy skin
- feel thirsty
- start to breathe more quickly but in a shallow way, perhaps gasping for air
- have a weak, rapid pulse.

A person who has internal bleeding will also display many of the symptoms above, though there will be no obvious signs of bleeding.

The aim of first aid when a casualty is losing blood or is suspected of having internal bleeding is to limit the loss of blood from the casualty's circulatory system. The first aider should do the following:

- Summon help and get a first-aid kit as soon as possible. If possible they should wear disposable gloves to avoid contact with the casualty's blood.
- Lie the casualty down as they may faint and it will be easier to elevate their wounds from this position.
- On an external wound the immediate first aid is to apply direct pressure to the wound, unless there is an object embedded in the wound.
- If there is an object in the wound, pressure should be applied either side of it. The object should not be removed as it may be acting as a plug that prevents further bleeding.
- A dressing should be applied to an external wound where there is no object embedded in it.
- To minimise the risk of infection, the first aider should either wear protective gloves or ask the person to apply pressure with their own hand to the top of an external wound.
- If possible, the wound should then be raised so that it is physically above the casualty's heart. This will help to reduce the blood flow to the area and will slow down blood loss.

Case study

Bill Williams, aged 71, is always keen to help friends and neighbours with their gardens. He has a lot of experience and a shed full of gardening tools at his disposal. Adam, Bill's next door neighbour asked Bill whether he could trim the higher part of the garden hedge for him. Bill pointed out that a step ladder and some assistance would be needed but he could certainly do it. In fact, he was free at that moment so he suggested that he and Adam could do it straight away. The accident happened when Bill tripped over the step up to Adam's front door. Bill was holding a pair of hedge trimmers in one hand and had a step ladder under the other arm. In his hurry to get into Adam'a house, Bill caught his foot on the step and pitched forward. His head hit the door handle quite hard, causing him to fall to his knees and cry out. Adam noticed a cut on the top of Bill's head that was bleeding a lot.

- What should Adam do first in order to help Bill?

- Describe how Adam should deal with the bleeding from the wound on Bill's head.

- How could Adam minimise the risk of cross-infection between himself and Bill?

- The casualty should also be monitored and treated for shock (see below).

- The casualty should then be taken for further emergency aid as necessary.

If the person is suspected of having internal bleeding, the following first aid actions are appropriate whilst waiting for emergency services to arrive:

- Lie the casualty down and raise their legs slightly but avoid moving the casualty otherwise.

- Offer reassurance and ask about areas of pain.

- Loosen any tight clothing but also protect the person from getting cold.

- Check the person's pulse and respiration every 10 minutes.

- Do not give the person anything to eat or drink as further treatment may be required.

- Monitor and treat the person for signs of shock.

If the casualty has lost a limb, finger or toe in the accident, the amputated body part should be wrapped in plastic then padding and kept as cold as possible. It may be possible for a surgeon to reattach it later if the blood vessels are preserved as a result of swift action.

Shock

First aiders are taught to treat accident casualties for **physiological shock** if they have suffered burns, scalds or bleeding. Shock occurs when a person's store of oxygen and their blood supply are redirected to their essential internal organs by their body. In severe cases of shock the blood supply to some organs can stop. The signs and symptoms of someone who is in shock are that they become pale, cold and clammy. They will also have a fast pulse that could be weak, they will feel cold and may complain of feeling extremely thirsty. Shock is dangerous but can be prevented and managed. A first aider who suspects a casualty is going in to shock should:

- Lay the person down and then place their legs in an elevated position (if possible). This will assist blood flow to their internal organs.

- Keep the person warm with blankets or clothing but not give them anything to eat or drink as they may need further emergency treatment.

- Continue to observe and monitor the person, checking their ABC and responses.

- Reassure the casualty until help arrives.

Fractures relating to limbs and body

Fractures are broken bones. They tend to occur more easily in older people than in children or younger adults because a person's bones become less dense as they grow older. An older person's bones may also be affected by osteoporosis, arthritis and general wear and tear due to the ageing process.

The signs and symptoms of fractures are:

- Swelling, pain and difficulty with movement in a limb or another area of the body

- The sound of an obvious snapping noise if you are present when the fracture occurs

- Bone protruding through the skin, together with bleeding, where the limb has fractured and torn open the skin

- A person's limb becomes floppy, lacks power or is held at a bizarre angle

- If the individual is very pale and clammy they may also be in shock.

A first aider needs to respond quickly but carefully to any incident where a casualty experiences a fracture. The aim of first aid in fracture situations is to stabilise the situation, minimise pain and possible infection and prevent further injuries from occurring to the casualty. A first aider who responds to a fracture situation should:

- First make an initial assessment using the emergency response procedure and avoid moving the casualty unless this is absolutely necessary for their safety.

- Provide comfort and reassurance for the casualty.

- Request help from emergency services if the person has broken a leg, arm or is unable to move themselves.

- Steady and support the injured limb to stop further movement that might cause tissue, ligament or nerve damage.

- If the casualty is bleeding, press a clean dressing over the wound and then bandage on and around the wound to stop blood loss.

- If the person has a broken leg, put padding between their knees and ankles and bandage their good leg to their bad leg at the knees and ankles. Anything that is soft, including pillows, rolled up blankets, coats and clothing are all suitable forms of padding. This will form a splint that will immobilise the broken leg.

- If the person has a broken arm, improvise a sling to keep the injured arm supported and close to the body.

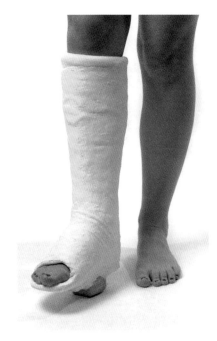

Fractures require specialist treatment.

Case study

Lizzie Birch is an 84-year-old lady living in residential home. Lately she has become confused at night and is also prone to falls if she gets out of bed. Kelly, one of the night staff, saw that Lizzie was quite restless just after midnight. She also noted that cot sides have been put on Lizzie's bed but are not in use. When she asked about this Kelly was told that the cot sides have been left down in case Lizzie tries to climbs over them in a confused, sleepy state. During the night a crashing sound is heard from Lizzie's room. Kelly, who is also a first aider, arrived first to find Lizzie lying on the floor with her left leg at an unusual angle to her body. Lizzie was also moaning in pain and indicated that she could not move to get up. At this point Kelly saw that Lizzie had turned very pale and was cold and clammy to touch.

- Referring to signs and symptoms, identify the health emergencies that Kelly should respond to here.

- Putting your points in priority order, describe the main actions Kelly should take to provide first aid for Lizzie in the situation described.

- What could go wrong if Kelly tries to lift or pull Lizzie to her feet?

- Monitor the casualty for signs of shock and stay with them until help arrives. If the person becomes unconscious, check their ABC and follow the resuscitation sequence (see DR ABC above) if any further problems occur.

- Do not give the casualty anything to eat or drink in case they require further treatment in hospital.

Loss of consciousness

Loss of consciousness can occur for many reasons. Whatever the cause, a first aider should follow the emergency response procedure. After assessing danger and seeking a response from the casualty, the first aider should carry out an initial assessment of the person's ABC (airway, breathing, circulation).

If the person is not breathing it is vital that the first aider either calls or asks someone else to call an emergency ambulance. The casualty must be given artificial ventilation quickly. If the first aider is trained to do this and the situation is safe, they should proceed to administer rescue breaths and chest compressions

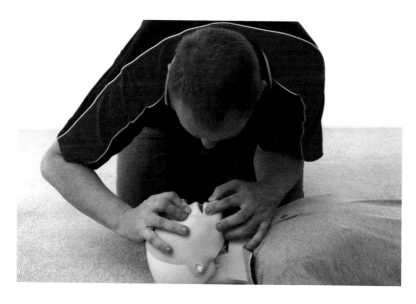

Preparing to give rescue breaths.

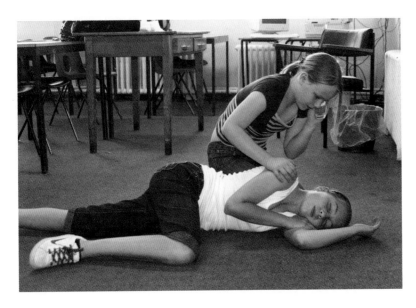

The recovery position.

immediately. The casualty's brain function will begin to deteriorate without oxygen after three minutes and their other organs will also be affected. Delays in treatment can lead to death.

If the unconscious person is breathing, they should be placed in the recovery position.

The recovery position is used to prevent a casualty from choking through airway obstruction However, if the first aider suspects that the casualty also has a head, neck or back injury they should not be moved unless there is a risk they might otherwise choke.

Breathing difficulties

Adults usually take between fourteen and sixteen breaths (respirations) per minute. Infants and children have a faster breathing rate than this. Infants under one year of age typically take between thirty and sixty breaths per minute whilst a six-year-old could normally take between eighteen and thirty breaths. Where a person is breathing normally their skin will look fresh and oxygenated and the correct colour for that person. The person's chest should move evenly and rhythmically and there should be no wheezing or excess noise from breathing.

The human airway starts at the nose and throat and ends in the lungs. If the airway is blocked, by mucus, vomit, swelling, foreign objects or by the tongue relaxing against the back of the throat, for example, the person will be unable to breathe and their lungs will be starved of oxygen. An individual in this situation is likely to die in a matter of minutes.

If a person's airway is blocked they will choke. As a result they are likely to have difficulty in speaking and breathing and may also be coughing or spluttering. In severe cases of choking the casualty may turn a blue-grey colour (drained of their usual skin colour) because an obstruction in their airway is preventing them from obtaining oxygen. This can lead to loss of consciousness. The first aid for choking is to:

- Reassure the casualty.
- Sit them down leaning forward.

Case study

Charisa Symons, aged 30, had decided to take her two-year old twins, Alistair and Jamie, to visit her sister Lana who lived about 200 miles away. Charisa had made sure that the twins were safely strapped into car seats and that they had a book to look at as she drove along. Because the traffic was slow, Charisa pulled over to give the children a drink and some pieces of apple to eat. When she strapped them back into the car seats and started driving again she didn't realize that Alistair still had a piece of apple in his hand. He put this into his mouth but couldn't swallow it. Charisa noticed that Alistair had gone quiet and that he looked grey in the face. She then realized that he was choking on the piece of apple and immediately stopped the car by the side of the road.

- Bearing in mind the DR ABC procedure, what do you think Charisa should do now?

- Describe the signs and symptoms of choking.

- What first aid procedures should Charisa use to help Alistair?

- Instruct the casualty to cough hard to remove any blockage from their airway.

- If this fails, the first aider should give up to five sharp slaps between the person's shoulder blades with the flat part of their hand whilst taking care to support the person's head.

The procedure should stop as soon as the obstruction is cleared. If the back slaps fail to clear the obstruction, five abdominal thrusts (the Heimlich manoeuvre) should be given and the procedure repeated until help arrives. If the person becomes unconscious the first aider may have to attempt to give artificial ventilation.

Dealing with an asthma attack

Asthma is an allergic response to **allergens** that cause irritation and inflammation in the bronchi or large air passages in the lungs). The bronchi become obstructed with mucous and the inflammatory response that occurs is a result of these irritants. Usually a person's bronchial inhalers will help to reduce swelling and when the allergens (such as dust, animal hair, pollens or aerosols) are no longer present the casualty should recover.

Where a person's inhaler has little or no effect, a first aider should summon help immediately. The person should be asked to sit leaning forward, preferably with their arms and upper body supported against a table and/or a pillow. They must be given plenty of space so that they do not feel overcrowded. The first aider should try to identify the allergen and ensure that it is not

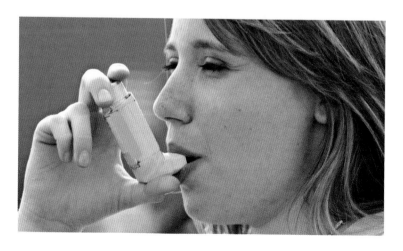

Using a bronchial inhaler.

within the vicinity of the casualty. It may be a good idea to open a window or to guide the person to a different room if they are able to walk there. The first aider can also help the person to use their inhalers whilst waiting for assistance to arrive. If the person becomes unconscious then the ABC procedures will become a priority and the casualty will need to be dealt with accordingly.

Dealing with anaphylactic shock

Anaphylaxis is a sudden, allergic reaction to allergens. Anaphylactic shock occurs when the body responds to an allergen (such as a bee sting or nuts) by releasing chemicals that cause a drop in blood pressure and constriction or narrowing of the airways causing wheezing, breathing difficulties and abdominal pain. The initial sign of anaphylactic shock is swelling and itching in the area where the allergen has entered the body. This might be on the arm if it is a bee sting or in the throat if it is food-based. Shortly afterwards a raised, itchy rash spreads across the body, the person's face and soft tissues begin to swell and breathing becomes difficult. It is likely that the person will become very agitated and may then collapse into unconsciousness as their blood pressure drops suddenly.

Emergency treatment with an injection of adrenaline is necessary to relieve the tissue swelling that is causing the person breathing difficulties. Many people who are aware that they are at risk of anaphylaxis because of an allergy carry pre-loaded adrenaline auto-injectors that may be referred to as an 'EpiPen'. If they are able to give themselves or are given an adrenaline injection in their thigh muscle promptly most people recover from anaphylactic shock. However, anybody who has had an anaphylactic reaction should go to hospital for examination and observation as they may need further treatment when the adrenaline injection wears off.

First aid and the law

Care practitioners and their employers are required to understand and put into practice the Health and Safety (First Aid) Regulations 1981 in the setting where they provide care services. These regulations require employers to:

- carry out risk assessments to identify the level of first aid provision required
- provide appropriate first aid equipment and facilities
- train and appoint staff to give first aid should employees get injured or fall ill at work
- have an effective means of recording accidents or incidents that require first aid intervention.

The types of first aid equipment needed, the number of first aiders required and the precise contents of first aid boxes are not specified by the regulations. Instead, care organisations have to decide what is adequate in relation to the circumstances of their care settings. Risk assessments and assessments of first aid needs that take into account workplace hazards, the size of the care setting and the vulnerabilities of people who spend time there as service users, visitors and staff are conducted to work this out.

Knowledge Check

1 Identify four different types of health emergencies where first aid might be required.

2 What is the difference between a burn and a scald?

3 Outline the first aid that should be provided to a person who experiences a burn or a scald.

4 What should a first aider do if they are called to see a casualty who has a bleeding arm wound with a large piece of glass embedded in it?

5 What is physiological shock and how would you know if a person is suffering from it?

6 Identify three signs or symptoms of a fracture?

7 When should an unconscious person be placed in the recovery position?

8 What is the first aid procedure when a person is choking and unable to breathe?

9 Describe the causes, symptoms and first aid for anaphylactic shock.

The first aid box

All employees should know the location of, and have access to, a first aid box in their workplace. Ideally the employer should appoint a trained first aider to check and replenish the various items contained in the first aid box on a regular basis. Many of the items have 'best before' dates on them and should be replaced within these time limits. So, what should a first aid box contain? There is no legal or mandatory list of contents. The employer's assessment of first aid needs should determine what each box contains. However, in practical terms, the Health and Safety Executive advises that each first aid box should contain:

- a leaflet giving guidance on first aid
- twenty individually wrapped sterile adhesive dressings (assorted sizes)
- two sterile eye pads
- four individually wrapped triangular bandages (preferably sterile)
- six safety pins
- six medium-sized (approx 12cm x 12cm) individually wrapped unmedicated wound dressings
- one pair of disposable gloves.

Scissors, sachets or a container of normal saline (0.9%) and adhesive tape are often also part of first aid boxes.

A workplace first aid kit.

First aid, incident reporting and record-keeping

The Health and Safety Executive recommends that employers should provide appointed first aiders with a book in which to record any accidents, incidents or health emergencies in which first aid intervention was required. The purpose of this is to help the employer and the appointed first aiders to identify trends that might point to a need for better control and management of health and safety risks. This record also provides useful information for future assessments of first aid needs. Useful information that might be recorded in the first aid book includes:

- the date, time and place of an incident
- the name and job of the injured or unwell person
- details of the injuries or illness and any first aid provided
- what happened to the person immediately after being given first aid – went home, went back to work, went to hospital, for example
- the name and signature of the first aider or the person who dealt with the incident.

In practice, a designated first aider or another appointed person usually takes responsibility for looking after the first aid book though it is the employers overall responsibility to ensure that efficient and accurate record-keeping is carried out. Whilst the Health and Safety Executive only advises employers to provide a first aid book or record-keeping system, there is a legal requirement to report accidents and ill-health at work under the Reporting of Injuries, Disease and Dangerous Occurrences Regulations (RIDDOR) 1995.

Knowledge Check

1 What responsibilities do the Health and Safety (First Aid) Regulations 1981 impose on care organisations?

2 Describe the kinds of items that should be in the first aid boxes that are provided in care settings.

3 Why is it helpful to make a record of all accidents and incidents that occur in a care setting requiring first aid assistance?

4 What kinds of information about first aid incidents should be recorded?

Chapter Checklist

The box below provides a summary of the areas covered in chapter 17. Tick the areas that you feel you understand and would be confident answering exam questions about. If there are any areas that you don't understand or are not confident about, you will need to return to them before you begin your exam revision.

The principles of first aid ☐

The five-step 'DR ABC' procedure ☐

Managing casualties in emergency situations ☐

Calling emergency services ☐

Common first aid situations
    Burns and scalds ☐
    Wounds and bleeding ☐
    Physiological shock ☐
    Fractures ☐
    Loss of consciousness ☐
    Breathing difficulties ☐
    Asthma attack ☐
    Anaphylactic shock ☐

Legislation relating to first aid ☐

Contents of the first aid box ☐

First aid incident reporting ☐

Assessment Guide

Your learning in this unit will be assessed through a one hour written examination.

The examination will consist of a series of short and longer answer questions covering all aspects of this unit. You will need to show that you understand:

● The principles of first aid

● How first aiders respond to emergency situations and manage casualties

● How to provide information to emergency services

● The signs and symptoms of a range of common health emergencies

● The basic first aid response for common health emergencies

● Legislation affecting first aid provision

● The expected contents of a first aid box

● First aid incident reporting requirements.

Chapter 17 provides full coverage of all of the topics you may be asked about in the examination.

Chapter 18

Recognising and reducing potential risks to safety

Key issue: How to recognise potential risks to people who use services and care workers and how to provide protection for those using the setting

The final chapter in this unit focuses on identifying and reducing risks to health and safety in care settings. You need to understand the importance of identifying:

- A range of potential risks that can occur in care settings
- The places in a care setting where these potential risks often occur
- The possible consequences of each type of risk.

Chapter 18 also explores how safety features could help to reduce the various risks, how to follow safety procedures and how to use safety equipment. Conducting risk assessments, knowing and following health and safety laws and regulations and implementing security procedures all help to reduce the risks people face in care settings.

Hazards and risks to health and safety in care settings

Health, social care and early years services are provided in a range of settings that include:

- service users' homes
- residential and nursing homes
- day care centres
- nurseries
- community-based surgeries and health centres
- schools
- hospitals
- hospices.

Every care setting has its own combination of physical characteristics and care facilities. Bedrooms, bathrooms, kitchens, corridors, stairs, recreational rooms, gardens, and perhaps lifts, are familiar features of care settings. Specialist care settings may also have clinical and treatment rooms or other less common facilities. All of these facilities, and the work that goes on in a care setting, should enable care practitioners to provide high-quality care for individuals. However, despite having such positive potential, care settings are also places that contain hazards and potential health and safety risks.

Working in any environment that has people, equipment, illness, disease and disability and a lot of work pressures can be risky! One of the golden rules of care work is that the health and safety of service users, colleagues and anybody else present in a care setting should be paramount. As a result, awareness of health and safety issues and principles is a basic competence required of all care practitioners.

Risks and hazards in care settings

Health and safety in care settings is generally achieved through preventive measures such as risk assessment, safe care practice and the correct use of safety systems and procedures. Hazards and risks to health and safety can arise from several different sources (see figure 4.9).

A hazard is anything that can cause harm. Hazards in care settings include:

- *Faulty electrical appliances*, switches, overloaded sockets, frayed flexes, power surges. All can lead to fires, burns and electrical shocks, for example

- *Faulty gas appliances and gas leaks* can lead to fires, explosions, breathing difficulties, unconsciousness and asphyxiation

- *Water leaks* result in wet floors, walls and carpets as well as rotten floorboards. All of these things cause accidents and injuries if people slip or trip. If there is contact between water and electricity there is also a danger of electrocution.

- *Kitchen hazards* include sharp knives, cooking appliances, pot handles hanging over the edge of the cooker, slippery floors, contaminated food.

- *Living room and bedroom hazards* include worn or badly fitted carpets, loose rugs, poorly placed furniture, floor length curtains, clothes or bed linen left on the floor, trailing flexes, poor lighting, electrical appliances, fires without guards

- *Bathroom hazards* include hot water, wet slippery surfaces and floors, electrical items near water

- *Stairs* are hazardous if they lack hand rails, are steep or have poorly fitted, loose carpets.

- *Working areas* that are cramped and draughty with poor lighting.

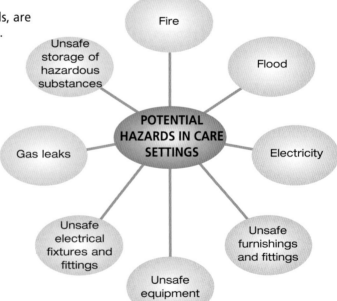

Figure 4.9 – Potential hazards in care settings.

A **risk** is the chance of harm being done by a hazard. **Risk assessment** is the process of evaluating the likelihood of a hazard actually causing harm. The areas in care settings where risks are often highest are:

- community rooms and lounges
- bedrooms
- kitchens
- community areas such as halls, entrance areas and stairs
- play areas (inside and outside)
- bathrooms.

Fire hazards and evacuation procedures

There may be a number of different fire hazards in a care setting, including:

- faulty electrical and gas appliances, gas leaks and open fires
- blocked fire exits and escape routes
- fire alarms that don't work or which people can't hear
- unsafe, loose or flammable furnishings (these must now be fire resistant)
- people smoking cigarettes, cigars or pipes indoors or using lighters and matches.

Every care setting should have a fire policy and an evacuation procedure. There should also be a range of safety features including marked fire exits, smoke alarms and no smoking signs within the building. Primary and secondary care workers usually receive basic fire safety training as part of their induction when they start their job. It is in everybody's interests that people working in a care setting are familiar with the fire policies, procedures and equipment in case of a fire or gas emergency.

Fires and gas leaks are very dangerous though it is very rare for a hospital or care home to have to evacuate in-patients or residents. However, all care settings should prepare for this unlikely possibility by developing a fire policy and practicing an evacuation procedure. Fire procedures tend to include the following kinds of advice:

- Alert people in the immediate area – shout 'Fire' and/or activate the alarm system.
- Call the fire service on 999.
- Remove people from immediate danger to a nearby area or external evacuation area.
- Close doors and windows as you leave to contain the fire.
- Use designated fire exits, closing doors behind you – and never use lifts.
- If evacuation is needed, gather people at the designated assembly point and tell them not to return until instructed to do so.
- Carry out a head count to check that everyone is accounted for.
- Only if it is safe and you feel capable, try to tackle the fire with safety equipment available. This could be a fire blanket or extinguishers. You need to use the correct type of extinguisher to tackle a fire safely (see figure 4.10). However, never take a risk with your own or other people's life.

An example of fire safety equipment.

Figure 4.10 Types of fire extinguisher.

Extinguisher	Type	Colour	Uses	Not to be used
Electrical fire	Dry powder	Blue marking	Burning liquids Electrical fires	Flammable metal fires
	Carbon dioxide	Black marking	Electrical fires Burning liquids Flammable liquids	
	Vapourising liquid	Green marking	Electrical fires Burning liquids Flammable liquids	
Non-electrical fire	Water	Red marking	Wood, paper, textiles, fabric	Burning liquid Electrical fire
	Foam	Cream / yellow	Burning liquid	Electrical or flammable metal

Gas leaks are also rare but dangerous events in care settings. The health and safety policies of a care organisation should provide details of what to do in the event of a gas leak occurring. Gas leak procedures tend to include the following kinds of advice:

- If gas is smelled, check that all gas appliances are switched off.
- Open doors and windows for ventilation.
- Don't use matches or lighters or switch on electrical appliances that might spark and cause an explosion and fire.
- Evacuate the area as quickly as possible.
- Phone the fire service and the gas emergency number from outside the building.
- Switch off the gas mains if this can be done from outside of the building.

Unsafe equipment

Care practitioners use a range of equipment to make their work easier. For example, they use hoists, bath boards, wheelchairs and electronically operated beds in order to take some of the physical strain out of moving service users. Personal protective equipment such as aprons, gloves and masks are also examples of health and safety equipment.

The equipment used by care practitioners needs to be in good condition and should only be used by people who have received appropriate training. Examples of equipment hazards that present health and safety risks to individuals and care practitioners include:

- mobility aids that are the wrong size or which do not work properly
- faulty or damaged lifting equipment
- brakes and hydraulics on beds that do not work properly
- computer display screens and keyboards that are badly located, poorly serviced or over-used
- blades and syringe needles that are stored or disposed of incorrectly
- unlabelled, incorrectly labelled or leaking bottles and containers

- old and faulty electrical and gas-fuelled appliances
- excessively full or faulty waste disposal equipment.

Care practitioners should always check the equipment that they intend to use to ensure it is safe and free of hazards. They should not use equipment that is faulty or which they have not been trained to use. Faulty, unsafe equipment should be reported and removed from the care setting.

Unsafe storage of hazardous substances

A range of substances that are potentially hazardous to health are present in care settings. These include various cleaning agents, such as disinfectants and detergents, medicines, art and craft materials (paints, glues and clay, for example) and sterilising fluids. Substances can be hazardous because they are toxic (poisonous), corrosive (burning) or irritants. Hazard symbols should be printed on bottles, packets and canisters to indicate the kinds of dangers they pose.

The Control of Substances Hazardous to Health (COSHH) Regulations 2005 state that all hazardous substances must be correctly handled and stored to minimise the risks they present. The COSHH file that must be kept in each care setting provides details of:

- the hazardous substances that are present
- where they are stored
- how they should be handled
- how any spillage or accident involving them should be dealt with.

Knowledge Check

1 What do the terms 'hazard' and 'risk' mean?

2 Identify three types of hazard that are present in care settings.

3 Describe three types of health and safety hazard that might be found in a care home kitchen.

4 Explain why loose carpets and rugs are a health and safety hazard in a care home for older people.

5 Identify three different fire hazards that could be found in a care setting.

6 Outline the kind of advice that is likely to be included in the fire procedure of a care setting.

7 If a small non-electrical fire started in the kitchen of a care home, which type and colour of fire extinguisher could be used to tackle it?

8 Give three examples of unsafe equipment that would present health and safety hazards in a care setting.

9 Identify three different types of hazardous substances that can often be found in care settings.

10 Explain why hazardous substances have to be handled and stored correctly.

Risk assessment

Care organisations are, by law, required to carry out formal risk assessments of their care settings. **Risk assessment** aims to identify potential risks to the health, safety and security of care practitioners, service users and visitors to a care setting. Risk assessment recognises that a range of care activities, equipment and the way a care setting is organised can be hazardous but that steps can be taken to minimise or remove the risk of people experiencing harm. The ultimate aim of a risk assessment is to ensure that people use care settings without coming to any harm. The Health and Safety Executive has identified five stages of a risk assessment. These stages and their purpose are identified in figure 4.11.

Figure 4.11 The stages of risk assessment.

Stage	Key questions	Purpose
1. Look for hazards	● What are the hazards?	● To identify all hazards
2. Assess who may be harmed	● Who is at risk?	● To evaluate the risk of hazards causing harm
3. Consider the risk – whether existing precautions are adequate	● What needs to be done? ● Who needs to do what?	● To evaluate risk control measures ● To identify risk control responsibilities
4. Document the findings	● A summary of the hazards and risks	● To record all findings and the risk control plan
5. Review the assessment and revise if necessary	● Is risk controlled? ● Are further controls needed?	● To monitor and maintain an accurate and up to date risk control system

The Management of Health and Safety at Work Regulations 1999 place a legal duty on employers to carry out risk assessments in order to ensure a safe and healthy workplace. The risk assessments that are produced should clearly identify:

● The potential hazards and risks to the health and safety of employees and others in the workplace

● Any preventive and protective measures that are needed to minimise risk and improve health and safety

Care practitioners can also carry out their own ongoing risk assessments in their everyday work. Basically this involves:

● being alert to possible hazards

● understanding the risks associated with each hazard

● reporting any health and safety concerns that are identified.

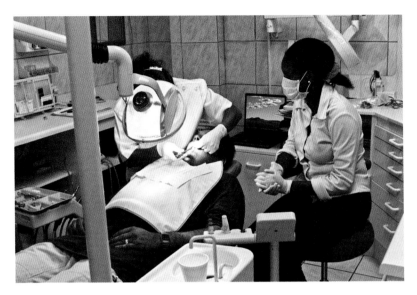

Risk areas that need to be assessed and planned for by care practitioners as part of their everyday work include risks associated with:

- moving and handling service users and equipment
- hazardous chemicals (such as cleaning fluids, disinfectants and sterilising fluids)
- medicines
- infection control
- personal security.

Security in care settings

Personal safety and security at work are increasingly becoming issues for care workers. Care settings are typically thought to be safe environments where people are cared for and not harmed. However, because of the threat of intruders and of increasing levels of violence and aggression towards care workers, the security of buildings and personnel need to be taken very seriously. In most care settings security provisions are designed to protect:

- personal safety
- property
- personal details and confidentiality
- service users from leaving buildings unless it is safe for them to do so.

There are two different types of security breach in care settings – external and internal security breaches. External security is breached when an unauthorized person gets into a care setting. Care organisations use a variety of methods to minimise the risk of external security breaches including:

- Developing security and incident policies and procedures and training staff to follow and apply them
- Having security guards and receptionists who check the identification of everybody entering a care setting
- Using identity card systems

Over to you!

Using a scale of 1–5 where 1 is the highest risk and 5 is the lowest risk, identify the main hazard in each of the following situations, estimate the risk and then briefly describe how the risk could be minimised.

- The playgroup kitchen floor has just been washed and is still wet
- A laundry bag half full of dirty linen has been left at the top of the stairs outside a hospital ward
- An elderly resident's window has been left wide open to air her room in a nursing home
- The scissors have been left out on the craft room table at the learning disability day centre
- A workman fitting a new security pad to the front door of the nursery has left the door wide open and unattended whilst he goes to his van for some tools.

- Fitting CCTV to monitor entrances, exits and corridors in care settings
- Fitting electronic code pads on doors, window guards and high level door handles to combat unauthorized entry risks.

Care practitioners can help to maintain high standards of security by:

- understanding the security and incident policies and procedures that apply in the care setting
- knowing how to operate any alarms or security systems that are provided
- wearing an identification badge and carrying any alarms that are provided for security purposes
- asking visitors to identify themselves and show some official identification badge or letter before letting them into the care setting
- locking doors and windows that are supposed to be locked for security purposes
- letting people know where they are and what they will be doing. This is especially important for care practitioners who work alone and visit people at home
- signing in and out of work if the care setting uses a sign-in book for employees.

CCTV is used in larger care organisations.

Care practitioners also need to remind service users living at home that they should never let unknown callers in. It is always important to check the identity of callers whilst using a security chain across the door in case they are bogus and pretending to be the Police or maintenance people, for example.

Inadequate security in a care setting puts the health and safety of everybody present at risk. The Health and Safety at Work Act 1974 places a duty on workers to take care of their own security, the security of others and to report security hazards to managers.

Internal security breaches are more difficult to spot than external breaches. They tend to involve the theft of money or belongings from service users or staff members or the theft of confidential information from service users' files or the care organisations computer systems. Service users' money should always be protected by a record-keeping system and shouldn't be held in large amounts on the premises. Care organisations generally have internal procedures for checking, recording and storing money and valuables. The marking of clothes and other possessions is also helpful to protect against theft.

Knowledge Check

1 What is the main purpose of a risk assessment?

2 Describe the five main stages of a risk assessment.

3 What can care practitioners do to make their work with service users as safe as possible?

4 What happens when there is an external security breach in a care setting?

5 Identify five different ways in which care organisations try to protect the security of staff and service users.

Health and safety legislation

The health and safety responsibilities of employers and employees result from the wide range of legislation that governs health and safety in workplaces generally. A number of laws also exist covering health and safety issues that are specific to care settings. Legislation is necessary to ensure that safe working practices are followed when caring for individuals and to protect the care practitioner.

The Health and Safety at Work Act 1974

This is the main piece of health and safety law in the UK. It affects both employers and employees. Under this Act, care practitioners share responsibility for health and safety in care settings with the care organisation that employs them. The care organisation is responsible for providing:

- a safe and secure work environment
- safe equipment
- information and training about health, safety and security.

In short, care organisations must provide a work environment that meets expected health and safety standards. They must make it possible for care practitioners to work safely. Care practitioners in turn have a responsibility to:

- work safely within the care setting
- monitor their work environment for health and safety problems that may develop
- report and respond appropriately to any health and safety risks.

To meet their legal responsibilities, care organisations:

- carry out health and safety risk assessments
- develop health and safety procedures, such as fire evacuation procedures
- provide health and safety equipment, such as fire extinguishers, fire blankets and first aid boxes
- ensure that care settings have safety features, such as smoke alarms, fire exits and security fixtures (electronic pads on doors and window guards, for example), built in to them
- train their employees to follow health and safety procedures and use health and safety equipment and safety features appropriately
- provide a range of health and safety information and warning signs to alert people to safety features such as fire exits and first aid equipment and to warn them about prohibited areas and not smoking, for example.

Care practitioners carry out their legal responsibilities by:

- developing an awareness of health and safety law
- working in ways that follow health and safety guidelines, policies and procedures
- monitoring the care environment for health and safety hazards.

Safeguarding and Protecting Individuals

Figure 4.12 The Health and Safety
at Work Act 1974.

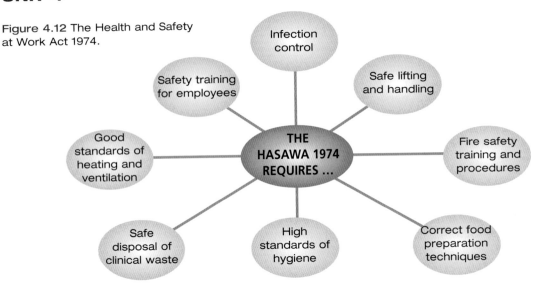

Infection control

Safety training for employees

Safe lifting and handling

Good standards of heating and ventilation

THE HASAWA 1974 REQUIRES ...

Fire safety training and procedures

Safe disposal of clinical waste

High standards of hygiene

Correct food preparation techniques

Figure 4.13 Health and Safety Regulations.

Regulations	Effects
Management of Health and Safety at Work Regulations 1999	This places a responsibility on employers to train staff in relation to health and safety legislation, fire prevention and moving and handling issues. They also require employers to carry out risk assessments and to remove or reduce any health and safety hazards identified. Employers must write safe working procedures based on risk assessments carried out.
Workplace (Health, Safety and Welfare) Regulations 1992	These cover a wide range of basic health, safety and welfare issues such as ventilation, heating, lighting, workstations, seating and welfare facilities.
Personal Protective Equipment at Work Regulations 1992	These require employers to provide appropriate protective clothing and equipment for employees.
Provision and Use of Work Equipment Regulations 1998	These require that equipment provided for use at work, including machinery, is safe.
The Manual Handling Operations Regulations 1992 (amended 2002)	These regulations cover all manual handling activities, such as lifting, lowering, pushing, pulling or carrying objects or people. A large proportion of workplace injuries are due to poor manual handling skills. Employers have a duty to assess risks of any activity that involves manual handling. They must put in place measures to reduce or avoid the risk. Employees must follow manual handling procedures and cooperate on all manual handling issues.
The Health and Safety (First Aid) Regulations 1981	These cover requirements for first aid provision.
The Health and Safety Information for Employees Regulations 1989	These require employers to display a poster telling employees what they need to know about health and safety. This includes the name of the employee health and safety representative; the name of the manager representative; the contact details of the Health and Safety Executive.
Reporting of Injuries, Diseases and Dangerous Occurrences Regulations 1995 (RIDDOR)	These require employers to notify a range of occupational injuries, diseases and dangerous events.
Noise at Work Regulations 1989	These require employers to take action to protect employees from hearing damage.
Control of Substances Hazardous to Health Regulations 2002 (COSHH)	These require employers to assess the risks from hazardous substances and take appropriate precautions.

- Dealing directly with hazards that present a health and safety risk where it is safe to do so
- Reporting health and safety hazards or the failure of safety systems or procedures to a supervisor or manager.

The Health and Safety at Work Act 1974 enforces minimum standards of workplace health and safety and establishes a framework for safe working. A range of regulations that apply to care settings have also been produced as a result of the 1974 Act. These are outlined in figure 4.13.

The Health and Safety Executive

The Health and Safety Executive is the body that monitors standards and enforces health and safety law in the workplace in England, Wales and Scotland. The Health and Safety Executive Northern Ireland has this responsibility in Northern Ireland. The Health and Safety Executive was created by the Health and Safety at Work Act 1974. One of its key tasks is to investigate all accidents in the workplace. The website of the Health and Safety Executive (www.hse.gov.uk) says that 'Our mission is to prevent death, injury and ill-health in Great Britain's workplaces'. The Health and Safety Executive can:

- enter premises to conduct investigations or carry out spot checks on health and safety
- conduct investigations into accidents and safety compliance
- take samples and photographs to assess health and safety risks
- ask questions about health and safety procedures and risk control
- give advice on how to minimise risk
- issue instructions that must be carried out by law
- issue Improvement and Prohibition notices.

The Health and Safety Executive is most likely to visit care settings where:

- there is evidence that health and safety is poor
- there are hazardous substances that should be properly stored and controlled
- a specific incident (accident, death or illness, for example) has occurred.

The purpose of Health and Safety Executive visits and investigations is to check that standards of workplace health, safety and welfare are satisfactory and to give advice on how risks to people being injured or becoming ill in the workplace can be minimised.

Knowledge Check

1 What responsibilities do employers have for health and safety under the Health and Safety at Work Act 1974?

2 Describe the health and safety responsibilities that employees have under the Health and Safety at Work Act 1974.

3 What does the law say about the provision and use of personal protective equipment in care settings?

4 How does RIDDOR 1995 affect health and safety in the care workplace?

5 What role do the Health and Safety Executive play in ensuring health and safety in care settings?

Chapter checklist

The box below provides a summary of the areas covered in chapter 18. Tick the areas that you feel you understand and would be confident answering exam questions about. If there are any areas that you don't understand or are not confident about, you will need to return to them before you begin your exam revision.

Potential hazards and risks to health and safety	❏
Location of hazards in care settings	❏
Safety features to reduce risks	❏
Fire hazards and evacuation procedures	❏
Unsafe equipment	❏
Unsafe storage of hazardous substances	❏
Risk assessment	
Reasons for risk assessment	❏
Five-step process	❏
Security in care settings	❏
Health and safety legislation	
Health and Safety at Work Act 1974	❏
Regulations	❏
The Health and Safety Executive	❏

Assessment Guide

Your learning in this unit will be assessed through a one hour written examination taken online.

The examination will consist of a series of short and longer answer questions covering all aspects of this unit. You will need to show that you understand:

- Different types of hazards and risks to health and safety in care settings.
- The likely location of hazards in care settings.
- The nature of fire hazards and ways of dealing with them.
- The risks posed by unsafe equipment.
- The risks associated with unsafe storage of hazardous substances.
- How risk assessments are carried out.
- Security risks in care settings and ways of minimising them.
- The main provisions of health and safety legislation.
- The role of the Health and Safety Executive.

Chapter 18 provides full coverage of all of the topics you may be asked about in the examination.

GLOSSARY

A

Absolute poverty – This occurs when people have insufficient income to meet their basic, daily living needs.

Abstract thinking – High level thinking ability that enables a person to think about issues, problems or situations that are hypothetical.

Acute problems – Health problems that have a sudden onset and which are usually short-term.

Ageing – The process of, and the changes that result from, growing older.

Allergens – Substances that cause allergies.

Ancillary roles – Indirect care work roles that usually involve organisational work such as administration or cleaning.

Anorexia Nervosa – An eating disorder in which a person maintains a very low body weight and has a distorted image of their body.

Anti-discriminatory approach – An approach to care practice that challenges instances of prejudice and unfair discrimination and aims to counter their negative effects.

Aseptic techniques – Procedures performed under sterile conditions to prevent infection.

Associative play – Play based on imitation and pretending.

Attachment relationship – An emotionally close relationship with a parent or carer through which an infant develops and expresses their emotions and a sense of security.

Autoclaving – Steaming equipment under pressure to sterilise it.

B

Balanced diet – A diet that contains adequate amounts of carbohydrates, fats, protein, vitamins and nutrients for healthy growth and activity.

Bereavement – Suffering loss as a result of someone dying.

Biomedical approach – The scientific approach to health used by the medical profession.

Blended family – A family containing stepbrothers and stepsisters that is created when two previously separate families merge into one unit.

Body Mass Index (BMI) – A system for assessing whether a person is a healthy weight for their height that is calculated by dividing a person's weight in kilograms by their height in metres squared.

Bonding – The formation of a very close emotional link between two people.

Bulimia Nervosa – A binge-eating disorder in which a person controls their weight and body shape typically by purging themselves of food soon after eating it.

C

Care needs – The reasons why an individual requires the help or support of health, social care or early years services.

Care package – The range of services and forms of support that are planned and organised to meet an individual's particular care needs.

Care values – The values and ethical principles that care practitioners apply to their work. These are based on beliefs about the proper way to treat service users. Confidentiality, respecting a person's beliefs and behaving in a non-discriminatory way are all examples of care values.

Carotid artery – A large artery found in the neck.

Catheter – A thin flexible tube that is inserted into the body to allow the introduction or withdrawal of fluids.

Charges – The amount of money required for a particular care service, such as a private dental consultation or a prescription.

Chinese herbal medicine – An ancient system of medicine of Chinese origin based on the use of herbs and plant products to treat a range of physical and psychological health problems.

Chlamydia – A curable sexually transmitted disease that has few obvious symptoms but which can damage a woman's reproductive organs.

Cholesterol – A fatty substance needed by the body and carried in the blood.

Chromosome – Long strands or packets of DNA.

Chronic conditions – Long-term or enduring health conditions that cannot usually be cured.

Client groups – Defined groups of people with similar care needs, such as 'children under five', 'adolescents' and 'disabled people'.

Code of practice – A document that provides guidance on ethically appropriate and recommended ways of behaving or dealing with situations.

Cognitive development – The development of thinking skills.

Cohabiting – Another term for 'living together' without being married.

Commissioning – This term refers to the acquisition or purchasing of care services on behalf of a local population of people.

Communication skills – The abilities and behaviours that allow people to understand and interact with each other.

Concepts – Abstract or general ideas.

Concrete operational thinking – The ability to use logical thinking to solve problems that apply to actual (concrete) objects or situations.

Confidentiality – The protection of personal or sensitive information to ensure that only those who are authorised to have access to it do so.

Conscience – An individual's sense of right and wrong.

Cooperative play – Forms of play in which children collaborate or work together for the same purpose.

Coronary heart disease – A health problem in which the circulation of blood to the heart is inadequate because of damage to arteries or heart muscle.

Cross-infection – The process of becoming infected by something (e.g bacteria) from a source other than the person themselves.

Culture – Common values, beliefs and customs or way of life.

D

Daily living skills – The range of practical skills needed to live independently.

Dementia-related illness – This term refers to a group of diseases where there is a progressive loss of brain function.

Department of Health – The government department responsible for planning and co-ordinating statutory health care provision.

Development – The process of acquiring new skills and capabilities.

Developmental norms – These are the points or 'milestones' when particular developmental changes are expected to occur or when skills and abilities usually develop.

DHSSPS – This is an acronym for the Department of Health, Social Services and Public Safety which has overall responsibility for health and care policy in Northern Ireland.

Dialysis – The process of cleaning the blood by passing it through a special machine.

Diastolic blood pressure – The second or bottom figure in a blood pressure result that shows the minimum pressure in the arteries between beats of the heart.

Disability – A lack of ability compared to the norm.

DNA – The abbreviation of deoxyribonucleic acid. It is a chemical ribbon that tells cells how to function.

Domiciliary care – Another term for home care.

E

Early years – This usually refers to children under 8 years of age, the care practitioners who work with them or the services provided for them.

Egocentric – This means being preoccupied with aspects of the 'self' whilst being insensitive to the needs and thoughts of others.

Eligibility criteria – These are the requirements or standards that must be met before a person is provided with a care service.

Emotional development – The emergence of feelings about self and others.

Emotional needs – These relate to the feelings people have and which are generally expressed through relationships with others.

Empathy – The ability to *see* and feel things from another person's point of view.

Emphysema – A disease of the lung that destroys the lung tissue and causes shortness of breath.

Empowering – A process of supporting and giving choice and decision-making powers to individuals or groups.

Ethnicity – A social profile that is used to classify people according to their social and cultural heritage and identification.

Expected life event – An anticipated event that occurs during an individual's lifetime that affects personal development.

Extended Services – A feature of children's services in which schools offer a range of additional leisure, child care and learning services that go beyond the provision normally expected of a school.

F

Fine motor skills – The manipulative movements an individual makes with their fingers.

Formal operational stage – The development of logical thinking skills during childhood.

Formal relationship – A relationship based on a set of rules, such as employer / employee.

Friendships – Co-operative and supportive, non-sexual relationships between people.

G

Gender – A term used by sociologists to describe the social and cultural attributes that are expected of men and women in a society.

Gender stereotypes – Expectations and images of women as 'feminine' and men as 'masculine'.

Genes – These are short stretches of DNA ribbon that are located in chromosomes.

Genetic inheritance – The genes received from biological parents.

Gross motor skills – Whole body movements, such as sitting up, walking or jumping.

Growth – An increase in size (mass or height).

Growth spurt – A short period of rapid physical change.

H

Hazard – A source of danger.

HDL cholesterol – High-density lipoproteins cholesterol is sometimes called 'good cholesterol' because it can remove cholesterol from the blood stream so that it is excreted from the body through the liver.

Health and Safety Executive – The Government body responsible for ensuring compliance with health and safety at work law and regulations.

Health care – Forms of physical care or treatment, usually focused on the body.

Health Improvement Plan – A series of targets and activities designed to improve the physical health and wellbeing of an individual.

Health monitoring – The process of measuring or checking the state of an individual's physical health.

Hierarchy of needs – The organisation of needs in terms of their level of importance.

Holistic – Looking at the whole person.

Hormones – Chemical substances secreted into the blood by certain glands that stimulate activity in other organs.

Hormone Replacement Therapy – Drug treatment that boosts hormone levels which is designed to ease the physical discomfort experienced by women who are undergoing the menopause.

I

Immunisation – The act of creating immunity by introducing a small, controlled dose of an infection into a person's body.

Informal sector – The term given to the large number of largely untrained and unpaid partners, friends and relatives who provide a range of care and support services for people who need care.

In-patient services – Services provided to people who are admitted to and live within an organisation such as a hospital, hospice or care home whilst receiving care.

Integrated Children's Services – Care services for children provided by health, social care and early years practitioners working in partnership.

Intellectual development – The emergence and improvement of thinking and language skills.

Intellectual needs – An individual's requirement for stimulation and learning opportunities.

Intervertebral discs – Discs that support and allow movement of the spine.

Invasive – This term is used to refer to a procedure, such as an operation, where something (e.g surgical instruments) enters the person's body.

K

Kwashiorkor – This is a childhood condition in which severe malnutrition results from a diet excessively high in carbohydrates and low in protein.

L

LDL cholesterol – Low density lipoprotein, also know as 'bad cholesterol' because it can become trapped in the blood vessels.

Learning disability – A condition that limits an individual's intellectual or thinking ability.

Life event – An event in an individual's life that has significance for or influence on their future development.

Life stages – The phases of growth and development that people pass through.

Local Authority – This is an administrative body, such as a County Council, City Council or Metropolitan Borough Council for example, that is responsible for early years, social care and education services at a local level.

M

Marasmus – A wasting disease caused by malnutrition or the inability to digest protein.

Material possessions – These are the goods, products and other physical items (car, house etc) that people own or possess.

Maturation – The gradual process of becoming physically mature or fully developed.

Means-testing – This involves assessing a person's income and wealth against a set of criteria to determine whether they are eligible for a specific service or benefit.

Menopause – The period of time during which the menstrual cycle wanes and gradually stops. Usually occurs between the 45th and 50th years of a woman's life.

Menstruation – Approximately monthly discharge of blood from the womb of a non-pregnant woman.

Migraine – A severe headache.

Monogamous – Being married to one person at a time.

Multi-agency working – Co-operation between care practitioners who work for different care organisations.

N

NHS – National Health Service.

NHS Direct – A 24-hour health advice and information service provided by the NHS.

NHS Trust – An organisation that provides health care services on behalf of the NHS in England and Wales.

Norms – Expected standards.

Nutrients – Naturally occurring chemical substances found in the food we eat. They include carbohydrates, fats, proteins, vitamins and minerals.

O

Obesity – A very overweight state, usually defined by a body mass index of 30 or more.

Object permanence – The awareness that objects continue to exist even when they are no longer visible.

Osteoporosis – A bone disease that leads to an increased risk of fracture.

Outpatient services – Care that involves attendance at a hospital clinic for brief investigations or treatment during the day.

Outsourcing – Purchasing services from an external organisation.

P

Parallel play – This happens when children play alongside but not directly with each other.

Partnership working – This term is used to refer to the arrangements that care organisations sometimes make to collaborate or work together in order to deliver care services to service users.

Peer group – Typically a group of friends of approximately the same age who *see* themselves and are seen by others as belonging together in some way.

Peer group pressure – The emotional and moral influence that a peer group can have on an individual's behaviour.

Permanent care needs – Ongoing or enduring requirements for assistance or support.

Percentile charts – Usually referred to as centile charts, these are used to record and compare the growth pattern of an infant.

Philanthropist – A wealthy person who voluntarily donates their money or other resources to welfare services for the benefit of others.

Physical needs – Health, development or care needs relating to the body.

Physiological shock – A serious, and sometimes life-threatening, condition in which insufficient blood flow reaches the body's tissues.

PIES – This stands for Physical, Intellectual, Emotional and Social needs.

Placenta – An organ rooted in the lining of the womb that supplies and links the baby's blood supply to the mother's blood supply, carrying oxygen and food to the unborn baby.

Policy – This is a written document that sets out an organisation's approach towards a particular issue.

Pollution – The introduction of contaminants into an environment.

Postcode lottery – This refers to the differing chances that people have of receiving care services depending on where they live. For example, some people don't get access to particular drugs or treatment when their neighbours do because they live in an area where the health authority does not fund the drugs or treatment concerned.

Poverty – A lack of resources, usually financial.

Prejudice – A strongly held attitude towards a particular group which will often persist even when shown to be unjustified or unfounded.

Pre-operational stage – A pre-logical stage of thinking that occurs between the ages of 2 and 6 in which children use a lot of imitation and imagination but can't solve problems logically.

Primary health care team – This term refers to the range of practitioners such as GPs practice nurses, community nurses and other health care staff who provide health care in community settings.

Primary practitioner – A care worker whose role involves working directly with service users in a care-giving capacity.

Primary socialisation – This is a social process carried out within the family. It involves the teaching and learning of social attitudes, values and the forms of behaviour that are acceptable in wider society.

Principled morality – This is a type of moral thinking that is based on self-chosen principles – such as justice or human rights – which some people develop and use to make judgements about right and wrong from late adolescence onwards.

Private practitioner – Care practitioners who are either self-employed or who are employed by a private sector care organisation.

Private sector – This is the collective term used to describe care businesses and self-employed practitioners who provide services on a commercial, profit-making basis.

Procedure – A document that sets out in detail the particular way in which a task must be carried out or an issue dealt with.

Professional referral – A request by one care professional for care services to be provided by another care professional.

Prosthesis – An artificial replacement for a body part, such as an artificial leg.

Puberty – The developmental period when secondary sexual characteristics develop and reproductive organs become functional.

R

Radial artery – The main blood vessel carrying oxygenated blood, found in the forearm.

Redundancy – The loss of a job because the job is no longer required or necessary.

Referral – This is the process used to obtain access to care services.

Reflexes – Involuntary and almost instant reactions to a particular stimulus.

Registered charity – A voluntary organisation registered with the charity commission.

Regulatory body – An organisation that maintains a register of qualified practitioners, gives guidance on professional ethics and removes those who are unfit to practice. Examples include the Nursing and Midwifery Council and the General Medical Council.

Relative poverty – This occurs when people live below the standard of living normally accepted in a particular society.

Retirement – The point where a person stops employment completely.

Risk – The possibility or likelihood of something happening.

Risk assessment – The process of identifying all the risks to and from an activity and the probability of them occurring.

Rural lifestyle – A way of life based in the countryside.

Screening – A strategy used in a population to detect a disease in individuals who currently don't have any signs or symptoms of the disease.

Secondary care – Healthcare services that are provided by hospital-based specialists for people with more complex or emergency health care needs.

Secondary practitioner – A job in a care organisation that involves providing organisational support rather than direct face-to-face contact with service users. An example would be the role of an accountant.

Secondary socialisation – Socialisation that occurs outside of the family. Typically socialisation influenced by friends, peer group, work colleagues and other significant adults.

Secretary of State for Health – The Politician who leads the Department of Health and is responsible for health policy.

Self – The essential qualities that make one person distinct or unique from another.

Self-concept – The combination of self-image and self-esteem that together produce a sense of personal identity.

Self-esteem – The sense of worth or value that a person attributes to themselves, their skills and their abilities.

Self-image – The way a person views themselves.

Self-referral – A direct request by an individual for health care services. Going to *see* a GP is an example of a self-referral.

Sensorimotor stage – The early stage of intellectual development in which basic learning occurs through the use of the senses and physical, or motor, activity.

Sensory impairment – Damage to or loss of one of the main senses – usually hearing impairment or visual impairment.

Service user – An individual who uses a health, social care or early years service.

Sexually transmitted disease – Diseases that are contracted through sexual contact.

Sexual orientation – This refers to the preference a person has for a heterosexual (opposite sex), homosexual (same sex) or bisexual (either same or opposite sex) relationship.

Sibling – This is another term for brother or sister.

Social care – Forms of non-medical support and assistance provided for vulnerable people.

Social class – There are many competing definitions of social class. Central to all definitions is the idea that a person's position in society is determined by their economic circumstances that will then influence their life choices, opportunities and future prospects.

Socially constructed – Something that is 'invented' or 'constructed' by people in a particular society.

Social development – The emergence and improvement of communication skills and relationships with other people.

Social exclusion – A term used to describe a situation where people are unable to participate fully in society for a number of related reasons often including poverty, unemployment, poor housing or homelessness, poor health and poor educational achievement.

Socialisation – This is the process of learning how our society works, its expectations and rules.

Social needs – These refer to an individual's need for interaction and relationships with others.

Social policy – The approach taken to changing or maintaining welfare issues in society.

Social Services Department – The part of a local authority, usually divided into Adult social services and Children's services, that commissions and provides social work, child protection and social care services.

Social Services Inspectorate – The part of central government that inspects social service provision in local authorities.

Social transition – The move from one phase of social development to another.

Solo play – Playing alone.

Solvents – Liquids or gases that are capable of dissolving other substances and which are sometimes abused by inhaling their fumes.

Specific needs – Care needs that result from particular health or developmental problems.

Statutory sector – The care sector that provides services that have to be provided by law. They are usually provided by public or government-controlled care organisations such as NHS Trusts or local authorities.

Stroke – A disturbance in the blood supply to the brain that can result in physical disability and mental impairment. The medical term for a stroke is cerebrovascular accident or CVA.

Sure Start Children's Centres – Government run and funded centres that provide early years support and services for young children and families.

Systolic blood pressure – This is the first figure in a blood pressure reading. It indicates the maximum pressure in the arteries when the heart beats.

T

Targeted services – Services that are designed and provided for people with specific health, social or developmental problems.

Temporary care needs – Care needs that result from short-term health, social or developmental problems.

Third-party referral – Referral to care services by someone who isn't a care professional, such as a friend, relative or employer.

Trepanning – A form of surgery in which a hole is drilled in the skull in order to release pressure or to release 'evil spirits'.

U

Unexpected life events – An event that occurs without warning – such as serious illness – that affects an individual's personal development.

Universal services – Services provided to meet general health and care needs, such as most GP services.

Unfair discrimination – The unjustified and less favourable treatment of a person or a group, perhaps as a result of prejudice.

Urban lifestyles – Ways of life that are based on living in a large town or city.

V

Vaccination – Giving a person the mild form of a disease, usually by injection, to make the immune to the disease itself.

Voluntary organisation – An organisation that is independent of government and which provides free or low cost care services on a not-for-profit basis. These organisations often rely on volunteer workers.

Voluntary sector – The care sector made up of voluntary and not-for-profit organisations that provide services free of charge or for a small, subsidised fee.

W

Wellbeing – A positive state of physical, intellectual, emotional and social health in which the person feels physically well and psychologically content.

Western societies – This term is generally used to refer to developed countries in Europe, North America and Asia.

INDEX

NOTES

NOTES